"Since Lewis and Hurd's *Lesson Study Steps by Steps*, teac
leaders who want to practise or are practising lesson study in
have been waiting for this book. In a subtle interplay of res
know-how, US and UK teachers, educators, researchers,
successfully implemented Collaborative Lesson Research
language, about a context that we can easily relate to."

Stéphane Clivaz, Professor of Mathematics Education,
Lausanne University of Teacher Education

"This is a great book for mathematics teachers and teacher educators who are seeking to
incorporate collaborative learning in their practice. This 'how to' of collaborative lesson
research provides a direct link between theory and practice in education. Most
importantly, the core focus of the book is the increased enjoyment and achievement
of students of mathematics."

Dr Aoibhinn Ní Shúilleabháin, Assistant Professor, *University College Dublin*

"With this lesson study guidebook, the editors and authors provide key contributions to
our understanding of how lesson study may be adapted and become sustainable in
countries outside Japan. The insights emerging from the Collaborative Lesson Research
approach to lesson study, implemented in different settings, offers an excellent resource
and makes this volume a must read for teacher educators, lesson study facilitators,
school leaders and researchers."

James Calleja, Collaborative Lesson Study Malta, *Faculty of Education,*
University of Malta

"Collaborative Lesson Research is a particular way of conducting lesson study that
highlights the key elements of this professional development process. This book presents
the experience of leaders, practitioners and participants in Collaborative Lesson
Research and is an essential support for those interested in getting involved as well as
in improving their experience in lesson study in the most powerful way."

João Pedro da Ponte, *Instituto de Educação, Universidade de Lisboa*

"This book is a great asset to teachers of students in any grade – and frankly any subject
– who wish to know, with assurance they can witness first hand, that their teaching is
impacting student learning in the way they hope. Read it alone if you must, but with
others if you can, as it will help bring learning to life in your school."

Sharon Dotger, *The Syracuse University School of Education*

The Mathematics Practitioner's Guidebook for Collaborative Lesson Research

This resource provides mathematics educators with tools for conducting Collaborative Lesson Research (CLR), a form of Lesson Study developed out of the original Japanese Lesson Study and intended to improve student and teacher learning. Renowned mathematics education researchers Akihiko Takahashi and Geoffrey Wake bring together educators across the US and UK with first-hand experience of using CLR in their schools.

Readers will learn the essentials for impactful Lesson Study directly from the scholars who coined the term, and benefit from the dual perspectives of math education researchers and teachers who have used CLR when reflecting on their own classroom pedagogy. These contributors define CLR and provide examples of successful CLR using real-life case studies, as well as introducing pathways for getting started and practical suggestions for implementation into different school environments. Across these examples, readers will

- understand the essence of Lesson Study, considered as CLR, and its important features
- be advised what participants in CLR should expect to do (observing research lessons, designing lessons, teaching research lessons, facilitating post-lesson discussion, etc.) and provide guidance and support with this enactment
- be advised on how to develop, embed, and sustain CLR communities
- preview potential outcomes over time from undertaking CLR

Supplementary materials that include research lesson proposals, plans, and links to videos of research lessons to support readers in understanding CLR are also included.

Ideal for practicing teachers, teacher leaders, teacher educators, and professional developers involved in mathematics teaching, this book offers first-of-its-kind entry points for CLR. Its combination of theory and practice will empower educators to implement this increasingly popular vehicle for understanding students' learning of mathematics.

Akihiko Takahashi is an Associate Professor at DePaul University, USA, where he teaches mathematics and mathematics education. He coined and introduced Collaborative Lesson Research in 2016 to distinguish an authentic Lesson Study from various forms of "Lesson Study" used worldwide.

Geoffrey Wake is a Professor of Mathematics Education at the University of Nottingham, UK, where he leads the work of the Centre for Research in Mathematics Education. He is a co-founder of the Collaborative Lesson Research group in the UK, which seeks to foster and support lesson study practices and practitioners.

Studies in mathematical thinking and learning
Series Editor: Alan H. Schoenfeld

The Mathematics Practitioner's Guidebook for Collaborative Lesson Research

Authentic Lesson Study for Teaching and Learning

Edited by Akihiko Takahashi and Geoffrey Wake

Routledge
Taylor & Francis Group

NEW YORK AND LONDON

Designed cover image: © Getty Images

First published 2024
by Routledge
605 Third Avenue, New York, NY 10158

and by Routledge
4 Park Square, Milton Park, Abingdon, Oxon, OX14 4RN

Routledge is an imprint of the Taylor & Francis Group, an informa business

© 2024 selection and editorial matter, Akihiko Takahashi and Geoffrey Wake; individual chapters, the contributors

The right of Akihiko Takahashi and Geoffrey Wake to be identified as the authors of the editorial material, and of the authors for their individual chapters, has been asserted in accordance with sections 77 and 78 of the Copyright, Designs and Patents Act 1988.

ISBN: 978-1-032-45077-3 (hbk)
ISBN: 978-1-032-45075-9 (pbk)
ISBN: 978-1-003-37527-2 (ebk)

DOI: 10.4324/9781003375272

Typeset in Sabon
by MPS Limited, Dehradun

Contents

Figures

Tables

Boxes

Introduction

School-based professional development for mathematics teachers is not commonly seen in the United States and the United Kingdom. Professional organisations such as the National Council of Teachers of Mathematics (NCTM) in the United States and the National Centre for Excellence in the Teaching of Mathematics (NCETM), Association of Teachers of Mathematics, Mathematical Association in the United Kingdom, and universities provide learning opportunities such as conferences, workshops, and summer programs for those who are enthusiastic about learning new teaching materials and pedagogical ideas. However, many teachers aren't able to take these opportunities and many are only able to teach mathematics every day by reading resource books, teaching guides, and other materials after their school day ends.

In contrast, schools in Japan offer their teachers professional development opportunities regularly and within their own schools. Ongoing professional development opportunities are built into their regular school days, and teachers in the same school building are expected to collaborate in improving their teaching and learning as a part of their professional duties.

When two books, *The Teaching Gap* (Stigler & Hiebert, 1999) and *Knowing and Teaching Elementary Mathematics* (Ma, 1999), became popular among teachers and educators, the mathematics education community started paying more attention to the importance of continuous teacher professional development for all teachers of mathematics. It was realized that teacher preparation is crucial but needs to be more comprehensive to nurture students in developing mathematical thinking and problem solving. Researchers argue that professional development for mathematics teachers should be built into teachers' everyday schedules (e.g., Lewis & Tsuchida, 1998; Ma, 1999; Stigler & Hiebert, 1999) in order for teachers to implement ideas from research and update their teaching practice to address issues in teaching and learning as they arise over time.

To respond to such suggestions, researchers and educators worldwide have been trying to use *Jyugyou kenkyuu* (Japanese Lesson Study), the primary form of professional development approach commonly used among schools in Japan, to replicate Japan's success in implementing ideas from research in their classrooms. However, adopting Japanese Lesson Study in schools in other countries has not always, if ever, been smooth. Even though teachers and schools are convinced that Lesson Study has contributed to improving and updating teaching and learning in Japan over the years, the school education system and culture in other countries are not the same as in Japan. Many researchers and teachers have tried implementing Japanese Lesson Study in various ways for over a decade now. Some take some parts of Lesson Study, and some try to faithfully adapt it as much as possible. Among those early adaptors of Japanese Lesson Study, some schools and teachers in the United States and the United Kingdom are tirelessly seeking a way to establish a continuous school-based professional development structure for mathematics teachers using a form of Japanese Lesson Study designed for schools and teachers outside Japan.

This book is a collection of the effort of 22 teachers, educators, and education researchers in the United States and the United Kingdom who have been working hard to design and conduct innovative professional development opportunities for all the teachers in their schools. Chapter 1 provides background information about how and why Collaborative Lesson Research (CLR) was proposed as an opening of this book. Chapter 2 reports cases from the United States and the United Kingdom on how CLR contributed to establishing sustainable professional development for practicing teachers in their schools and districts. To establish a professional development structure within a school system, Chapter 3 provides critical information for getting started with CLR, including two major pathways to introducing CLR to encourage teachers to become interested in trying a new endeavour for school-based professional learning. Chapter 4 is for school leaders and policymakers to guide how to build capacity to be ready for implementing CLR. Chapter 5 is a collection of reports from the field about what teachers and teacher educators have learned from CLR. It can be a good resource for educators seeking an impactful professional opportunity for their schools and districts. Finally, Chapter 6 suggests a possible next step after reading this unique book written by teachers and educators in the field of mathematics education.

The ideas from this book can be used in schools outside Japan to help establish a structure for supporting mathematics teachers in becoming lifelong learners to continuously improve teaching and learning.

Akihiko Takahashi, Geoffrey Wake

References

Lewis, C., & Tsuchida, I. (1998). *A lesson is like a swiftly flowing river*. American Educator (Winter 1998), 12–51.

Ma, L. (1999). *Knowing and teaching elementary mathematics: Teachers' understanding of fundamental mathematics in China and the United States*. Erlbaum Associates, Incorporated, Lawrence.

Stigler, J., & Hiebert, J. (1999). *The teaching gap: Best ideas from the world's teachers for improving education in the classroom*. Free Press.

Acknowledgements

As readers of this volume will recognise it is based on an amazing amount of work that is undertaken by the contributors that is based squarely in their professional lives. Their involvement in collaborative lesson research has taken hold of their passion for learning, and they and the colleagues that they have worked with over the years have done much to improve their professional learning, and importantly the learning of the students. We would like to acknowledge this commitment, energy, expertise, and support of all involved and recognise the support of the schools and organisations they work for and importantly their students for their unsolicited engagement in collaborative research.

Most of all, of course, we thank the contributing authors, who have given us such wonderful insight into their experiences and have identified many interesting issues and questions that we need to consider as we continue to learn how best to work with collaborative lesson research in our different cultures and contexts.

Those writing from the United Kingdom would like to acknowledge the support over time of colleagues of the IMPULS Project at Tokyo Gakugei University from whom we have learned so much, but perhaps more importantly have inspired us to adopt and adapt Lesson Study into the models of collaborative lesson research we are working with today. We made initial contact with the IMPULS team when it was discovered that researchers were working with tasks that were developed in the United Kingdom as part of the Bowland Maths Project (www.bowlandmaths.org.uk). This led to some of the work that was initiated with Bowland Maths funding and which is the basis of some of what is reported here. In particular, we would like to thank Sachi Hatakenaka who, working for Bowland, has been a massive support to many of us over the intervening years. Further to that initial inspiration we also would like to acknowledge the Nuffield Foundation which provided further funding in the early days with a grant for the Lessons for Mathematical Problem Solving (LeMaPS) project which allowed that work to continue. More recently the collaborative lesson research community has been creative in the sources that they have found to support their work. To these hidden people, schools, Academy Trusts, local authorities, charitable organisations, and so on, we also extend our thanks.

In addition to the above support, the U.S. contributing authors would like to give thanks to the generous public and private organisations whose financial support helped make the CLR work described in this volume happen. Critical support came from the Bill & Melinda Gates Foundation and the McDougal Family Foundation.

Contributors

Rosa Archer, Manchester Institute of Education, University of Manchester

Mike Askew, University of Witwatersrand

Brigid Brown, Oakland Unified School District

Stefanie Burke, Maths Adviser, Devon Education Services

Rashida Carter, San Francisco Unified School District

Karen Cortez, San Francisco Unified School District

Paul Crossley, Director of Redhill College of Leadership and Development

Shelley Friedkin, San Francisco Unified School District

Jeffrey Goodwin, Independent Consultant working in Primary Schools

Marie Joubert, Centre for Research in Mathematics Education, University of Nottingham

Sarah Leakey, Teacher, Highland Council

Joshua Lerner, Peirce School of International Studies

Catherine Lewis, School of Education, Mills College at Northeastern University

Jacqueline Mann, Teacher, Spires Academy, Canterbury

Thomas McDougal, Lesson Study Alliance

Courtney Ortega, Oakland Unified School District

Luke Rolls, University of Cambridge Primary School

Bob Sawyer, Director of Schools in the Diocese of Hallam South Yorkshire

Akihiko Takahashi, College of Education, DePaul University

Ruth Trundley, Maths Adviser, Devon Education Services

Geoffrey Wake, Centre for Research in Mathematics Education, University of Nottingham

Matt Woodford, Nottingham Institute of Education, Nottingham Trent University

Foreword

It's generally true that to improve any skill, reflecting on your personal experience of carrying out that skill is crucial, and learning from experts and collaborating with others to share and analyse experiences will accelerate improvement.

To improve a skill as complex as teaching mathematics it would therefore seem natural that teachers should develop their professional learning by working collaboratively, considering mathematics education research, and observing and analysing mathematics lessons. Mathematics teachers and education researchers collaborating in this way is routine practice in Far Eastern jurisdictions such as Japan, Shanghai, and Singapore, which consistently show the highest levels of performance in international comparisons of mathematics education. However, despite the success of this approach in the Far East, it is certainly not standard practice in the West.

The practice whereby classroom teachers of mathematics and other mathematics education experts work collaboratively to share knowledge through planning, observing, and analysing lessons together to continually develop their teaching skills is helpfully referred in this book as "Collaborative Lesson Research" (CLR).

In my role as Director of the National Centre for Excellence in the Teaching of Mathematics (NCETM) in England, I visited Shanghai in 2014 to investigate how maths was being taught there. The visit was motivated by Shanghai's outstanding performance in mathematics in PISA 2012. In Shanghai, I certainly saw some excellent maths teaching, but what struck me most was how mathematics teachers were working collaboratively to continually improve their teaching. Key aspects of this collaborative working were teachers designing lessons together, observing one another's lessons and discussing lessons in detail. Furthermore, this practice was happening both within and between schools and was supported by research-informed expertise from Shanghai Normal University. It was clear that this CLR process is fundamental to Shanghai's success in mathematics education.

That initial visit to Shanghai led to a programme of teacher exchanges between England and Shanghai for primary and secondary maths teachers each year from 2014 to 2019. A key purpose of the exchanges was for English teachers to experience CLR in action. Teachers from England observed lessons and then took part in detailed discussions of those lessons with Chinese teachers and other mathematics education experts. The teachers from England who were involved in these discussions described the experience as the most valuable professional development of their careers.

Building from the experience of the England-Shanghai teacher exchanges, and considering education research more widely, the NCETM has ensured that teacher collaboration underpins its national professional development programmes. The NCETM's Teaching for Mastery programme, a key element of our work, includes teachers from different schools being supported to collaborate in "Teacher Research Groups" where they participate in lesson design and observation and discuss lessons in detail as a key part of their professional development.

In England, school organisation and the time available to teachers to take part in professional development make CLR approaches challenging to implement. The NCETM is finding ways to adapt CLR to our circumstances, but we are still some way from embedding CLR as a standard element of continuous professional development for mathematics teachers.

My description of the CLR process described above is simplistic. This book explains CLR in detail, beginning by describing "Japanese Lesson Study" a highly developed system of continuous professional development that underpins mathematics teaching in Japan. CLR is not Japanese Lesson Study, but the authors have been informed by Japanese Lesson Study practices. The book defines the essential elements of CLR and goes on to discuss how CLR can be adapted in the context of different education systems, with valuable evidence from practitioners who are finding ways to implement CLR in their own contexts. It provides both a high-level guide and opportunities for insight into deeper issues relating to CLR and how it can be implemented. We will use it to help to inform the work of the NCETM.

A key feature of CLR is teachers of mathematics working in "collaborative learning groups," as described in the Royal Society's "Professional learning for all teachers of mathematics" report (2016). This fosters teachers' ongoing professional learning, helping them to continuously improve their specialist skills to teach mathematics. Working in this way not only improves teaching, so improving the mathematics education of young people, it also provides a stimulating and enjoyable experience for teachers. Engaging with colleagues to improve your teaching is hugely rewarding and CLR provides an excellent vehicle for this.

CLR practices have a key role to play in improving teaching and learning in mathematics and this book can help mathematics educators everywhere to develop ways to implement CLR in their own contexts. I recommend that all mathematics educators should read this book.

Charlie Stripp, NCETM Director

A note from the series editor

Collaborative Lesson Research (CLR), a generalization of Lesson Study, can be transformative.

Why the phrase? Because, in fact, there's no one form of Lesson Study. The best-known form of Lesson study (at least in the West) is exemplified by the way LS is practiced in Japan, but there is a widely practiced version in China that differs along key dimensions, and other nations have their own well-developed forms. The term "Collaborative Lesson Research" is intended to capture the essence across various models. The key idea is that when professional learning communities engage over time with deep ideas of mathematical pedagogy – not in the abstract but by building lessons and carefully examining what happens – teaching can improve and student learning can increase a great deal. Engaging in this work is a wonderful experience for teachers, and the students reap the benefit in terms of learning gains.

CLR is deceptively simple. In Japan, for example, lesson study is undergirded by cultural tradition and a set of tacit understandings. Typically the work begins with the serious study of curricular goals and the examination of attempts to teach them: what is the important mathematics, what have people tried, to get it across; what can we build on from the literature, what might we want to change? Goals for student learning are explicit. Lesson design is a careful, iterative process, with each part of the lesson put together with the expectation that students will engage in specific ways and learn specific things as a result. Once the lesson is designed, one member of the teaching community teaches the lesson on behalf of the whole community. Others observe "close up" – are the students acting and learning as we expected? Then there are a series of commentaries, including a key commentary by an outside expert, and a collective reflection. It's this whole process that produces teacher learning.

In the U.S., I've seen groups of teachers get together (on their own time!) to try their hand at lesson study. Unaware of the tradition of studying the mathematics and the curriculum, they took a troublesome topic and asked, "how can we design a good lesson to get at this topic?" They worked hard, and did indeed design a good lesson. Their evaluation of the lesson was on the order of "That went pretty well. The kids seemed engaged."

My point? That was a good experience, but it wasn't CLR, and it couldn't possibly deliver the benefits of CLR when it's done right. This book, in a very reader-friendly way, unpacks the CLR experience so that it can be experienced in powerful ways. My hope is that teams of teachers who use it will reap the benefits that deep and meaningful planning, enacting, and reflecting on mathematics lessons can provide.

Alan Schoenfeld
University of California, Berkeley – March 2023

Part 1

Collaborative Lesson Research

A form of Lesson Study to encourage
teachers to work collaboratively

1.1   Collaborative Lesson Research

Akihiko Takahashi and Thomas McDougal

Challenges in using Lesson Study

Researchers and educators worldwide have been trying to use *jyugyou kenkyuu* (Japanese Lesson Study), the primary form of professional development approach commonly used in schools in Japan, to replicate Japan's success in implementing ideas from research in their classrooms.

US researchers published articles and books, including "A Lesson Is Like a Swiftly Flowing River" (Lewis & Tsuchida, 1998) and *The Teaching Gap* (Stigler & Hiebert, 1999), that reported on how Japanese mathematics and science classrooms had been shifted from teach-by-telling instruction to a student-centred instruction by engaging students in solving problems and hands-on investigations. They argue that *jyugyou kenkyuu*, a unique professional development approach using live classroom observation, may be the fundamental driver enabling Japanese schools to implement ideas from educational research, particularly in mathematics and science. *Jyugyou kenkyuu* attracted researchers and educators in many different countries who were looking for effective teacher professional development programmes to support their own teachers.

Since the beginning of this international movement, the term "Lesson Study" (Stigler & Hiebert, 1999; Yoshida, 1999) has been widely used instead of the original Japanese term, *jyugyou kenkyuu*. "Lesson Study" has also come to be used to describe activities that vary significantly from what Japanese educators would recognise as *jyugyou kenkyuu*.

One likely reason why lesson studies[1] outside Japan may vary so much from what is practiced in Japan is the lack of a clear definition of *jyugyou kenkyuu*. At the beginning of the Lesson Study movement, in the early 2000s, even Japanese researchers and teachers could not identify the critical elements of *jyugyou kenkyuu*. As Fujii (2014) reported, Japanese teachers would say it is "like the air", so ubiquitous as to be unnoticeable. In fact, Japanese schools and teachers have a variety of professional development activities that use live classroom observation, each with a different purpose and organised differently. Both US- and Japanese-based researchers have tried to identify their different affordances (Lewis, 2000; Murata & Takahashi, 2002; Takahashi, 2000). Table 1.1.1 shows the common professional development opportunities available for typical Japanese teachers. All of them use live classroom observation, but Japanese teachers and researchers do not all agree on which ones should be considered *jyugyou kenkyuu*.

The lack of consensus about what qualifies as *jyugyou kenkyuu* even among Japanese teachers and researchers made it difficult for those without first-hand experience to understand not only the process but also the purpose of *jyugyou kenkyuu*. As a result, they had a hard time faithfully replicating the process by reading case studies. Another challenge

DOI: 10.4324/9781003375272-2

Table 1.1.1 Types of Japanese teacher professional development use live classroom observations

	School-based LS 校内授業研究	District-wide LS 授業研究会	Cross District LS 公開授業研究会	Demonstration Lesson 師範授業
Purpose	Teacher research	Teacher research	Teacher research	Dissemination of exemplary practice
Participants	Teachers from the school (closed)	Teachers from the school district (closed)	Conference participants (open to the public)	Teachers in the school/district
Planning	Team of teachers from the school	Team of teachers from the district	Volunteer group or individual (experienced teacher)	Usually individual (experienced teacher)
Research lesson	Held in the students' classroom	Held at the students' school but maybe a different room to accommodate more participants	Held at a conference venue	Location varies
Teacher	The classroom teacher who regularly teaches the students	The classroom teacher who regularly teaches the students	A guest teacher who has never taught the students before, or the classroom teacher who regularly teaches the students	Guest teacher who has never taught the students before
Post lesson discussion	Discussion among all the teachers from the school	Discussion among all the teachers from the district, or panel discussion	Panel discussion	None; perhaps a Q & A session

was the fact that Lesson Study requires that teachers engage in a series of intensive activities, unlike most teachers' professional development at the time. It requires teachers and schools to allocate extra resources, including time and human capacity. Some teachers and schools felt they could not implement *jyugyou kenkyuu* as the literature described it, but still wanted to try it in order to improve their students' mathematical thinking skills (e.g., Hart et al., 2011). So, some schools and teachers modified Lesson Study to fit within the constraints of their school schedule and available resources.

Fujii (2014) studied how lesson studies had been done in several African countries and found that many essential parts of *jyugyou kenkyuu* were not done as Japanese teachers do them, or were omitted. The same problem can also be seen in the United States and other countries. Such modifications reduced the effectiveness of those lesson studies, and participants were usually not motivated to continue. For example, lesson studies in the United States are often conducted as an ad hoc professional development programme run by external funding, and many of those Lesson Study programmes ended immediately after external funding ended (e.g., Akiba & Howard, 2021).

Successful Lesson Study

Although many early adaptations resulted in ineffective and non-sustainable lesson studies, some schools outside Japan started to use Lesson Study as their primary form of mathematics professional development. These schools used ideas from later research about Lesson Study conducted in elementary schools in Japan. One of those ideas was to use school-wide Lesson Study as part of a multiple-year research project to implement new national curriculum standards effectively (Lewis & Takahashi, 2013; Takahashi & McDougal, 2014). Another was about how outside experts support school-based Lesson Study by providing suggestions and comments to summarise the learning from a research lesson and post-lesson discussion (Takahashi, 2014). And there were also new insights into how to design a research lesson (Fujii, 2016; Takahashi, 2011; Watanabe et al., 2008). Takahashi and McDougal (2016) studied several successful cases of Lesson Study conducted among public schools in Chicago and argued that the following features seemed important for Lesson Study to be effective:

1 Teachers engage in Lesson Study to gain knowledge and promote the development of expertise in teaching. They do not do seek a "perfect" lesson.
2 Lesson Study is structured and has the support of the school or even district leadership.
3 Teachers spend significant time doing *kyouzai kenkyuu* (researching teaching materials, discussed below) to develop a plan for the research lesson.
4 The entire process of preparing and conducting a research lesson spans several weeks.
5 Knowledgeable others are part of the Lesson Study project. They give advice during lesson planning and during the post-lesson discussion.

(Takahashi & McDougal, 2016)

Lewis et al. (2022) conducted further study to establish carefully designed support for establishing a school-wide Lesson Study among US schools. They found that the following are common factors shaping effective and sustained Lesson Study:

1 Teacher agency.
2 Access to a sound instructional vision that values student thinking and makes it visible.
3 Teachers' content study and access to content expertise.
4 Site-developed strategic management structures. The central role of teacher agency in sustainability is one implication of the study.

(Lewis et al., 2022)

Taken together, the above studies suggest that, first, a successful Lesson Study should be a teacher-led initiative with strong support from the school administrators. Second, teachers should understand that Lesson Study is a type of teacher research and a collaborative effort among teachers who share a common issue they want to overcome. To guide teachers outside Japan towards a practice that is effective and enduring, Takahashi and McDougal (2016) coined the term *Collaborative Lesson Research* (CLR), which they defined as a form of Lesson Study having certain elements and characteristics, based on case studies of successful use of Lesson Study in Japan and the United States.

CLR: A powerful kind of Lesson Study

The new term, *Collaborative Lesson Research*, was created to describe a specific successful kind of Lesson Study, particularly to guide those who have never experienced professional development that uses live classroom observation. In CLR, educators collaboratively plan, teach/observe, and reflect to study teaching and learning. By definition, CLR must have the following:

1 A clear research purpose
2 *Kyouzai kenkyuu* ("study of materials for teaching")
3 A written research proposal
4 A live research lesson and post-lesson discussion
5 Knowledgeable others
6 Sharing of results

These characteristics define CLR as more similar to *jyugyou kenkyuu* as practiced in Japan than many lesson studies seen outside Japan. More important, it has had some success in schools in the United States and the United Kingdom. The following explanations of these six critical elements are based on Takahashi and McDougal (2016).

A clear research purpose

The driving force behind CLR is the educators' desire to overcome an issue in teaching and learning. For example, if a team of teachers has been experiencing difficulty helping students develop a solid conceptual understanding of fractions, that can be an issue to overcome.

The research focus of CLR usually has two layers. One layer is teaching specific content: how can we design a lesson so that students can learn a certain mathematical concept or skill better? The topic of the research lesson is usually presented as a challenge for students or teachers. The second layer is a general teaching-learning goal. It must be a big goal, one that goes beyond any specific topic or grade level, and it may even apply to several school subjects. This goal is called the *research theme*.

A research theme has two parts. The first part is a long-term desired outcome for students. The second part is an idea about how to achieve the long-term desired outcome through everyday teaching. Many of the schools we have worked with have decided that their long-term desired outcome (i.e., the first part of their research theme) is to develop students' persistence in the face of challenging problems. Their idea for how to achieve that (the second part of their research theme) is to use an instructional approach called Teaching through Problem Solving (TTP), in which students attack problems that are beyond what students have previously learned. The challenge for teachers, now, is to design lessons to implement this idea, and that becomes the unifying goal of a school-wide CLR effort. (See Chapter 3.5 for additional discussion and examples of research themes and of TTP.)

A clear research purpose is important for motivation. When teachers review the results from assessment tasks and find what their students are having trouble with, they are excited to work together with other teachers on the problem. When the research theme can be used for all grade levels, teachers understand how important it is to watch research lessons with students older or younger than their own. They can contribute to their professional community.

Kyouzai kenkyuu, *"study of materials for teaching"*

In the words of *Adding It Up* (National Research Council, 2001), the teaching and learning of mathematics is "the product of interactions among the teacher, the students, and the mathematics":

The pedagogical challenge for teachers is to manage instruction in ways that help particular students develop mathematical proficiency. High-quality instruction, in whatever form it comes, focuses on important mathematical content, represented and developed with integrity (p. 315).

Thus, it is crucial for the effective design and implementation *of any lesson* that the teacher be clear and knowledgeable about the specific mathematics they want their students to learn, about the ways that mathematics might be taught, and about the condition of their specific students.

The Japanese term *kyouzai kenkyuu* refers to the process of investigating (1) the mathematics, (2) pedagogical options for teaching that mathematics, and (3) the condition (or likely condition) of the students (Takahashi & Yoshida, 2004; Takahashi et al., 2005). Japanese teachers understand that *kyouzai kenkyuu* is a necessary part of everyday lesson planning. Though textbooks can serve as a guide, even a well-designed textbook needs to be interpreted in a way that is appropriate for the particular circumstances of the teacher and students. Knowing how to use a textbook effectively for different groups of students is crucial professional knowledge that teachers need to acquire on the job.

In Lesson Study, Japanese teachers typically begin *kyouzai kenkyuu* by reviewing the standards and their textbook, including related standards and the treatment of related topics in later grades, in order to understand clearly what mathematics students are expected to learn. They will also study the treatment of related content in prior grades to know what experiences the students will have had prior to the lesson, upon which new knowledge can be built. Then, they research teaching and learning issues, such as common misunderstandings of the mathematical concept perhaps by reading journal articles. They may examine textbooks other than their own to broaden their knowledge of possible instructional approaches. Finally, they consider the tools, materials, tasks, and activities that they could use, in order to choose those which they think will work best for their students.

Through *kyouzai kenkyuu*, teachers deepen their understanding of the mathematics they are teaching as well as their "pedagogical content knowledge" (Shulman, 1986; Ball et al., 2008). This is important because, it is safe to say, no teacher starts out with all the pedagogical content knowledge they will need to teach mathematics effectively; they will need to acquire most of it on the job. New teachers, especially, have much to learn. *Kyouzai kenkyuu* is a way to learn it, and conducting *kyouzai kenkyuu* together with colleagues as part of CLR is especially powerful.

For teachers who do not know how to conduct *kyouzai kenkyuu* – and this will be the case especially for most new teachers – Lesson Study provides a valuable opportunity to learn either from more experienced colleagues or from a *knowledgeable other* (discussed next) who can serve as a guide to the planning team. Teachers can also learn by reading research lesson proposals developed by other teachers and seeing what those teachers did as part of their *kyouzai kenkyuu* and what they learned as a result.

There are many materials in Japan to help teachers do *kyouzai kenkyuu*. Fewer high-quality materials are available to teachers in America (Lewis et al., 2011). Therefore, many of the teachers we work with in America rely upon a translation of a popular Japanese textbook series and their teaching guides. A small but growing database of research lesson reports, most of which can serve as good examples of *kyouzai kenkyuu*, is available at https://LSAlliance.org.

Early reports in English about Japanese Lesson Study, such as *The Teaching Gap* (Stigler & Hiebert, 1999), either ignored or failed to emphasise *kyouzai kenkyuu*, but we include it as a critical part of CLR because of its importance for both teacher and student learning.

A written research plan

A CLR planning team creates a written document, called the *lesson research proposal* (see Appendix 2.4.1 for an example). The term *lesson plan* is often used in lesson studies, but we avoid this term to make it clear that this document is not like a plan for an everyday lesson. CLR is teacher research, and the proposal for a research lesson should make an argument, based on previous experience and the careful study of available resources, for testing the planning team's idea for a new approach to teaching and learning. The lesson research proposal says what the team learned from *kyouzai kenkyuu* and explains their ideas about classroom instruction. It includes the learning goals for a unit, a rationale of the unit and lesson design, and a detailed teaching-learning plan for one particular lesson within the unit (the *research lesson*). It explains the design of the unit and research lesson. It also clearly explains how the research lesson connects to the research theme and learning goals. A lesson research proposal will be several pages long.

As part of finalising the plan for the research lesson itself, the team should conduct a run-through of that lesson, which some call a "mock lesson", in which one person plays the role of the teacher while other teachers play the role of (well-behaved) students. The purpose is to fine-tune details of the lesson, such as how the problem and other information will be presented, which student ideas will be discussed and how, and how the lesson will be concluded. The mock lesson is discussed further in Chapter 3.5.

A live research lesson and post-lesson discussion

One member of the team teaches the research lesson to his or her own students while the planning team and other members of the CLR community observe. The people watching collect data about how teacher leads the class, e.g., how she or he presents tasks and facilitates discussions, and how the students respond, especially as relates to the research theme and learning goals. It can be useful to make a video recording of the lesson. However, in CLR, people need to see the lesson from many viewpoints, so many people must actually watch the lesson live with their own eyes.

After the research lesson, the people who watched share the data they collected and discuss what the data means. The main goals of the discussion are to better understand teaching and learning and establish shared understanding about the research theme. Some lesson studies refer to this activity as a "debrief", but we believe that term is misleading. The original Japanese term, *kenkyuu kyougikai*, means more than "debriefing" and is closer to "research colloquium". Therefore, we suggest using the term "post-lesson discussion" in CLR to emphasise the importance of having a fruitful, multi-directional discussion.

Knowledgeable others

The post-lesson discussion typically concludes with an expert commentary by a *koshi*, sometimes referred to as a knowledgeable other or final commentator. The *koshi* should be someone who is not in the planning team and usually comes from outside the school, who is knowledgeable about teaching and learning related to the topic and the research theme, and also an expert in Lesson Study. The *koshi* is important in CLR for helping the team go beyond what they know. He or she will watch the research lesson and, at the end of the discussion after the research lesson, may be invited to provide expert commentary. That commentary will usually highlight the most critical events from the research lesson relative to the learning goals and the team's research theme, and make connections between the research lesson and new knowledge from research and standards. The *koshi* also gives advice to the CLR community about steps they can take to accomplish their research theme (Takahashi, 2014; Watanabe & Wang-Iverson, 2005).

Ideally, a CLR community has another knowledgeable other who helps during the planning process. That person can suggest useful resources for the team's *kyouzai kenkyuu*, such as research papers or results from CLR work at other schools. They can also give advice and feedback on the research proposal.

Both the *koshi* and a knowledgeable other who helps during planning must have a lot of knowledge about the subject matter and topic. And they must also be familiar with the school's curriculum and students. An experienced teacher or a content coach who often works at the school can be these kinds of knowledgeable other. These roles are discussed further in Chapter 3.5.

Share results

As research, CLR generally results in new knowledge of teaching and learning that deserves to be shared with the wider education community. Simply inviting people from outside of the planning team to watch and discuss the research lesson is one way that CLR teams can share their results. Research lessons to which outsiders are invited are called public research lessons; public research lessons are an important part of the professional development system in Japan and should be viewed similarly outside Japan. Also, the team can create a report comprising their research lesson proposal with a summary of the post-lesson discussion and the expert commentary. Such a report can be extremely useful to other educators.

The cycle of CLR

The purpose of CLR is to investigate critical issues in improving teaching and learning. Because the issues are rarely simple, multiple research lessons are usually needed to resolve them. Japanese schools typically have several research lessons in a year and continue for two-three years under one research theme. Thus, CLR should ideally involve most of the teachers in a school, and its cycle may continue for at least two years with three to six research lessons addressing the same research theme each year. This is the reason why the common factors we discussed earlier, including teacher agency and structured support from school administrators, are critical for effective CLR.

Later chapters in this book will describe efforts to implement CLR at different sites around the world. Some of these efforts may not yet qualify as full-fledged CLR, but they all treat Lesson Study as an ongoing project of teacher research for the purpose of improving instruction.

Note

1 Lesson Study (singular, capitalised) refers to the English translation of *jyugyou kenkyuu,* commonly seen among Japanese schools. Lesson studies (plural, lower case) refer to modified versions of Lesson Study seen among schools outside Japan.

References

Akiba, M., & Howard, C. (2021). After the race to the top: State and district capacity to sustain professional development innovation in Florida. *Educational Policy*, 08959048211015619. 10.11 77/08959048211015619

Ball, D. L., Thames, M. H., & Phelps, G. (2008). Content knowledge for teaching: What makes it special? *Journal of Teacher Education, 59*(5), 389–407. 10.1177/0022487108324554

Fujii, T. (2014). Implementing Japanese Lesson Study in foreign countries: Misconceptions revealed. *Mathematics Teacher Education and Development, 16*(1), 65–83. http://www.merga.net.au/ojs/index.php/mted/article/view/206

Fujii, T. (2016). Designing and adapting tasks in lesson planning: A critical process of Lesson Study. *ZDM*, 1–13. 10.1007/s11858-016-0770-3

Hart, L. C., Alston, A., & Murata, A. (Eds.). (2011). *Lesson study research and practice in mathematics education*. Springer.

Lewis, C. (2000, April). Lesson Study: The core of Japanese professional development. New Orleans: Special Interest Group on Research in Mathematics Education American Educational Research Association Meetings.

Lewis, C., Perry, R., & Friedkin, S. (2011). Using Japanese curriculum materials to support Lesson Study outside Japan: Toward coherent curriculum. *Educational studies in Japan: international yearbook: ESJ, 6* (Classrooms and Schools in Japan), 5–19. http://ci.nii.ac.jp/naid/110009328438/en/

Lewis, C., & Takahashi, A. (2013). Facilitating curriculum reforms through lesson study. *International Journal for Lesson and Learning Studies, 2*(3), 207–217.

Lewis, C., & Tsuchida, I. (1998). A lesson is like a swiftly flowing river. *American Educator* (Winter 1998), 12–51.

Lewis, C. C., Takahashi, A., Friedkin, S., Liebert, S., & Houseman, N. (2022). Sustained, effective school-wide Lesson Study: How do we get there? *Vietnam Journal of Education, 6*, 45–57.

Murata, A., & Takahashi, A. (2002). *Vehicle to connect theory, research, and practice: How teacher thinking changes in district-level Lesson Study in Japan*. ERIC/CSMEE Publications.

National Research Council (2001). *Adding it up: Helping children learn mathematics*. National Academy Press.

Shulman, L. S. (1986). Those who understand: Knowledge growth in teaching. *Educational Researcher, 15*(2), 4–14.

Stigler, J., & Hiebert, J. (1999). *The teaching gap: Best ideas from the world's teachers for improving education in the classroom*. Free Press.

Takahashi, A. (2000). Current trends and issues in lesson study in Japan and the United States. *Journal of Japan Society of Mathematical Education, 82*(12), 15–21.

Takahashi, A. (2011). The Japanese approach to developing expertise in using the textbook to teach mathematics rather than teaching the textbook. In Y. Li & G. Kaiser (Eds.), *Expertise in mathematics instruction: An international perspective* (pp. 197–219). Springer.

Takahashi, A. (2014). The role of the knowledgeable other in Lesson Study: Examining the final comments of experienced Lesson Study practitioners. *Mathematics Teacher Education and Development, 16*(1), 4–21. http://www.merga.net.au/ojs/index.php/mted/article/view/204

Takahashi, A., & McDougal, T. (2014). Implementing a new national curriculum: A Japanese public school's two-year Lesson-Study project. In A. R. McDuffie & K. S. Karp (Eds.), *Annual perspectives in mathematics education (APME) 2014: Using research to improve instruction* (pp. 13–21). National Council of Teachers of Mathematics. http://books.google.com/books?id=nHiEngEACAAJ

Takahashi, A., & McDougal, T. (2016, July). Collaborative lesson research: maximizing the impact of lesson study. *ZDM Mathematics Education, 48*(4), 513–526. 10.1007/s11858-015-0752-x

Takahashi, A., Watanabe, T., Yoshida, M., & Wand-Iverson, P. (2005). Improving content and pedagogical knowledge through Kyozaikenkyu. In P. Wang-Iverson & M. Yoshida (Eds.), *Building our understanding of lesson study* (pp. 101–110). Research for Better Schools.

Takahashi, A., & Yoshida, M. (2004, May). How can we start lesson study?: Ideas for establishing lesson study communities. *Teaching Children Mathematics, 10*(9), 436–443.

Watanabe, T., Takahashi, A., & Yoshida, M. (2008). Kyozaikenkyu: A critical step for conducting effective lesson study and beyond. In F. Arbaugh & P. M. Taylor (Eds.), *Inquiry into mathematics teacher education, Association of Mathematics Teacher Educators (AMTE) monograph series* (Vol. 5, pp. 131–142). Information Age Publishing.

Watanabe, T., & Wang-Iverson, P. (2005). The role of knowledgeable others. In P. Wang-Iverson & M. Yoshida (Eds.), *Building our understanding of lesson study* (pp. 85–91). Research for Better Schools.

Yoshida, M. (1999). *Lesson study: A case study of a Japanese approach to improving instruction through school-based teacher development* [Dissertation, University of Chicago]. Chicago.

1.2 Issues in adopting and adapting Lesson Study

Geoffrey Wake

> For Japanese educators, Lesson Study is like air, felt everywhere because it is implemented in everyday school activities.
>
> (Fujii, 2014, p. 68)

The above quote by Professor Fujii, of Tokyo Gakugei University, has become increasingly used in writing and discussion about the place of Lesson Study in the lives of teachers in Japan. It illustrates how Lesson Study is a fundamental part of their professional lives: it is an important part of what it means to be a teacher. Lesson Study provides an important part of professional learning throughout their careers. This places the learning of both students and teachers firmly central to "teacher work". It's not good enough to ensure student learning as a teacher: we also need to consider our own learning throughout our career. I presume that not many of us would argue against such a statement, but why are lesson studies, or more specifically Collaborative Lesson Research the way of achieving this? And how can we adopt and adapt the Japanese model of Lesson Study to work in a different socio-cultural setting in distant countries?

1.2.1 Japanese Lesson Study: Why the interest?

To be frank, the attainment of Japanese students in international tests in mathematics, such as the OECD's PISA programme[1] is primarily responsible for the interest in Lesson Study that has been generated around the world. As educators sought to understand how they might replicate the high level of mathematical proficiency that was clearly evident in Japan, Stigler and Hiebert in the volume *The Teaching Gap* (1999) reported outcomes of a video study that examined teaching in three countries: the United States, Japan, and Germany. Distinct differences in teaching and lesson structure in Japan compared to the other two countries led to a focus on Lesson Study that facilitated teachers' learning in Japan where the process of Lesson Study led to teachers' learning about both pedagogical and didactical issues in mathematics teaching. The focus of this collaborative learning is teacher knowledge, both of individuals and communities (Wake, 2023), in relation to the mathematics and how, as teachers, we engage students with mathematical knowledge and understanding.

It is also perhaps not surprising that Japanese Lesson Study has attracted the attention of educators around the world – as a professional learning experience it connects directly with the core business of teachers, that of teaching in classrooms. It is not by chance that it meets all the key features of good quality professional development that research points us to. Research suggests that high-quality professional learning activity is as follows:

DOI: 10.4324/9781003375272-3

- *Experiential*: stimulating and drawing on teachers' experiences
- *Sustained*: cycles of planning, predicting, enactment, and reflection
- *Grounded*: practical, well-resourced; related to context and culture
- *Safe*: teachers able to speak their minds, permission to take risks
- *Collaborative*: involving networks of teachers and administrators
- *Informed*: by outside expertise and research
- *Provocative*: involving both pressure and support
- *Focused*: attentive to the development of the mathematics itself

(See, e.g., Guskey & Yoon, 2009; Joubert & Sutherland, 2009; Villegas-Reimers, 2003.)

Lesson studies have proved attractive to educators from across the world and many have considered adopting or adapting the Japanese model in some way to engage teachers in their countries in programmes of professional learning. Personally, I have been part of a group(s) attempting to do this from 2012 onwards. As part of a team of university researchers and curriculum developers at the University of Nottingham, our initial contact was with colleagues in Japan who carried out similar work in relation to mathematical problem solving and modelling. Engaging in Lesson Study with our colleagues at Tokyo Gakugei University, we had an opportunity to observe how teachers were working with students on tasks that were designed in England and adapted for use in Japanese classrooms. We soon explored the potential of doing likewise here in England and have consequently become involved since that time in including modified versions of Lesson Study in many of our research projects. In the rest of this chapter, I reflect on some of the issues we have met in attempting to adopt and adapt Lesson Study to support teacher learning in our own country (the United Kingdom). These reflections are far from exhaustive: I first consider some issues in relation to learning more generally but which seem important because they underpin my own understanding of why CLR works in the way that it does. I go on to consider some of the main features of the process of CLR before focusing on the question of what it is that we wish to adopt or adapt. Finally, I consider, what for me often seems to be omitted in discussions of making CLR work: that of the important role of the *broker*.

1.2.2 Socio-cultural context and learning

All Lesson Study/CLR communities have a shared purpose in general terms – they have the purpose of developing professional knowledge – teacher learning is central to the activity. But what do we mean by "learning"? Throughout my own work, with both students in schools and with teachers, I have taken a socio-cultural view of learning. I consider that learning involves more than knowledge that resides in the individual. I take the broader view that it is collectively distributed and constructed. I am particularly drawn to the model of learning that Etienne Wenger (1998) proposes in relation to communities of practice. Fundamental to Wenger's thinking is the idea that learning is about practice (i.e., being able to do something as part of a collective – the community), developing identity (i.e., becoming someone who identifies as a participant in the practice of the community), making meaning of the practice(s) of the community, as they become part of, and active as a participant in it. Throughout this volume, the authors of the different chapters consider that as teachers, lesson studies can become part of our practice in ways that facilitate an expanded notion of teaching and teachers in ways that encompass professional learning which I recognise as being in line with Wenger's model of learning.

Of course, lesson studies or CLR will be just a part of our professional and wider lives: we live in ways that bring together our participation in multiple communities (of practice).

As individuals, we understand our self as being an amalgam of the identities that these different experiences provide, and these in turn reflect the culture and infrastructures in which we live and work.

I can only start to imagine what it is like to be a teacher in Japan – if I think about all the unknowns I have about living and working in Japan and how these will impact teaching, the practice of Lesson Study becomes a conundrum. As an outsider, there is so much we don't know, and we even don't know what to ask about, if we want to understand teachers' and students' behaviours in the cultural context of Japan. If you have the privilege of observing a research lesson in Japan, you might like to reflect on the way in which teachers interact with one another, likewise students, and both more widely in other parts of the school day. For example, what about hierarchies in the school system and society more generally? How do the resulting relationships between teachers impact Lesson Study as a collaborative endeavour? On one visit to Japan, I and another researcher interviewed teachers, head teachers, university educators, school leaders in schools, at prefecture level, subject association leaders, and so on, to get a sense of the infrastructure that supports Lesson Study activity in slightly different formats. This gave just a sense of some of the similarities, but mainly differences between lesson studies in our different countries and the structures and cultures that can act to support or challenge implementation of our different manifestations of Lesson Study.

On reflection, developing a flexibility and pragmatism that is sensitive to your own national setting is important as you work to develop a model of Lesson Study as a professional practice: it seems better to have an adapted model that works for you and colleagues than aiming to replicate what you might observe of what works in Japan. Almost without exception, only cultural natives can have the knowledge and sensitivities to sufficiently understand what might work in their country setting. It is important to be aware of the issues that this raises as we endeavour to develop a model of CLR that works for us.

1.2.3 Lesson Study, CLR, or something else?

If you are reading this as someone who is new to the idea of lesson studies or CLR, it may be the case that you believe that there is one model of Lesson Study in Japan that is practised everywhere. This, inevitably perhaps, is not the case. There are many ways of operationalising Lesson Study – even in Japan. Perhaps the model that is most prevalent in Japan is that practised within a single school. This sits within an annual research theme, with teachers seeking to answer the questions they have in relation to this theme in the research lessons that are part of their Lesson Study cycles. However, there are many different variations of such Lesson Study that connect individuals and communities of teachers within and across schools. For example, in addition to the within-school model lesson studies may be (i) organised by subject associations, (ii) as part of a university-led research group exploring potential curriculum innovation, (iii) as an annual open house Lesson Study in which a school shares their within school learning more widely, (iv) as demonstration lessons, with many teachers attending, to disseminate certain ways of teaching more widely at a prefecture or even national level, and so on.

In working to adopt and adapt Lesson Study in schools in Chicago, USA, my co-editor, Akihiko Takahashi and his colleague Tom McDougal, in response to Lesson Study being used as a term to describe many different models of (non-Japanese) lesson studies, have coined the term *Collaborative Lesson Research* to distinguish this as being closer to the Japanese model than some, and as a way of capturing the importance of collaboration, lessons and (teacher) research as being essential ingredients. In Chapter 1.1, they identify six essential elements of CLR. Here, I emphasise that the term CLR itself implies that it:

- is **collaborative**: teachers and other educators come together to consider their professional knowledge
- involves collaborative observation of a lesson
- has **research** as central: there is a question about professional practice about teaching in classrooms that the CLR group seeks to answer

Further to these features, I would also emphasise that CLR requires:

- joint engagement by the group, prior to the lesson to consider the proposal for the lesson and to consider what the teacher will do and their students' likely resulting responses
- post-lesson discussion in which there is collaborative reflection on what happened

There is one other feature of our Lesson Study work that I would highlight: there being some outside (to the group) expertise in addition to the wealth of knowledge that members of the group bring to their activities. Ideally this "knowledgeable other" has both knowledge of CLR as well as knowledge of the subject area/focus of the group. We have found this very helpful in stimulating thinking in the group, especially thinking about how to keep the momentum of the group moving forward. This is particularly important as a group works to become more firmly established; however, that can prove particularly problematic as I highlight below.

1.2.4 Adopting vs adapting

There is only one-letter difference between the words adopt and adapt but they imply very different activities. I have met the same issue and a similar conundrum about the use of words in discussion about whether we can *transfer* mathematical practices from one problem context to another or do we need to *transform* them. Again, two similar words, but the second word in each case, adapt and transform, suggest that we need to do more to make something work in the new context. Lesson Study, as practised in Japan, is not transportable intact. Although we do need to ensure that we don't lose its essential features, we have to make adaptations, take ownership of the process, and ensure it "fits in" and works for us. Fundamentally, this is a matter of careful (re-)design.

Seleznyov (2018), in her review of the translation of Lesson Study beyond Japan, provides insight into the form that adaptations of LS take that are reported in the research literature. As might be expected, the features of Lesson Study that are most successfully translated into practice in other countries are those that are most central to the "research lesson" of the Lesson Study cycle: that is the collaborative observation and post-lesson discussion. On the other hand, the processes of engaging in *kyouzai kenkyuu* and the involvement of outside expertise are most frequently omitted. This will be for different reasons in the different countries of the studies surveyed by Selezynov's research, which raises questions for those involved in adapting Lesson Study for use in our own settings to consider how we might effectively engage in these aspects of the Japanese model of Lesson Study.

Although day-to-day practice in school mathematics classrooms can look very similar in countries around the world, this all takes place within a wide range of overarching school systems and structures: and importantly expectations of what constitutes a mathematics lesson by the important stakeholders of students and their parents. We, as teachers, have many other demands in our work in preparing for, and carrying out, classroom teaching. For example, we have to prepare students for examinations, choose resources to work with, develop sequences of lessons, and so on. We all have lessons as central to our work, but how do we expand that work to include lesson studies? How do we collaborate with others? Either within school or across schools?

This is where we have to be creative and consider how we can make structures and systems work for us in ways that help us meet the essential features of CLR, or at least as many as we can without ending up with an impoverished model. In my experience in the United Kingdom and more widely across Europe, at any moment in time, there are many initiatives in mathematics education that basically seek to develop teaching in ways that lead to improvements in student learning. CLR, or a slight variation of this, can often add value to these initiatives: primarily by bringing teachers together to share their developing expertise. For example, in the United Kingdom, there is currently much interest in ensuring that teaching becomes more evidence-led or research-informed. Our research group at the University of Nottingham has been working with partnership schools to consider how we might better connect research and lessons. In this work, we have included a number of CLR cycles. These are adapted from a standard or "pure" model of CLR by including additional workshops to provide time for teachers to engage with at least some of the appropriate research in the areas of variation theory and the use of representations. These provide an opportunity to engage in a structured way in a form of *kyouzai kenkyuu*. We also embedded our cycles of CLR in the wider project that included a mini-conference to which we invited teachers and researchers more widely allowing an opportunity to disseminate our learning and CLR more substantially.

In another variation, we embedded a modified version of CLR within a large-scale trial of new approaches to teaching. We write about this in more detail in Chapter 2.2, but here note how fundamentally teachers were not directly involved in the lesson planning process. Whilst this seems contrary to the essential ingredients of CLR that I identified earlier, we did ensure that all participants had opportunities to engage fully in understanding the intentions of the lesson designs and even teach the lesson before attending the research lesson that was part of the CLR cycle. In this way, we were able to adapt the model of CLR in ways that ensured as many teachers as possible were able to benefit from the experience.

In these different adaptations of the CLR model, we have been able to ensure that we have widened our CLR base whilst meeting expectations of both funders and participants in these different aspects of our work.

1.2.5 Very important people: Brokers

Lesson Study is an activity that is for and depends on, people: it's a socio-cultural activity that occurs over time. As such, there are key people who make sure it works. They have a shared vision and purpose: as part of this they want to come together regularly in pursuit of joint activity. Etienne Wenger terms such groups, *communities of practice*. Central to any community of practice is that Wenger considers it as a learning community and its participants as learners. He takes a socio-cultural view of learning and points to practice, identity development, making meaning, and developing a sense of community as being the key elements of such learning. These important underlying aims seem particularly aligned with the intentions of CLR.

Here I want to emphasise the important role that someone with particular enthusiasms and talents needs to fill. In Etinenne Wenger's discussion of *Communities of Practice*,he identifies such people and uses the term brokers to indicate their essential role as key networkers. They have a clear vision of what they are aiming to achieve and have the wherewithal to facilitate the emergence and development of the Lesson Study community in the particular context in which they work. Their particular talent is one that is often especially pragmatic and innovative as they often know how to ensure that the new community is able to get support from leadership and can attract the provision of the necessary resources that the group needs. For example, as many others throughout this handbook comment, CLR as a quality experience for teachers and other educators requires time for teachers to work together. It appears that in Japan, where Lesson Study is well-established, patterns of teachers' work provide for them to come together to take part in collaborative planning, observation, and reflections. How can this be achieved in an environment of competing priorities?

It is my observation that the CLR community can benefit immensely from a broker who can work out how to ensure that CLR can be seen as a potential answer to other current issues, problems and questions, and consequently has the potential to gain the support of leadership and the resource that will ensure it gets off the ground. Ideally, it's presented as the answer to problems that are considered of the moment and of utmost importance. Brokers can make this happen because of their knowledge of context and because they are networked into and beyond school leadership. This often allows them to gain access to sources of funding that may support the group: for example, it can provide funding to pay for teachers who can deputise for others so that they might be released from their own teaching to attend research lessons in their own or other schools. They are knowledgeable about, and advocates for, CLR and can provide guidance and support to groups as they make their journey from initiation through development to becoming well established.

In my experience, brokers are people who can turn challenges into opportunities. By necessity, the world of Lesson Study is full of such optimists!

In summary, it has been our experience, here in the United Kingdom that whilst current systems and structures might seem to be difficult to work within to establish CLR as a mode of deep professional learning, it is possible if we consider adaptation rather than adoption. We need to be creative and flexible to ensure that we stay true to the essential features of CLR/Lesson Study as much as possible, but to adopt a level of pragmatism to get things working. Identifying key *brokers* who can help in this regard seems important, if not essential. It is often their knowledge and enthusiasm as well as the networks that they span that can help get things up and running.

Note

1 https://www.oecd.org/pisa/aboutpisa/

References

Guskey, T. R., & Yoon, K. S. (2009). What works in professional development? *Phi Delta Kappan*, 90(7), 495–500.

Joubert, M. V., & Sutherland, R. J. (2009). *A perspective on the literature: CPD for teachers of mathematics*. National Centre for Excellence in the Teaching of Mathematics.

Seleznyov, S. (2018). Lesson study: An exploration of its translation beyond Japan. *International Journal for Lesson and Learning Studies, 7*(3), 217–229. 10.1108/ IJLLS-04-2018-0020

Stigler, J., & Hiebert, J. (1999). *The teaching gap: Best ideas from the world's teachers for improving education in the classroom.* New York: Free Press.

Villegas-Reimers, E. 2003. *Teacher professional development: An international review of the literature.* Paris: International Institute of Educational Planning, UNESCO.

Wake, G. (2023). Designing lesson study for individual and collective learning: Networking theoretical perspectives. *International Journal for Lesson and Learning Studies, 12*(1), 7–20. 10.1108/ IJLLS-08-2022-0111

Wenger, E. (1998). *Communities of practice: Learning, meaning, and identity.* New York: Cambridge University Press.

Part 2

Exemplary Collaborative Lesson Research

2.1 A case study of school-wide Collaborative Lesson Research
Lake View High School in Chicago

Thomas McDougal

In 2016, the math department at Lake View High School (LVHS) was like a lot of high school math departments in the United States. Most instruction was teacher-centered direct instruction. Despite pockets of excellence, good ideas and effective practices remained siloed with individual teachers because there was no culture of collaboration. Teachers taught with their doors closed and didn't discuss much of what went on behind them. Even if there had been collaboration, there was no shared consensus about what good math teaching looked like. Instead, there was a common feeling among the teachers that the teaching was fine, but the students were not capable of doing challenging mathematics. In fact, some were trying to persuade their new principal, Dr. Paul "P.J." Karafiol, that there should be a distinct course in between the regular track and the team-taught classes (which had a specialized teacher to support diverse learners). Karafiol refused to do so unless they could produce a curriculum for the course that would prepare the students for the standardized achievement tests that students take in their last year of high school. The teachers never did.

In the spring of 2017, with encouragement from Karafiol, three math teachers and an assistant principal attended the Chicago Lesson Study Conference. In the following school year, the math department began using Collaborative Lesson Research (CLR) to examine their teaching.

Five years later, it is a very different math department. In their department meetings, teachers regularly present to each other about practices that are working for their students, and those practices are getting picked up by others. There is a culture of what the principal calls "critical collaboration", a willingness to share ideas and argue about whether those ideas are good ones. The teaching of mathematics has become more problem-solving-oriented and less teacher-centered. They have decided as a department that they want to cultivate more mathematical discourse among the students. The teachers even gather socially out of school, and when they do, in Unander's words, "They do math".

This chapter describes the evolution of CLR at this one high school as a model of how CLR can be introduced and spread department-wide or even school-wide as a structure to support improvements in teaching. The steps, missteps, and experiences at this school provide valuable lessons to educators interested in introducing CLR elsewhere. The following section describes the evolution of CLR at Lake View, while later sections will reflect on the impacts of CLR and lessons learned from the Lake View experience that could guide other schools seeking to implement CLR.

The chronology

Table 2.1.1 contains a summary of CLR activities at Lake View.

DOI: 10.4324/9781003375272-5

Table 2.1.1 A timeline of Collaborative Lesson Research activities at Lake View High School in Chicago

Year	Activities and key personnel
2016–2017	May: Chicago Lesson Study Conference (Unander, Rosenberg, Johnson, Vast-Binder)
2017–2018	May: Research Lesson (Geometry): Probability as a ratio of areas (Rosenberg)
	May: Chicago Lesson Study Conference (Unander, Boes, Cimaglia, Wittenwyler, London, Lis)
2018–2019	Nov.: Research Lesson (Geometry): Sum of exterior angles (Tamburello & London)
	Feb.: Research Lesson (Algebra 1): Intersections of graphs/systems (Cimaglia)
	Mar: Research Lesson (Geometry): Similarity (Johnson & Wittenwyler)
	May: Chicago Lesson Study Conference (Stein, Mah, Unander, Sovell, Bringer, Tamburello, Montana)
2019–2020	Nov.: Research Lesson (Geom) Perp bisector … paper folding (Unander)
	Dec.: Research Lesson (English) Dog in the Nighttime/Courage
	Jan.: Research Lesson (Algebra 1) Rates of change (Lis)
	Feb.: Research Lesson (Algebra 2) Complex numbers (Brown)
	Feb.: Research Lesson (World Studies) Creoles & revolution in Lat. Am. (Fehr, Gioia)
	Additional research lessons and the Chicago conference canceled due to Covid

In the 2016–2017 school year, the geometry team had begun experimenting with a new curriculum that was more problem-based than their previous one. Despite the challenges of implementing this new approach, the teachers were pretty sure this was an important improvement over what they had been doing. But the department chair, Erin Unander, who also taught geometry, felt that the department was stagnating due to a lack of collaboration.

In February 2017, her principal forwarded to her an announcement about the upcoming Chicago Lesson Study Conference. "This might be a great place to send folks to think about working on complex tasks", he wrote. Karafiol had had experience with Lesson Study at a previous school, but he was being deliberately low-key about introducing it as a new principal.

Unander was initially skeptical. According to the announcement, the conference seemed oriented towards elementary school teachers: it was going to feature a lesson for ten-year-old students and a lesson for eight-year-old students. The relevance of the event to high school mathematics was not obvious. Nonetheless, she brought the idea to her department, and, ultimately, she chose to attend along with two other geometry teachers and an assistant principal.

They were not disappointed. "Once the lessons started", Unander recounted, "it didn't matter that it was elementary school. You were seeing students working on a problem, talking about their ideas, very much what we were trying to get in our lessons". Even more important, in the panel discussions, the teachers who had planned the research lessons described exactly the kind of teacher collaboration that she and her colleagues were hungry for. "It was such an amazing experience", she said. "To hear teachers talk about planning together, about students, about mathematics … It was wonderful".

They were excited to try this themselves. The following winter, the school administration provided two days of substitute coverage so that the entire geometry team – seven teachers, including Unander – could meet at a nearby coffee shop to plan their first research lesson.

The first lesson was in February 2018. The lesson they chose was based on a lesson in their new textbook on estimating the area of a closed curve. In their research lesson proposal, they noted the challenges they were experiencing as they tried to push students to be more independent:

As we have moved to a curriculum that has a heavier emphasis on student discovery and student thought, ... [we] see a lot of students shutting down prior to engaging with the task and a lot of stalling out as the tasks push them to think deeply about the subject. As a geometry team, we want to expand our ability to build and maintain a classroom that is conducive to student problem solving.

The results of their first research lesson were not what they hoped for. Although they had hoped to observe student perseverance and critical thinking, they hadn't thought clearly about what the indicators of those would be, and so the observers were unable to provide good evidence of what was happening "inside the students' heads". Based on what was observed, they believed that direct instruction, which was given after some students had presented their own methods, had not advanced student thinking and may have devalued the student ideas.

In their second research lesson, the geometry team explicitly thought about how to make student thinking visible and felt the lesson was more successful than the first in that regard. In the post-lesson discussion, however, they realized that the level of cognitive demand was low, and realized that was probably a common problem they needed to fix:

As a team we have made great progress during this cycle of lesson study in our approach to eliciting and using student thinking in the classroom. ... That being said, these practices will only take the class as far as the mathematics at hand in the lesson. As a team, we need to trust our students with cognitively rigorous tasks, believe that they will rise to the challenges that we present them, and support them through the challenge without removing the cognitive demand ... .

Thanks to significant logistical support organized by the school administrators, all teachers from the math department were freed to observe both research lessons and participate in both post-lesson discussions. Although some of them were uneasy about the critical scrutiny each lesson received, the members of the planning team reassured their colleagues that this was what they wanted, and there was at least tentative interest from the algebra team in trying Lesson Study.

In May 2018, the school again sent Unander to the Chicago Lesson Study conference along with five teachers from the algebra team. This time, in addition to a lesson for eight-year-old students, there was one algebra lesson, albeit with twelve-year-old students. As before, however, the topic or grade level of the lessons was less significant to the Lake View teachers than the level of discussion they got to observe about teaching and student thinking. They also had opportunities to talk one-on-one with teachers who were already involved in Lesson Study. This experience helped solidify the algebra team's commitment to follow the geometry team's lead.

In the following year, the geometry team conducted another two research lessons, and the algebra team did one. An interesting feature of the research lesson by the Algebra team is that they explicitly incorporated some ideas from a school-wide powerful instruction practice, Reading Apprenticeship, as a way to address an overall goal of raising the level of student mathematical discourse.

Teachers in other departments were hearing from the math teachers about this process that they both enjoyed – even though it was hard work – and that they thought was helping them get better. And Erin Unander was seeing exactly those changes in the dynamics of her department that she and some of her colleagues had hoped for. Teachers were talking informally about their lessons and about teaching much more than before they had started CLR. The administration also noticed these changes, and interest grew in expanding CLR into the other departments. So, when Unander again attended the Chicago Lesson Study Conference in May of 2019, the chair of the English department attended as well, along with the assistant principal who oversaw English and four math teachers from the Algebra 2 team. Fortunately, this conference had a humanities research lesson with age 12 students in addition to several mathematics lessons, which gave the AP and the English chair a chance to see how CLR worked outside of mathematics.

Following this experience, the school administrators and department chairs created a plan for the 2019–2020 school year to have two research lessons each in English and Social Studies, plus two each in Algebra, Geometry, and Algebra 2.

Each team did in fact complete one research lesson – a total of five – just before the COVID-19 pandemic led to a shutdown of in-school learning in Chicago. For the next two and a half years, the teachers at LVHS – like most teachers in Chicago generally, were too stretched, first with trying to adapt to online instruction, then with dealing with the social-emotional impacts of the pandemic on their students. Only in the fall of 2022, as this is being written, do teachers feel like they might have the capacity to plan research lessons again.

Reflecting on the Lake View experience

Impacts of CLR

With each grade-level team, the act of planning their first research lessons was like a seed that sprouted the next year, in the form of a noticeable increase in day-to-day collaboration and changes in teaching. Teachers talked more intentionally with each other about their students – not just kvetching but analyzing their thinking and learning. They talked about their unit plans and lesson plans; they thought more critically about what each piece of their lessons was supposed to accomplish. They developed joint formative assessments. The algebra team developed a common course calendar and began using the algebra text from the same problem-oriented curriculum that the geometry team was using. Across the department, the teachers got used to observing each other. When he visited the math classes, Karafiol could see that students were being given more opportunities to figure things out for themselves. In the research lessons, the teams began to focus on cultivating student discourse, and that carried over into their everyday lessons as well. "We are doing such a better job of anticipating student responses", says Unander, and thus planning to address student difficulties.

All of the teachers appreciated the unique opportunity to have a full day to talk about teaching and about the contents. As one of the social studies teachers said, "It's an opportunity to step back from day-to-day teaching and think bigger". The social studies chair, Rachel Allmen, characterized the experience as providing a "north star", an ideal that can guide daily planning and give you a clearer target to strive for in daily lessons. Michael Lis, a veteran teacher on the algebra team who taught their research lesson in the third year, wrote that Lesson Study pushed his colleagues and him to think more critically and carefully about their lessons: "Why are we doing that?" he wrote. "Should we be doing that? How can we do that even better?"

Teachers wanted to see each other teach; previously there was no structure for it. Some (though not all) were also hungry to have their colleagues observe *them*, in a non-evaluative way. "The only time anyone came into our classroom", Unander said, "was for a learning walk or to do an evaluation". Although some teachers were initially uncomfortable with

Table 2.1.2 Lake View math teachers who participated in Lesson Study and the awards they received

Name	Award	Award date
Erin Unander	Golden Apple	2018
Stephen Cimaglia	Promising New Teacher (Illinois Council of Teachers of Mathematics)	2019
John Brown	Knowles Teaching Fellowship	2020
Peter Smith	Promising New Teacher (Illinois Council of Teachers of Mathematics)	2022

the critical spotlight of the post-lesson discussions, the teachers who taught the research lessons, and their colleagues on the planning team, were grateful for the feedback. "I liked hearing the perspectives of everyone else", Lis said. "That's so rare in teaching".

There is some outside validation of the positive impacts of lesson study on the department. Five teachers involved in teaching or planning research lessons were later recognized at the state or national level for their teaching and leadership (see Table 2.1.2). Dr. Karafiol proudly claims he now has "the best math department in the city". Acknowledging that there were other factors that contributed to the department's growth, he nonetheless credits Lesson Study as providing a structure that jump-started collaboration and supported innovation.

Transferable lessons learned

The experience at Lake View High School provides a path to CLR that other schools should be able to follow, along with a few missteps that other schools should avoid. The effort was encouraged and supported by the administration but was largely driven by the teachers. The principal strategically introduced the idea via his "change agents" (as Karafiol put it), key members of the geometry team. He leveraged their work, and the work of later planning teams, by investing in substitutes so that other teachers could observe the research lessons, as a way to draw them into the conversations about teaching and to let them learn about Lesson Study itself. He himself attended almost every research lesson, which communicated to the teachers that this was something he valued. But it was the teachers themselves who persuaded their colleagues that, despite the hard work, Lesson Study was not only valuable but even fun.

Having an opportunity to observe someone else's research lesson, and to talk with the teachers involved, was crucial. The geometry team got that experience by attending the Chicago Lesson Study Conference. The rest of the department was able to get that experience in-house, as mentioned earlier. The conference continued to be valuable, however. Michael Lis wrote:

> I remember [the conference] very well and the feeling of community with other teachers from other parts of the state, country and the world (I think some people were there from Qatar …) was wonderful. I don't think it's ever possible to get enough of that. We're all so locked in our own rooms and departments, you forget about how you are really a part of a massive group with similar hopes and goals. It really rejuvenated us to experience it.

But a research lesson can be like the exposed top of an iceberg, revealing little about the process that led up to it. As often happens, the LVHS geometry team, as well as some of the later teams, thought they knew what to do when they started planning their own research lesson, but made some mistakes. One mistake some of the teams made was to choose a lesson that was too soon to allow enough time for the necessary planning, which is understandable given the dramatic difference in intensity between planning a research lesson vs. everyday lesson planning. They also underestimated the amount of detail they needed to provide in their research lesson proposal. But they were also in some ways overly ambitious. "We thought the research lesson had to be something grandiose", Unander said. Eventually, they came to understand, partly by seeing the lessons at the conference, that a research lesson could be based on a regular lesson in their textbook.

In the third year, they also began inviting a knowledgeable other – the author of this chapter – to join one planning meeting for an hour or two. Having an outside perspective from someone experienced in lesson study helped push their thinking around their lesson design and helped them craft better research proposals.

Finally, the LVHS teachers did not fully appreciate the purpose of Lesson Study. They viewed it as a way to experiment with some new teaching strategies and a way to jump start collaboration. While it undeniably served these needs, they failed to appreciate its utility as a long-term approach to meeting the infinite challenges in teaching. According to Karafiol, there was a feeling in 2022 that they had "done" lesson study and had moved on. Karafiol was urging them to keep using it with a revised research goal (i.e., research theme). "I told them, 'Lesson Study is like a car. Yes, you can drive for fun, but really a car is a way to get somewhere you want to go'".

Recommendations

The LVHS principal and the teachers interviewed for this chapter agree on the following important principles for developing school-wide CLR.

Administrators must understand and support the work

Conducting Lesson Study in American schools is a counter-cultural effort that requires realigning resources – mainly, freeing teachers to plan and attend the lessons. The administration needs to believe that this investment of resources is worthwhile and understand that the payoff may take some time. At LVHS, the principal knew Lesson Study already from his time at another school, but he also sent assistant principals to the Chicago Lesson Study Conference so that they, too, would understand it. Then, either he or an assistant principal, or both, attended the research lessons, which was both a way to monitor the work and to communicate that they thought the work the teachers were doing was important.

Let the teachers be the main messengers. Let it grow organically

At LVHS, as at other schools, teachers were the best messengers when it came to convincing their colleagues to try Lesson Study. Although the principal introduced the idea initially, he was careful to position it as a possible solution to a problem the teachers were already wrestling with, and careful to let it be their choice. He also strategically introduced it to persons he thought might be the best "change agents". Unander wrote in an email, "[Karafiol] never forced us to do it but supported us 100%. He would visit us at our planning meetings and offer support. LS never felt like a mandate or something we felt pressured to do".

Have teachers (and administrators) observe research lessons elsewhere first

Observing someone else's research lesson is a low-investment way to learn about Lesson Study, to generate interest, and to give teachers a concrete vision of where they are going. Ideally, the observers would also have an opportunity to talk directly with teachers who have been doing Lesson Study. For LVHS, the Chicago Lesson Study Conference provided one opportunity for this, and all those who went found the experience energizing. Later, the in-house research lessons created easy opportunities for the entire math department and for teachers from other departments.

Provide teams with a guide, at least initially

Teachers need to understand both the purpose of Lesson Study and have an overview of the process. They need to know that their research lesson is meant to be a vehicle for exploring broader issues in teaching. They should identify a motivating research theme for their research lessons; ideally, this research theme should be constructed jointly by the whole department or school. Teams also need help understanding what is expected and setting a timetable for their work. All of this is difficult to understand from just observing a research lesson or reading an article. An experenced guide is crucial.

Enlist knowledgeable others

Having knowledgeable outsiders to give feedback during the planning phase and at the research lesson (i.e., final comments) significantly enriched the experience for the LVHS teachers. It was also helpful, especially in the beginning, to have someone experienced in Lesson Study serve as a sort of master of ceremonies for the research lessons themselves.

CLR had clear positive impacts on the professional culture in the math department at Lake View High School and on many individual teachers. Most important, it has changed the mathematics teaching that students experience there, making it more problem-based, more challenging, and more engaging. The lessons learned from the evolution of CLR at LVHS – starting with just a few of the geometry teachers, then spreading to the other math course teams and even to other departments – provide a guide for other schools, elementary or high schools, that may want to engage in CLR.

2.2   A case in Nottingham

Integrating lesson study into a research and innovation programme

Marie Joubert and Geoffrey Wake

In the United Kingdom, students who fail to achieve a pass mark in the public examination in mathematics taken at the age of 16 (GCSE) are required to attend mathematics lessons and re-take the examination in their further education (FE). These students are known as GCSE-resit students. Between 2018 and 2023, the government funded an initiative, the Centres for Excellence in Mathematics programme, designed, amongst other things, to improve the mathematical experience of these students.

The University of Nottingham was one of a number of partner organisations responsible for the project and our role involved organising, running and evaluating a randomised control trial of an intervention in which about 10,000 students were taught mathematics using a "mastery" approach. Another group of students were taught by teachers who had no intervention. The trial involved comparing examination results of those students who experienced the intervention and those who did not.

The students were in the classes of teachers who volunteered to take part in the trials. The teachers were randomly allocated to one of three groups, receiving the full intervention (41 teachers), partial intervention (29 teachers) and no intervention (53 teachers), respectively. In both the full- and partial-intervention groups, teachers were asked to adopt a mastery-teaching approach, and asked to teach at least one specially designed mastery lesson in each of five given time periods, or windows. They were further asked to adopt mastery approaches in all their mathematics lessons. Both groups took part in three days of professional development related to the teaching-for-mastery approach. This approach is described in a little more detail in Chapter 5.2.

The full intervention group additionally took part in a cycle of lesson study, once in each window, in small groups of three to six, which we called cluster groups: they used an adapted lesson study approach. The hypothesis underpinning this research design decision was that teachers who experienced the cycles of lesson study would develop a better understanding of teaching for mastery than those who did not, with a possible knock-on effect of their students achieving better results than those in the partial intervention group.

This chapter describes how our adapted lesson study approach was organised, what worked well, and the challenges we encountered.

2.2.1 Organisation of the lesson study

Prior to the trial, ten Lead Teachers were appointed to facilitate the cluster groups; these teachers had taken part in the pilot study for the trials and had some experience of both the teaching for mastery approach and the model of lesson study we were working to. They took part in two full days of professional development before the main intervention began

DOI: 10.4324/9781003375272-6

and one somewhere in the middle, to prepare them to run cluster meetings and to enhance their understanding of the teaching for mastery approach.

At the start of the intervention, all full- and partial-intervention teachers and all lead teachers participated in online professional development related to using the teaching for mastery approaches in teaching mathematics. Lead teachers and full-intervention teachers further took part in professional development designed to familiarise them with our lesson study model.

The intervention took place in one academic year; the five teaching windows were evenly spread throughout this period. The Lead Teachers organised their group's lesson-study meetings within this framework. It was decided in advance that the lesson-study meetings in Windows 3 and 4 would take place online, due to anticipated Covid-19 restrictions, but other than that, the Lead Teachers had autonomy in the organisation of the meetings. For the online meetings, one research lesson taught by a lead teacher was video recorded, with the camera on the teacher for whole-class teaching and on a pair of students, selected by the teacher, for students' individual activity or small group work.

2.2.2 A randomised control trial: Implications for the design of the lesson study activities

This section considers how the requirements of a randomised control trial influenced some of the design decisions we made. In the next section, examples are provided.

In a randomised control trial, participants in each group (in this case students) should have the same experience. All students of teachers who received the full intervention should have the same experience of mathematics, all those in the partial intervention should have the same experience which is slightly different to the experience of those in the full intervention group and all those in the control group should experience "business as usual". Here we are interested in the full intervention group.

The students in this group were to be taught mathematics using the teaching-for-mastery approach that we outline in Chapter 5.2. For the research there was a design decision about how to best achieve this: many lesson study groups design a lesson collaboratively, but the research team was of the view that the lessons, and importantly the teaching for mastery principles they embody, required greater levels of consistency than this could achieve. The option we adopted was to provide pre-designed teaching for mastery lessons; while this option potentially limits the benefits of taking part in lesson study, it was practical in terms of ensuring consistency in teaching approaches, and consequently in student experiences. The lessons could also be given to the teachers in partial intervention which limited, to some extent, at least, the ways in which teachers might interpret teaching for mastery and the ways in which students might experience this.

At the lesson study cluster meetings, Lead Teachers introduced the next lesson to be taught. They had been introduced to the lessons in their various professional development sessions, but there were still questions about how consistent they would be in passing that introduction on to the teachers in their cluster and what messages may be added or lost. Again, for the research, there was the tension of balancing the need for the Lead Teachers to have some autonomy in the cluster meetings with the need for a consistent experience for the teachers. We decided to produce materials (PowerPoint and written guidance) to support Lead Teachers in introducing the lesson. These materials for all the lessons can be found at: https://uniofnottm.sharepoint.com/:f:/r/sites/CfEM/Shared%20Documents/Research_trials/Research_trials_2020_2022/04_Professional_development_TT_and_LT/Cluster%203?csf=1&web=1&e=tPGzuj

A third, related tension, relates to the observation of the lesson. In lesson study, when teachers observe the research lesson, they do so with particular attention to the research questions developed within a research theme agreed by them the lesson study group. However, in our research, again with the intention of providing teachers with a uniform experience, we as the research team devised the research questions and the teachers did not contribute to developing them. We provided them with observation sheets https://uniofnottm.sharepoint.com/:f:/r/sites/CfEM/Shared%20Documents/Research_trials/Research_trials_2020_2022/04_Professional_development_TT_and_LT/Cluster%203?csf=1&web=1&e=tPGzuj which aimed to draw their attention to the teaching-for-mastery approach to help provide them with insights into issues that were the focus of the research questions for the lesson.

A vital aspect of the lesson study is the post-lesson discussion, to which there is often a contribution by an outside expert. However, the involvement of an outside expert would again perhaps introduce too much variation in the experiences of the participating teachers. This fourth design tension was addressed by asking the lead teachers to lead the discussion and providing them with guiding questions for them to use to structure the discussion.

2.2.3 Design decisions: What they tell us about lesson study

The previous section explained how the requirements of the randomised control trial resulted in some specific design decisions about how best to support a modified lesson study model. In summary, we provided participants in the full-intervention arm of the trial with examples: of pre-designed teaching for mastery lessons, materials to support the lead teachers, research questions and guiding questions for lead teachers.

Chapter 5.2 considers issues relating to the design of the research lessons in some detail. This chapter is more concerned with how we adapted the design of the lesson study so that it fitted with the research programme. The deliberate adaptations that we made serve to illustrate both how adaptations can ensure that a form of lesson study becomes central to teachers' experiences: in ways that may not have been possible if it weren't for the research programme and indeed the modifications that we made.

Importantly, at the heart of the mastery approach exemplified by the lessons we had authored, are five key principles, such as, for example, "develop an understanding of mathematical structure" and "develop a collaborative culture in which everyone believes that everyone can succeed". The lessons provided detailed guidance for teachers about not only what they and the students should do at each stage of the lesson but also how the lesson structure and its activities exemplify and contribute towards the key principles. We reflect on some of these issues of design in more detail in Chapter 5.2; however, here we remark that our adaptation that took some of the decisions that we make in typical lesson study practices out of the hands of the lesson study group, meant that we could perhaps make a more effective start than may have been possible otherwise. Our experiences of working with groups starting out on a lesson study journey is that, because it introduces a number of new experiences, and indeed a new community into the busy lives of teachers, it takes both considerable levels of support, and indeed time for teachers to get involved. It is a "slow burn". When introducing lesson study we may wish to make adaptations that scaffold the work of the new and emerging community by taking away some of the flexibility that lesson study as a process offers. For example, defining with some clarity the

Lesson 4 Explore 2

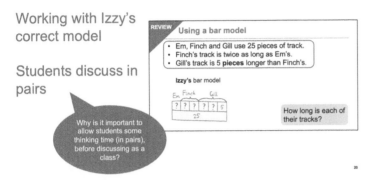

Figures 2.2.1 Questions designed to engage teachers with the design of the lesson.

research theme, the research questions, and the general underlying principles of what will be worked on/researched in the lesson study cycles.

The guidance and support materials for the lead teachers included two main sections, as explained above. The first was a detailed introduction to the forthcoming lesson, on PowerPoint, with accompanying notes. This included: a discussion of the structure and content of the lesson; a range of questions designed to engage the teachers with the design of the lesson and the mastery principles; and a discussion of likely student responses. Figures 2.2.1 and 2.2.2 give two examples from the introduction to a lesson designed to promote algebraic thinking, of the sorts of questions included.

Teachers were also asked to take the role of students and try out the student activities themselves. When the cluster meetings took place online, an electronic version of the student activity was provided, using Jamboard, Desmos Classroom or interactive worksheets. Figure 2.2.3 shows one of the slides from the Desmos activity teachers were asked to work through to familiarise themselves with the student task. It follows a drag-

Lesson 4 Explore/discuss 3 - Main student activity

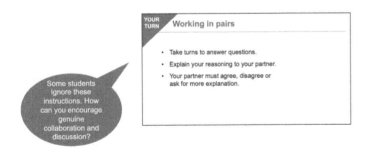

Figures 2.2.2 Questions designed to engage teachers with the design of the lesson.

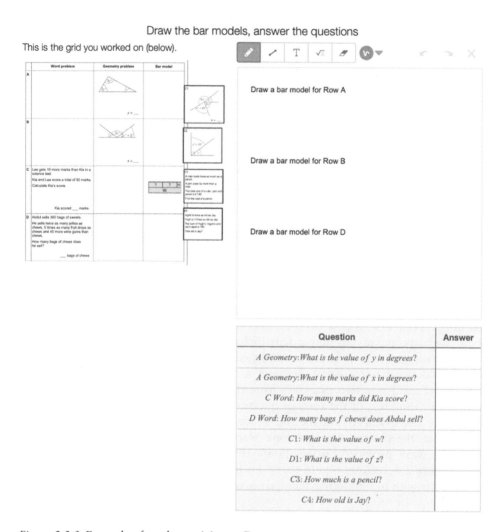

Figure 2.2.3 Example of teacher activity on Desmos.

and-drop activity in which teachers dragged four cards onto the appropriate cell on a background grid.[1]

In terms of the observation of the lesson at the cluster meeting, each lesson included two research questions, one with a pedagogic focus and one with a mathematics focus. At the heart of the mastery approach used in the trial are five mastery key principles and the questions were designed to emphasise these key principles. The research questions used in the algebraic thinking lesson are as follows:

- Pedagogic focus: in what ways does the teacher develop and bring the lesson to a close to support a culture where everyone believes everyone can succeed?
- Maths focus: in what ways do students use representations to access the structure of mathematical problems?

For the teacher guidance, the following list of questions, again related to the algebraic thinking lesson, was provided to help the lead teacher structure the post-lesson discussion:

- How well did students appear to understand how to use the rules given to determine the length of the different walls and train track?
- How did the students talk about finding the base value?
- What did you notice about the way the students drew bar diagrams?
- What did the students do when they were asked to discuss the geometry diagrams?
- Where did students appear to get stuck, or have difficulties?
- How did the class discuss the completed grid and to what extent did they move beyond checking the answers? Did they appear to be making connections between the word problems, the geometry diagrams and the bar models?

2.2.4 Comments, reflection, and discussion

An implementation and process evaluation of the trial took place, and the data for the evaluation included case studies of six full-intervention teachers, two from each of the three cluster groups. These six teachers were observed teaching all five research lessons to one of their classes and at cluster group lesson study meetings. The six teachers and the three lead teachers of their cluster groups were interviewed. A focus group meeting of five lead teachers also took place after the intervention. All teachers were surveyed at the end of the intervention.

The observation data suggests that the lesson study meetings were broadly in line with the guidance given in the support materials.

Both the trial teachers and the lead teachers appeared to benefit from the process. They found it valuable to meet and talk about their experiences of teaching a particular lesson. As one lead teacher explained,

> I think the fact that they get to talk to each other and exchange their own experiences and have a chat about 'that worked for me' or 'well it didn't work for me'. Allows them to reflect a little bit more as well, and maybe make some changes.
>
> (LT2, interview 3)

Almost all the six teachers and the three lead teachers reported that they particularly valued the opportunity to observe another teacher teaching a lesson. Some of them referred to what they learned in terms of teaching, such as the trial teacher who mentioned developing perseverance:

> But it is the most amazing experience to be able to watch someone else teach, and I think Andrew's lesson in particular really showed me value of perseverance, particularly with students who appear to be disengaged.
>
> (TT157, interview 2)

Others mentioned the value of observing students closely, such as the lead teacher who explained:

You are able to see the interaction between the students, you are able to see how they're behaving with the material and that's what hopefully they *(the trial teachers in his group)* got out of it.

(LT3, interview 2)

Finally, while it may not be usual or common for lesson study (or a version of lesson study) to be incorporated into a randomised control trial, our research has shown that it is possible and that teachers benefitted from taking part and reported that they enjoyed it.

Note

1 The activity can be found here: https://student.desmos.com/join/8amk72

2.3 A case study

The important role of the knowledgeable other in supporting planning teams in SW England

Ruth Trundley

Introduction

This section will explore the experience of lesson study from the perspective of the Devon Maths team, a team of four advisers that I am privileged to lead. We work with all those involved in learning and teaching mathematics, mainly in primary schools (learners from 4 to 11): locally (Devon has more than 300 primary schools); nationally and internationally. Our work involves providing professional development and tailored support, leading and participating in research projects, and developing materials. All of our work has a focus on mathematical thinking.

The team's earliest involvement with lesson study was as part of the National Numeracy Strategy (NNS) which was a government-funded initiative in England from 1999 to 2011. The inclusion of lesson study in the NNS approach was heavily influenced by the publication of *The Teaching Gap* (Stigler & Hiebert, 1999) and by Pete Dudley, who was director of the Primary National Strategies from 2006 to 2011. Our understanding was that with lesson study we should focus on: teaching an observed lesson; collaborative post-lesson discussion, with the intention of identifying ways to improve the lesson; reteaching the lesson; and observing the impact of the changes made. The "improve and reteach" elements could happen multiple times in a lesson study cycle.

We were unaware of how different our approach was to Japanese practice until 2016, when we had the opportunity to speak with and listen to three experts in Japanese lesson study: Akihiko Takahashi, Toshiakira Fujii, and Keiichi Nishimura. We were immediately aware of two key differences between our practice and the approach in Japan. The first of these differences was the minimal time and attention we gave to teacher learning prior to the research lesson. Connected to this was the focus on adapting the lesson to then reteach it, potentially aiming to perfect the teaching of the lesson. This was addressed with passion by Fujii during his talk, where he stated:

Re-teaching is disrespectful of the students' right to the best education one can provide them. Having the thought of re-teaching at the back of one's mind is like making the first class a pawn in order to improve classroom teaching. This benefits teachers and lesson plan makers at the expense of the children.

Fujii (2016)

Readings, including Fujii (2014) and Takahashi and Mcdougal (2016), participation in the International Math-teacher Professionalisation Using Lesson Study (IMPULS) programme in 2017 and working with the Collaborative Lesson Research UK (CLR UK) group supported us to start developing a different approach to lesson study.

DOI: 10.4324/9781003375272-7

We immediately made changes within an action research project we had planned, extending the time spent on learning prior to the research lesson and removing re-teaching. The lesson study cycles we then led and experienced as part of this project were more closely matched to the Japanese approach. We recognised that this approach resulted in more opportunity for professional learning, provoking teachers to reveal (to themselves and others) what they really think and understand about both mathematics and mathematics teaching and learning. These early experiences of CLR presented challenges, which led us to identify adaptations we needed to make, mainly because of our professional, cultural, geographical and education contexts.

Multi-school planning teams

As a team of maths advisers, we are not school situated and much of our work within professional development programmes and research projects involves teachers from multiple schools. Working with multi-school planning teams means thinking differently about how to identify a research theme. We use the following:

- Themes to address local issues identified by the maths team, often arising from work with mathematics subject leaders across Devon. For example, in 2021 we initiated three cycles of CLR; the research theme, *building communities that encourage mathematical behaviours by providing opportunities to reason and by supporting oracy,* emerged from local teachers who identified it as a result of considering the impact of the previous 16 months of COVID disruption.
- Themes linked to a research project. For example, in 2019 we supported a cycle of CLR as part of an international research project looking at student understanding of structured number lines. The research question was: *What are the key elements to understanding number lines as representations of the number system and how does this understanding support children to make decisions when calculating?*

Support for the planning team (role of the knowledgeable other)

Our early experiences led us to identify that support for the planning team is essential; in Japan, where lesson study is established, schools have teachers who are highly experienced both in the classroom and in participating in lesson study and so planning teams do not usually need the support of an external knowledgeable other. We are working in a context where there is little existing experience of lesson study in schools so one of our main roles is to support the planning team. We made mistakes early on by offering too many new elements for teachers to focus on at the same time. As the cycles were part of a research study and the CLR approach was new to the teachers, they were grappling with understanding: the research area; collaborative lesson research; teaching through problem-solving; and the mathematics content. One of the ways we have addressed this is by working on mathematics content (subject knowledge) at the start of each cycle.

Mathematics content

We quickly recognised that, unlike in Japan, we cannot assume a shared understanding of the mathematics content amongst teachers in a planning team. We decided that the first part of any CLR cycle should be working on subject knowledge together; teachers together exploring their own understanding of the mathematics. We have found this adjustment has been hugely beneficial and is now an established part of our approach.

An example of this can be seen within our research project *Understanding Structured Number Lines* (Trundley & Burke, 2019). The research team identified that few of the children in the study made the decision to solve subtractions such as 82 − 77 by considering how close the numbers were together. This became the focus of a CLR cycle; in the first meeting of the planning team, the teachers worked on the maths together. They considered the following problem:

In a supermarket bottles of orange juice cost £1.90 each.
  There is a special offer: **Buy two bottles for £3.50**
  How much money do you save if you buy two bottles today rather than one bottle today and one bottle next week?

- What calculations did you do? Write them down?
- Why were these the calculations you needed to do?
- How did you choose to work them out?
- What different calculations might people have done?

None of the teachers recorded the subtraction £3.80 − £3.50 as the second calculation they were solving. When the adviser asked the teachers what they would need to put into a calculator to solve the problem, they made the connection.

During the exploration of the mathematics in this teaching sequence, the planning team explored problems involving subtraction where the numbers are close together. When these were solved by teachers using addition, they were also represented symbolically as additions; the calculation identified was not the calculation that matched the problem but the calculation that matched the method chosen for solving the problem. (p. 35)

The teachers then considered four different subtractions involving pairs of two-digit numbers and identified the decisions they were making about how to solve each one. They then discussed the understanding behind how they decided to solve 82–77. Critical to both this research project, and to planning for the research lesson, was appreciating that understanding subtractions can be solved by thinking about how close the numbers are together is key to making decisions about how to calculate a subtraction.

Kyouzai kenkyuu

We have found that having worked on the maths together first, members of the planning team are better placed to engage with literature focussed on what is known from research about the teaching and learning of the chosen area of mathematics. We suggest readings for the planning team; these reflect the research theme and the area of mathematics chosen, often directly linked to the discussions that emerge whilst working on the mathematics together. For example, in the CLR cycle above, following the first session the planning team were given a book chapter examining structures of subtraction (Haylock & Manning, 2014). The second meeting began with exploring and reflecting on this reading which then informed examination of curriculum materials and decisions for the lesson proposal.

The curriculum and curriculum materials available to schools differs greatly between England and Japan. In Japan, all schools use one of the six state-approved textbooks. These textbooks have been developed over time by a collaboration of university professors and schoolteachers and through lesson study. The books reflect a stable curriculum that has a carefully thought-out progression of mathematical concepts both within grades and across grades. In contrast, schools in England draw on a variety of different materials to support mathematics teaching, and work from a national curriculum that lacks carefully planned progression in mathematical ideas. Teachers are heavily influenced in their teaching of mathematics by high-stakes assessment in primary schools and high-stakes inspections.

When working with teachers from multiple schools in a planning team, we encourage them to consider curriculum materials available freely to all teachers and linked to the national curriculum in England, such as the *Mathematics Guidance: key stages 1 and 2* (DfE, 2020) and the *Curriculum Prioritisation in Primary Maths* materials (NCETM, 2021). With single school cycles we work with the curriculum materials used by teachers in the school. In many of these cases, the materials do not support a teaching through problem-solving approach, and we explore how we can support the planning team to consider this approach, in the context of the materials they are using, wherever possible.

Assessment

Assessment acts as a bridge between the exploration of subject knowledge/curriculum materials and planning the research lesson; it is a vital part of our lesson study process, helping to shape the teaching sequence and focus the planning team on the mathematics and understanding of the mathematics. Spending time collating and analysing responses, discussing the children's papers, provokes teachers to think about the understanding behind responses and the implications for teaching. For example, Table 2.3.1 shows questions from a whole school CLR cycle in 2018, part of the second phase of *Supporting children to be active and influential participants in mathematics lessons through effective use of assigning competence and pre-teaching* (Trundley et al., 2017).

The planning team recognised that many of the learners had not secured an understanding of fractions relevant to previous years. Both questions 2 and 3 revealed that few of the learners understood that a fraction could be bigger than one. Question 2 had been designed to be deliberately open; the majority of responses to this question were smaller than one and many were smaller than one half. As a result, the planning team decided to begin the sequence with revisiting and securing this understanding, with the research lesson focussed on counting in fractions to go beyond one.

Table 2.3.1 Assessment questions and responses

Question	Correct	Partly correct	Incorrect
What is a fraction?	27%	55%	18%
Write down a big fraction	9%	45.5%	45.5%
Is a fraction always less than 1?	5%	14%	81%

Research lesson

We have devised a simple format for planning teams to use for the flow of a research lesson, as shown in Figure 2.3.1.

The focus on anticipating student responses (influenced by the work of Stein et al., 2008) has been one of the most important elements of CLR in our experience, shifting attention from considering only what the teacher will "do" to include the sense the learners might make of the mathematics, their mathematical thinking, and the implications of this in shaping the lesson. We find that when responses are anticipated it leads to changes in what is planned for the teacher to say and do. Our role at this stage of the cycle is to avoid being drawn into making any of the decisions but instead to support the process by asking questions, prompting anticipation of student responses, and pushing for all decisions to be collaboratively explored and explicitly agreed.

To aid observation of a research lesson, we use the same format with an additional column so that observers can make notes of what they see learners say and do (see Figure 2.3.2). This informs the post-lesson discussion.

When working with small groups we take a grounded narrative approach (Coles, 2019, Nemirovsky et al., 2005), in the post-lesson discussion, beginning with agreeing what happened through the flow of the lesson; with larger groups this is not practical, but we do expect comments to start from what was actually observed (see chapter 5.4).

At the end of the discussion, we sometimes have a second knowledgeable other acting as final commentator. We are still novices in this role ourselves; we take the opportunity to undertake it across the team where possible so that we can learn together and occasionally others from outside of the team take on the role. This has not been a priority to date and most often there is no final commentator. However, we ask all participants to reflect and share what they are taking from the experience, what thinking it has provoked and the implications for teaching and learning mathematics (see Chapter 5.4).

Flow of the lesson	
Research theme:	
Maths Focus:	
What will the teacher **say and do**? What will be recorded and how (plan for the board)?	What do we think the children **might** say and do?

Figure 2.3.1 Flow of the lesson proforma.

Flow of the lesson		
Research theme:		
Maths focus:		
What will the teacher **say and do**? What will be recorded and how (plan for the board)?	What do we think the children **might** say and do?	What **happened**?

Figure 2.3.2 Flow of the lesson proforma for observers.

Further developments

The geography of our region, especially when working with multi-school teams, can be a challenge and we have begun experimenting with supporting planning teams online. We have also utilised working online to provide opportunities for early career teachers. Novice teachers in Japan are not expected to be part of a planning team at the start of their teaching careers but they participate in lesson study through observing research lessons and post-lesson discussions. We wanted a similar opportunity for our novice teachers and have found the following online model works well:

- Explore the maths that will be the focus of the research lesson (supported)
- Read the lesson proposal (independent)
- Discuss observations (supported)
- Observe lesson recording (independent)
- Observe live post-lesson discussion between experienced teachers (supported)
- Review lesson and lesson proposal (independent)
- Discuss observations (supported)
- Final reflections (independent)

We also work within the local maths hubs; government-funded organisations with the core purpose of helping schools and colleges lead improvement in mathematics education in England, supported by the National Centre for Excellence in the Teaching of Mathematics (NCETM). We have been able to introduce principles of CLR into our work in our local hub, focussing on collaborative planning for lessons that will be observed, anticipating student responses and shaping lessons around these responses. Work Group leads have also had the opportunity to be part of planning teams for full cycles of CLR. One of our cycles was recorded and is used by the NCETM on one of their national programmes. This year for the first time we have introduced full CLR within one maths hub programme.

Developing our approach to CLR has influenced all areas of our work. Where we can engage with full CLR cycles we do; often these are still within specific research projects. In other areas of work, such as our year-long Developing Reasoning programmes and maths hub Work Groups, we incorporate aspects of CLR. Common to all of these contexts is: the teacher learning prior to the lesson is always allocated considerably more time than that given to the other elements of the cycle; the planning of the lesson is preceded by work on both content and pedagogical subject knowledge; the flow of the lesson has a focus on anticipating student responses; observation of the lesson focuses on the learners; and post-lesson discussion considers how the teaching decisions made had an impact on the learners.

The reason why we remain so committed to this approach is summed up by Fujii (2016):

> *Lesson study is not just about improving a single lesson. It's about building pathways for ongoing improvement of instruction.*

References

Coles, A. (2019). Facilitating the use of video with teachers of mathematics: Learning from staying with the detail. *International Journal of STEM Education*, 6(5), 1–13. 10.1186/s40594-018-0155.

DfE (2020). Mathematics guidance: Key stages 1 and 2. *Non-statutory guidance for the national curriculum in England.*

Fujii, T. (2014). Implementing Japanese lesson study in foreign countries: Misconceptions revealed. *Mathematics Teacher Education and Development, 16*, 65–83.

Fujii, T. (2016). Japanese Lesson Study in Mathematics: Critical role of external experts presentation at UCL Institute of Education on 6th September 2016.

Haylock, D., & Manning, R. (2014). *Mathematics explained for primary teachers* 5th ed. London: Sage Publications.

NCETM (2021). *Curriculum prioritisation in primary math*, NCETM.

Nemirovsky, R., Dimattia, C., Ribeiro, B., & Lara-Meloy, T. (2005). Talking about teaching episodes. *Journal of Mathematics Teacher Education, 8*(5), 363–392.

Stein, M., Engle, R., Smith, M., & Hughes, E. (2008). Orchestrating productive mathematical discussions: Five practices for helping teachers move beyond show and tell. *Mathematical Thinking and Learning, 10*(4), 313–340. 10.1080/10986060802229675.

Stigler, J., & Hiebert, J. (1999). *The teaching gap: Best ideas from the world's teachers for improving education in the classroom.* New York: The Free Press. http://lst-iiep.iiep-unesco.org/cgi-bin/wwwi32.exe/[in=epidoc1.in]/?t2000=011347/(100).

Takahashi, A., & Mcdougal, T. (2016). Collaborative lesson research: Maximizing the impact of lesson study. *ZDM Mathematics Education, 48*(4), 513–526. 10.1007/s11858-015-0752-x.

Trundley, R., & Burke, S. (2019). Understanding Structured Number Lines. Phase 1 report. Education and skills websites – Understanding-Structured-Number-Lines-phase-1-report-July-2019.pdf – All Documents (sharepoint.com).

Trundley, R, Wreghitt, C., Edginton, H., Eversett, H., & Burke, S. (2017). Supporting children to be active and influential participants in mathematics lessons through effective use of assigning competence and pre-teaching. Final report. Education and skills websites – Supporting-children-to-actively-participate.pdf – All Documents (sharepoint.com).

2.4 Collaborative lesson research in the San Francisco Bay Area

The learning opportunities provided by public research lessons

Catherine Lewis, Courtney Ortega, Brigid Brown,
Karen Cortez, Rashida Carter, and Shelley Friedkin

Introduction

We look at the work of three schools in the San Francisco Bay Area that have used Collaborative Lesson Research (CLR) – a rigorous form of school-wide Lesson Study – to build Teaching Through Problem-solving in Mathematics. We examine public research lessons conducted by the three schools, with a focus on the potential of public research lessons to support improvement in a school, region, and beyond.

The Lesson Study ecosystem in Japan

In Japan, public research lessons are one important way that knowledge spreads across settings. For example, university-affiliated laboratory schools and national subject matter associations host public research lessons (usually annually) to test out innovations to curriculum and instruction (Lewis & Tsuchida, 1997, 1998). These research lessons may be viewed and discussed by a thousand or more educators, whose participation is supported via headsets, large video screens, and reproductions of student work. Likewise, large public research lessons are hosted by "Designated Research Schools" that apply for public grant funding to pioneer changes in the national Course of Study; these schools disseminate their grant-funded work through large public research lessons. Smaller-scale public research lessons are conducted by district-based Lesson Study teams and individual schools engaging in CLR, whose work often focuses on local adaptation and spread of research-based innovations.

In Japan, these various settings for Lesson Study play complementary roles in the development, testing, and spread of innovations (Lewis, 2014, 2015). For example, subject matter associations and university-attached demonstration schools often introduce and test ideas from research conducted within or outside Japan and propose changes to the national Course of Study. District and school research lessons (such as those conducted in CLR) allow local educators to show how research-based ideas can be adapted to local needs – for example, to settings with many students from historically discriminated groups or settings where teaching through problem-solving is challenging because students already "know" mathematical procedures from attending after-school examination-focused schools. CLR plays a pivotal role in system-wide reform in Japan, by allowing teachers to adapt and test innovations with their own students and collaborate to refine them. Educators in different settings learn about each other's work through the network of district-based and university-based educators schools invite to serve as outside final commentators, *koshi*, on research lessons (Lewis, 2014). It is not uncommon for university professors in Japan to be introduced at conferences with accolades about the number of schools where the professor has provided final commentary on research lessons – sometimes 60 or more schools per year!

DOI: 10.4324/9781003375272-8

Collaborative lesson research in the San Francisco Bay Area

In late 2014, our team obtained funding to initiate CLR in 1–2 sites in each of three urban districts and to develop video and print resources to support the further spread of CLR. This chapter focuses on the three elementary schools in the San Francisco Bay Area that chose to use Teaching Through Problem-solving schoolwide as their focus for CLR: School A in Oakland Unified School District; and Schools H and M in San Francisco Unified School District. All three schools serve low-income, historically underserved student populations, as shown in Table 2.4.1. Schools began building Lesson Study in 2015, using materials and processes now found online (LSGAMC, 2022a); School M had one existing Lesson Study team. The work generally began with teachers creating a Research Theme to capture their long-term vision for student development (see the process at LSGAMC, 2022b). Over the next three years, teachers learned about Teaching Through Problem-solving through videos, written materials, presentations, and feedback on research lesson plan drafts and final commentary on research lessons; many of these resources are now available online (LSGAMC, 2022c,d).

Figures 2.4.1 to 2.4.3 show the mathematics SBAC scores from 2014 (before CLR work began) through 2019; project funding ended in 2018. Tables 2.4.1 and 2.4.2 provide school and district demographics. As the figures and table show, these CLR schools served a greater proportion of low-income, historically underserved students than their respective districts and were substantially more effective in building equity of mathematics learning for these students than were their respective districts. In fact, School M was a three-sigma positive outlier in mathematics SBAC growth in 2018–2019 (i.e., greater than 99.7% of district schools).

Table 2.4.1 Demographic information for Schools M and H and SFUSD (2018–2019)

	Black	*Latinx*	*Asian*	*White*	*English Learner*	*Low SES*	*Homeless Youth*
School M	24.9%	51.6%	2.2%	2.7%	41.8%	84.0%	16.0%
School H	9.3%	41.7%	30.0%	1.0%	59.3%	84.5%	19.5%
SFUSD	6.6%	27.4%	34.1%	14.7%	28.6%	54.4%	3.9%

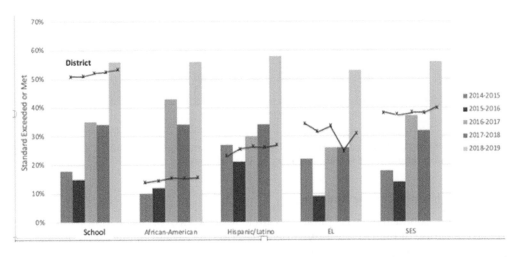

Figure 2.4.1 School M Mathematics Smarter Balanced Assessment Scores (SBAC), 2015–2019 by Subgroup; district scores shown by X-marked lines.

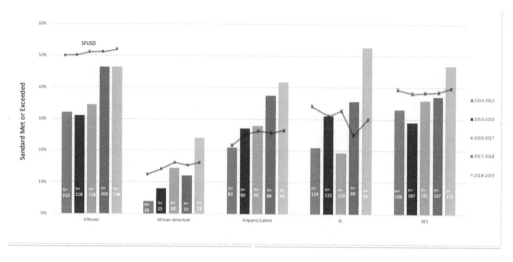

Figure 2.4.2 School H Mathematics Smarter Balanced Assessment Scores (SBAC), 2015–2019 by Subgroup; district scores shown by X-marked lines.

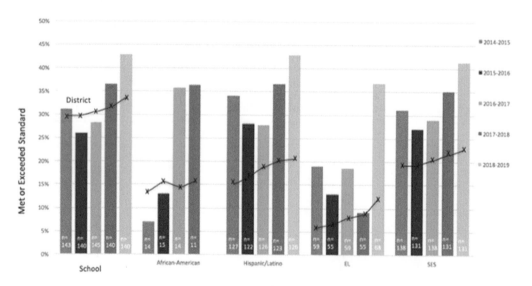

Figure 2.4.3 School A Mathematics Smarter Balanced Assessment Scores (SBAC), 2015–2019 by Subgroup; district scores shown by X-marked lines.

Public research lessons at the three sites

All three sites conducted large public research lessons two or more times during the 2015–2018 period of funded work. We briefly describe the earliest public research lesson at each site and explore its learning opportunities.

Table 2.4.2 Demographic information for School A and OUSD (2018–2019)

	Black	Latinx	Asian	White	English Learner	Low SES
School A	6.3%	89.5%	1.0%	2.1%	70.6%	92.0%
OUSD	23.9%	46.2%	11.8%	9.9%	31.2%	73.0%

School A

January 2016 public research lesson conference for regional and statewide mathematics networks

Less than a year into its work, School A and OUSD agreed to host two public research lessons as part of a 2-day convening of a 10-district mathematics consortium dedicated to enacting the Common Core State Standards in Mathematics (CCSS-M; NGACBP & CCSSO, 2010). Coaches and academic officers from the 10-district consortium attended elementary and lower secondary public research lessons presented by OUSD Lesson Study teams. The Teaching-Learning Plan for the elementary public research lesson can be found in Appendix 1. The plan is called "Lesson Study Cycle Discussion Guide", reflecting the team's use of the document to guide their Lesson Study cycle. Comments by event participants (captured in discussion records and post-lesson written reflections) reveal several types of learning.

Learning about mathematics content and instruction

The team's plan (Appendix 1), captures much knowledge about the mathematical topic and its teaching-learning. The research lesson and unit target students' conceptual understanding of place value within multi-digit addition and subtraction. As teachers explain in the Teaching-Learning Plan, the third graders successfully represented numbers to 1000 in multiple ways (e.g., using base ten blocks and place value charts), yet "students still were not able to grasp the reason for why these models were useful". The team notes that students struggle to explain why regrouping is needed, and typically subtract one by one (rather than using tens). For that reason, the team wanted to design a lesson "to bridge the gap between 2nd and 3rd grade"– to support students in moving from using concrete models for multi-digit addition and subtraction to understanding the algorithms (and their underlying ideas about place value). During a planning meeting the day before the research lesson, Akihiko Takahashi upended the team's planning by suggesting that they pose the problem of adding two 3-digit numbers using pictures of 356 and 432 cats (see end of Teaching-Learning Plan in Appendix 1), rather than by presenting numbers. As teachers themselves used the pictures to solve the problem during a mock-up lesson, they realised that the pictures could spark students to notice the connection between place value and the algorithm. Since counting the cats one by one would be very onerous, some students would be likely to count groups of tens and hundreds that would differ obviously in size and make visible the reason for combining like terms in the algorithm. Teachers actively embraced the new visual for the lesson, noting in their Teaching-Learning Plan: "The diagrams that we decided to use allow students to draw upon their prior learning to make sense of place value, and *why adding like place values is important*". (Italics added.)

Reconsidering supervisors' observation guidelines

The team studied CCSS-M and noticed that the phrase "concrete models or drawings" appears in Grade 2 CCSS-M standards for addition and subtraction within 1000 but disappears from Grade 3 standards; the team reproduced the following standards in their plan:

- 2.NBT.B.7 Add and subtract within 1000, using concrete models or drawings and strategies based on place value, properties of operations, and/or the relationship between addition and subtraction; relate the strategy to a written method.

- 3.NBT.A.2 Fluently add and subtract within 1000 using strategies and algorithms based on place value, properties of operations, and/or the relationship between addition and subtraction.

The plan's "Background and Rationale" argues that many grade 3 students were not yet connecting the concrete model to the algorithm, so the research lesson would "bridge the gap" between the "concrete models or drawings" expected in grade 2 and the "algorithms based on place value" expected in grade 3. During the post-lesson discussion, a district mathematics specialist commented that the use of drawings placed the grade 3 research lesson below CCSS-M grade-level expectations. Lively discussions – at the event and subsequent meetings – problematised the specialist's perspective, raising the larger question of how to design lessons that build a bridge from students' current understanding to the expected grade-level standard. Teachers commented that, if students need prior-grade concrete models to build a bridge to grade-level understanding, teachers should not be viewed as non-compliant with standards. Officers from many districts thus had the opportunity to consider the impact of standards-based evaluative frameworks they routinely used: was it simply to *check* whether grade-level content was taught, or to strategise ways to *build toward* grade-level understanding?

Considering the elements of high-quality site-based professional learning

A panel discussion on the day following the research lessons enabled mathematics educators from the networked districts to ask OUSD teachers and leaders about the essential components that make Lesson Study successful. One OUSD teacher commented on how much she learned from studying the curriculum content and writing a rationale for the lesson and unit design; in response, a visiting educator noted "So the knowledge is not in the program, it is in the teachers". Visiting educators also commented on the power of teachers' "ownership" of instructional hypotheses; their principled reflection on collected data; and their planning routines (e.g., anticipating student thinking) and instructional routines (e.g., mathematics journals) that support mathematical practices.

The role of outside knowledgeable others

We were surprised when, the day before the planned public research lesson, Akihiko Takahashi suggested that the teachers make a major change in their plan (to present the problem using pictures of cats, rather than numbers, and to allow students to solve it using self-chosen strategies rather than designating tools such as the place value chart). Our experience (before and after that intervention) is that Dr. Takahashi rarely makes such direct suggestions, since he wants teachers to experience agency over lesson decisions. We surmise that he made the direct suggestion because (1) he wanted teachers to have a good task for their public research lesson the next day and (2) his knowledge of the Japanese curriculum made the task and its likely impact very familiar to him, whereas the task probably was not available to teachers in their curriculum study. The decision seems to have paid off, since the task made students' thinking about place value quite visible. Team members later reflected that using a concrete counting task to build appreciation of place value was a big learning from their work, and the School A team greatly deepened their interest in CLR and Teaching Through Problem-solving following their public research lesson. The research lesson publicly positioned the teachers as authors and investigators of knowledge for the teaching profession, strengthening educators' identity in this regard.

Summary

Reading this account of the public research lesson seven years later, the research lesson instructor identified several shifts in her practice catalysed by the experience. Her reflections bring together the different types of learning – about content, professional learning, standards – highlighted in this section.

> I realised Lesson Study was not about refining and perfecting a single lesson (or even unit) but about building a shared and cohesive conceptual understanding of the math content among a team of teachers who then created opportunities for students to grasp the mathematics throughout their multi-year learning trajectory.
>
> Lesson Study allows a deep dive to touch on what's most important in terms of both the mathematical concepts and the philosophy of teaching. ... I saw the impact of the research not in a single lesson, but in the moment-to-moment decisions of my daily teaching, which moved closer toward alignment with these ideas, now surfaced.
>
> As an individual teacher, narrowly focusing on my own grade-level expectations kept me from understanding why my students were not yet mastering the concepts I was supposed to teach them.

School M

On 12 December 2017, School M held its first public research lesson, attended by about 80 educators from outside the school, including teachers and administrators from the district and beyond, mathematics specialists, a well-known mathematics curriculum author, and an author of the CCSS-M. The public research lesson video, Teaching-Learning Plan, and Pre-lesson Discussion are available online (LSGAMC, 2020e,f,g). In addition to the types of learning opportunities mentioned for the School A public research lesson, this research lesson offered several additional opportunities.

Joint, practice-based understanding of "problem-solving"

The public research lesson day started with a short presentation on Japanese Teaching Through Problem-solving (by Dr. Akihiko Takahashi) and on the district mathematics curriculum (by a district mathematics specialist). As the Participant Agenda explains (see Appendix 2 Participant Agenda, 12-14-17) a goal of the day was to "Deepen our understanding of how we teach through problem-solving within the [District] core curriculum". In their plan and public discussions, team members actively negotiated between their emerging ideas about mathematical problem-solving and the district curriculum. For example, team members expressed the belief that an authentic mathematics problem gives students the opportunity to develop a new mathematical understanding using their prior knowledge, and then explained how they refined the district curriculum unit on division to create sufficient time for students to construct each new interpretation of remainders. The team explained that students need a whole lesson to grasp why "6, remainder 3" is not always the correct answer to the expression $27 \div 4 = ?$. In the lesson, students develop a new interpretation of division with remainder in which the quotient is rounded up – specifically, the interpretation needed for the problem: How many 4-person roller coaster cars are needed to hold 27 students? Teachers described their efforts to "look at our curriculum through the lens of Japanese curriculum … " and also discussed an OECD-developed conceptual model of problem-solving (See Teaching-Learning Plan in Appendix A) to build a shared understanding of problem-solving; they stressed the final phase of re-contextualising the answer as an insight gained from the OECD model.

Pre-lesson discussion

SFUSD educators added a 40-minute pre-lesson discussion to the schedule for public research lessons, so the Lesson Study team could present the findings from their curriculum study and the rationale for their research lesson design and so attendees could read the Teaching-Learning Plan, learn about their role as data collectors, and ask clarifying questions. The pre-lesson discussion improved observers' data collection and so became a standard feature of SFUSD public research lessons, spreading to some other districts as well, through the Facilitator Agenda provided in Appendix 3. Public Research Lesson Protocol: Facilitator Script.

Classroom discourse routines to support problem-solving

The research lesson (available for viewing at LSGAMC, 2022g) revealed classroom discourse routines to support problem-solving. Students used their reflective mathematics journals to solve the problem, to explain their thinking to classmates, and to revisit prior interpretations of division remainder (the latter two without any prompting from the teacher). The teacher began the lesson by posting and reading four students' reflections from the prior day's lesson and briefly discussing them as a class in order to highlight mathematical ideas and norms that she hoped students might draw on during the lesson. (The teacher explained this routine practice and its purpose in the pre-lesson discussion with observers, found at LSGAMC, 2022f.)

Planned board use was another routine used to support discourse during the lesson; the board made student thinking visible in an organised way that allowed students to compare mathematical ideas (along with corresponding diagrams and expressions) as they asked questions or made arguments. Routines of student-led presentation and lesson summarisation allowed the new mathematics to be articulated by the students. Many outside observers commented appreciatively on these routines; for example, a teacher from a rural California school soon emailed that she had begun to use journals in her classroom the day after observing the public lesson, and she asked several practical follow-up questions about journal use (see resources at LSGAMC, 2022h).

School H

On 17 April 2018, School H conducted a public research lesson with an audience of about 80 educators present. The lesson video (LSGAMC 2022i) and Teaching-Learning Plan

(LSGAMC 2022j) are available online. In addition to the types of learning highlighted above, some additional learning opportunities were offered by this public research lesson. The lesson took place in a bilingual classroom, and the classroom teacher invited parents to the lesson. In addition, district department heads interested in the Lesson Study process, mathematics specialists from a local network and an author of the CCSS-M attended the lesson. The Lesson Study team noticed in their study of CCSS-M that "Grade 3 expectations … are limited to fractions with denominators 2,3, 4, 6 and 8;" (NGACBP & CCSSO, 2010, p.24). The team's Teaching-Learning Plan argued that students should "not be limited by these denominators and [should] begin seeing denominators such as 10 … Exposing them to the denominator of 10 will give them background knowledge of tenths so that when they begin working with decimals in fourth grade, they will understand that a number can be broken up into tenths". The grade 3 team was interested in tenths in part because they noticed (during a grade 4 research lesson) that students struggled when decimals were introduced. The grade 3 teachers became curious about how to lay a better foundation for understanding decimals.

Reconsider standards based on shared observation of practice

The research lesson posed a situation problem: an (imagined) disagreement between two teachers about whether ½ or 5/10 of a sandwich was more. The data collected during the lesson suggested that students could understand and compare tenths and that, in fact, students' familiarity with composing 10 made it relatively easy to see five as half of ten and reason that 5/10 is equal to ½ (easier than might be the case for other denominators). Phil Daro, an author of the mathematics Common Core State Standards, closely observed student learning during the public research lesson and found the team's ideas about adding tenths to the Grade 3 curriculum persuasive, but challenged the team to find more definitive indicators of student understanding of tenths. After seeing students draw incorrect inferences from homemade fraction strips, final commentators suggested that the team think further about tool choice and use in the lesson. What might be the difference between plotting fractions on a single number line rather than on two number lines that might have different proportions? What about using homemade vs commercial fraction strips (given the imprecision introduced by the former)? These discussions raised the question of what it means to understand equivalent fractions: what explanations and models demonstrate understanding of equivalent fractions? The exchange, at a public research lesson, between a team of elementary teachers who advocate for a modification of standards and an author of the standards would not be unusual in Japan. But in the United States, educators remarked on the power of the public research lesson as a forum for classroom teachers and a standards author to discuss possible refinement of standards, using jointly viewed student classroom learning as evidence.

Parent participation

Parents were invited to watch the public research lesson (though not the post-lesson discussion, when they joined their children for a celebration). Research lesson observation has become a valued part of family-school partnership at School H, allowing parents to see how students' mathematical thinking, writing and speech are encouraged, recorded, and valued during instruction. Participation in public research lessons has the potential to strengthen school-parent partnerships, particularly in schools where many parents are not familiar with U.S. schooling or did not have positive experiences of schooling. A teacher at School H notes that including parents as observers of research lessons has demystified the Common Core Standards and the shift to Teaching Through Problem-solving for parents, enabling them to better support their students. Some schools that initially included parents in research lessons discontinued this practice and instituted separate experiences for parents, since it was hard to simultaneously support teachers' research and parent involvement during the same research lesson.

New ways to build understanding of teaching through problem-solving

The public research lesson at School H allowed observers to see many tools and adaptations of Teaching Through Problem-solving for bilingual classrooms – for example, sentence frames and reflection prompts in Spanish–and strategies for newcomers to participate in their native language while building English fluency. In addition, School H students taught visiting educators about reflective mathematics journals during a short workshop following the research lesson. Each student brought their own reflective mathematics journal to show and explain to a group of about four educators and then fielded questions from the educators. Observers could see how Teaching Through Problem-solving is adapted to classrooms serving many English language learners and could see multilingual students positioned as experts teaching educators about Teaching Through Problem-solving.

Summary

Description of the first public research lesson conducted at each CLR site in the San Francisco Bay Area suggests the ways that public research lessons can support development and dissemination of knowledge for teaching, even in the early phases of CLR. For sites planning to conduct public research lessons, we recommend thinking strategically about the following.

Who will attend?

In addition to educators from within the school, the three public research lessons invited outside educators, including:

- Educators from a statewide network focused on standards-based mathematics instruction
- Site leaders from schools interested in building effective professional learning
- Mathematics curriculum and content specialists interested in understanding and using district curricular resources
- Classroom teachers, coaches, and district administrators interested in mathematics learning and/or changes in professional learning
- Curriculum and standards authors interested in use/refinement of these resources
- University-based educators interested in preservice or inservice learning

The range of participant roles suggests the various networks that might build and spread knowledge from Lesson Study through local or regional networks focused on mathematics, professional learning, education of English language learners, curriculum, etc.

What ideas will be made public?

The three public research lessons illustrate the range of ideas that are made available for public discussion and refinement. For example, these included:

- Knowledge about a specific mathematics topic and its teaching-learning
- Understanding what constitutes mathematical "problem-solving"
- Knowledge of classroom routines (such as board use and reflective journals) to make students' thinking visible
- Unit and lesson design to support mathematical problem-solving
- Understanding of the standards, their enactment in practice, and what to do if students do not yet have the requisite prior knowledge to solve grade-level problems
- Examination and questioning of the standards in practice with the goal of improving them

What changes in identity and professional learning culture are targeted?

Teachers' collective efficacy – their belief that teachers at their school can improve outcomes for students – greatly impacts student outcomes (Goddard et al., 2004; Hattie, 2012) and teachers develop collective efficacy in part through *vicarious* experience seeing colleagues improve. Public research lesson attendees can learn crucial direct and vicarious lessons about their power to affect student learning. In CLR schools, joint study of the curriculum, co-planning of the unit and lesson and discussion of data from the research lesson, all motivated by a shared schoolwide Research Theme, build a culture focused on "our" students (not "my" or "your" students) and the power of teachers to improve instruction. In addition to shaping teachers' collective efficacy, public research lessons have the potential to shape many other aspects of teachers' identity and professional learning culture, such as:

- Teachers' identity as investigators of practice and authors of knowledge for the profession
- Collegial expectations of high-quality lesson planning (e.g., studying content, curriculum, and standards, identifying the new learning within a lesson, anticipating student thinking)
- Adult learning routines that expect teachers to support and learn from one another and from students

We hope that, as other sites consider public research lessons, they will consider the outsiders they might invite, the ideas that might be made public, and the impact on professional community and identity that might result. Please add to our initial observations!

Note

1 This document is adapted from a lesson plan template developed by the Chicago Lesson Study Group. It is licensed to Lesson Study Alliance, Chicago, IL.

References

Goddard, R. D., Hoy, W. K., & Hoy, A. W. (2004). Collective efficacy beliefs: Theoretical developments, empirical evidence, and future directions. *Educational researcher*, *33*(3), 3–13.

Hattie, J. (2012). Visible learning for teachers: Maximizing impact on learning. Routledge, Taylor & Francis Group.

Lesson Study Group at Mills College (2022a). Conduct a Cycle. Downloaded November 12, 2022. https://lessonresearch.net/conduct-a-cycle/overview/

Lesson Study Group at Mills College (2022b). Develop a Research Theme. Downloaded November 12, 2022. https://lessonresearch.net/study-step/develop-research-theme/

Lesson Study Group at Mills College (2022c). Teaching Through Problem-solving: Overview. Downloaded November 12, 2022. https://lessonresearch.net/teaching-problem-solving/overview/

Lesson Study Group at Mills College (2022d). Teaching Through Problem-solving in Action. Downloaded November 12, 2022. https://lessonresearch.net/teaching-problem-solving/ttp-in-action/

Lesson Study Group at Mills College (2022e). Interpreting the Remainder in Division: Research Lesson Proposal G4. Downloaded November 12, 2022. https://lessonresearch.net/wp-content/uploads/2018/08/Research-Lesson-Proposal-G4-December-2017-1.pdf

Lesson Study Group at Mills College (2022f). Interpreting the Remainder in Division: Pre-Lesson Discussion. Downloaded November 12, 2022. https://lessonresearch.net/teaching-problem-solving/ttp-in-action/

Lesson Study Group at Mills College (2022g). Interpreting the Remainder in Division: Lesson. Downloaded November 12, 2022. https://lessonresearch.net/teaching-problem-solving/ttp-in-action/

Lesson Study Group at Mills College (2022h). Teaching Through Problem-solving: Journals. Downloaded November 12, 2022. https://lessonresearch.net/teaching-problem-solving/journals/

Lesson Study Group at Mills College (2022i). Grade 3 (bilingual): Compare 5/10 and ½ (Video) Downloaded November 12, 2022. https://lessonresearch.net/teaching-problem-solving/ttp-in-action/

Lesson Study Group at Mills College (2022j). SFUSD: Planning and Memorializing Template. Downloaded November 12, 2022 https://lessonresearch.net/wp-content/uploads/2018/08/20180417_Gates_SFUSD_Hillcrest_Grade3_LessonPlanNotesPostCycleReflection.pdf

Lewis, C. (2014). How do Japanese teachers improve their Instruction? Synergies of Lesson Study at the School, District, and National levels. *Board on Science Education Commissioned Paper.* http://sites.nationalacademies.org/DBASSE/BOSE/DBASSE_084388

Lewis, C. (2015). What is improvement science? Do we need it in education? *Educational Researcher,* 44(1), 54–61. 10.3102/0013189X15570388

Lewis, C., & Tsuchida, I. (1997). Planned educational change in Japan: The case of elementary science instruction. *Journal of Educational Policy,* 12(5), 313–331.

Lewis, C., & Tsuchida, I. (1998). A lesson is like a swiftly flowing river: Research lessons and the improvement of Japanese education. *American Educator,* 22(Winter), 14–17 & 50–52.

NGACBP & CCSSO (National Governors Association Center for Best Practices, Council of Chief State School Officers). (2010). *Common Core State Standards for Mathematics.* National Governors Association Center for Best Practices & Council of Chief State School Officers.

OUSD Lesson Study Cycle DISCUSSION GUIDE[1]

Name of the School: Acorn Woodland Elementary School
Names of Planning Team Members: Brigid Brown (3rd Grade Teacher), John Aragon (2nd Grade Bilingual Teacher), Leslie Detter (3rd Grade Teacher), Shelby Halela (2nd Grade SDC Teacher) and Monique LaCour (2nd Grade Teacher)
Date of Research Lesson: Tuesday, January 26, 2016
Grade/Course, Unit, Task/lesson: Grade 3, Unit: Addition & Subtraction, Lesson: Addition of Numbers within 1000
Instructor: Brigid Brown

PART 1: Research Theme and Theory of Action

Research Theme: Deepen students' conceptual understanding of mathematics through an inquiry-based approach

Theory of Action: If teachers apply an inquiry-based approach, then students will deepen their conceptual understanding of mathematics. This will result in students being able to apply their learning in multiple contexts and to justify their thinking by utilising or making connections between multiple representations. Conceptual understanding will also support procedural fluency, as students make connections and see patterns between content. Students will understand and apply algorithms effectively as a result of this conceptual foundation. In order for this type of learning approach to occur, classrooms must be socially and emotionally safe where mistakes are valued. Students must work collaboratively to develop skills of productive struggle, problem solving, communication, and stamina. Students must develop a growth mindset. Metrics that we can gather that show evidence of deepened conceptual understanding are (1) observations of students applying their learning in multiple contexts, (2) students justifying their thinking by utilising or making connections between multiple representations (3) recording the number of times students talk and the quality of that talk.

I hecka
math

OAKLAND UNIFIED
SCHOOL DISTRICT
Community Schools, Thriving Students

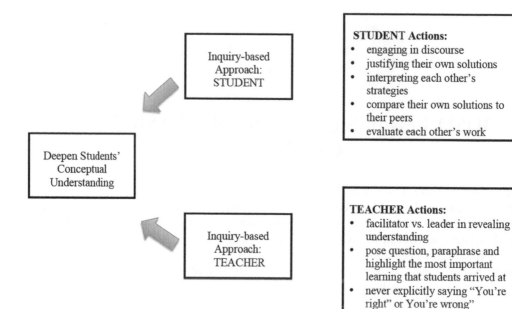

Data that we would like observers to gather, and questions that we hope the postlesson discussion will help us to address are:

- How do students represent the problem using visual representations?
- How do visual representations support student understanding of the concept of addition?
- How often and what is the quality of student to student talk? That is, Onewordanswers, justifying reasons, asking questions, building on others' ideas, revising thinking
- How are students engaging with one another's ideas? What propels them? What shuts them down? Which comments are building on prior thinking and which comments are in isolation?
- When students have an incorrect answer...

  o What is their body language? Do they continue to participate? Do they revise their thinking?

PART 2: Research and *Kyouzaikenkyuu*

Observing Dr. Takahashi during the Lesson Study Institute in August 2015 had a significant impact on our learning as a staff. We saw the importance of open-ended questions and how it supported students to engage with the math content and allow for multiple ways of solving a problem. We want to have students learn mathematics through problem solving.

It is important for students to have a solid conceptual foundation before they learn an algorithm. Students need to have a lot of experience with manipulatives and visual representations before they can understand an algorithm or procedure. The textbooks we have do not explicitly support students to make a connection between the concepts and particular algorithms, so teachers will need to make those connections clear. We also have found it valuable for students to use notebooks so they have a record of their mathematical thinking.

For this lesson, it was important that we understood the progression of understanding place value from prior grades, in order to identify the key learning regarding the conceptual understanding of the algorithm of adding multi-digit numbers. In lower grades, most students count one by one or skip count. When considering the algorithm for adding, if you know single-digit addition and subtraction, then you can count any number. Then, if you have a strong understanding of place value, students can apply this algorithm to multi-digit problems. So in this unit, we want to bring every student to grade-level understanding, even if they are still in 1st- and 2nd-grade understanding.

PART 3: Unpacking the Unit

Goals by middle of the Unit (Formative and Expert Tasks):

- Use place value strategies and models to represent addition problems
- Round 3-digit numbers
- Estimate the sums for addition problems
- Solve 1step and 2step addition problems

Goals by the end of the Unit (Summative Task):

- Use place value strategies and models to represent subtraction problems
- Estimate the differences for subtraction problems
- Solve 1step and 2step subtraction problems

Learning Goal	Learning Activities	Major Assessment Criteria
Represent a number using place value blocks Make place value drawings to represent numbers to 1000	Build numbers using base ten blocks. Use place value drawings: quick hundreds, quick tens and ones to represent numbers. i.e., 231 ⊟lll.	Students understand the value of the digits of a number and associate that value with a corresponding place value drawing

(Continued)

Learning Goal	Learning Activities	Major Assessment Criteria
Represent numbers to 1000 with base ten blocks in a variety of ways. Use place value drawings to represent the base ten blocks.	Trade one place value block for other place value blocks (i.e., ones for tens) Represent a number (i.e., 324) using base ten blocks in 3 different ways. (i.e., 3 hundreds, 2 tens, 4 ones, or 2 hundreds 12 tens and 4 ones or 1 hundred, 21 tens, and 14 ones). Represent the 3 different base ten block configurations using place value drawings	Students can decompose a number in a variety of different ways and represent that with base ten blocks and place value drawings.
Write numbers to 1000 in expanded form & use expanded form to add numbers	Build numbers using base ten blocks. Write addition equations that match the place value blocks. i.e., 538 = 500 + 30 + 8 Discuss the value of each digit. i.e., 538 = 5 hundreds, 3 tens and 8 ones Apply expanded form to addition of numbers, i.e., 123 +456 = 100 + 20 + 3 400 + 50 + 6 --------------------	Students can identify the value of each digit in a numeral and write a number in expanded form. Students can use the expanded form to add numbers.
*Solve addition problems using visual representations based on place value	**Solve 3-digit addition problem WITHOUT regrouping using place value drawings**	**Students can add multi-digit numbers, using strategies grounded in understanding of place value.**
Solve addition problems that requires regrouping using visual representations based on place value	Solve 3-digit addition problem WITH regrouping using place value drawings	Students can solve addition problems with regrouping using place value drawings
Apply the algorithm to solve addition problems	Solve 3-digit addition problem WITHOUT regrouping using conceptual model (place value drawing or manipulatives) and then use the algorithm to reinforce the mathematics. Solve 3-digit addition problem WITH regrouping using conceptual model (place value drawing or manipulatives) and then use the algorithm to reinforce the mathematics	Students can solve an addition problem by using the algorithm and make a connection from this procedure to a conceptual model
Solve subtraction problems using conceptual models based on place value	Solve 3-digit subtraction problem WITHOUT regrouping using conceptual model (place value drawing or manipulatives) Solve 3-digit subtraction problem WITH regrouping using conceptual model (place value drawing or manipulatives)	Students can solve an addition problem using conceptual tools like manipulatives and drawings

(Continued)

Learning Goal	Learning Activities	Major Assessment Criteria
Apply the algorithm to solve subtraction problems	Solve 3-digit subtraction problem WITHOUT regrouping using conceptual model and then use the algorithm to reinforce the mathematics Solve 3-digit subtraction problem WITH regrouping using conceptual model and then use the algorithm to reinforce the mathematics	Students can solve a subtraction problem by using the algorithm and make a connection from this procedure to a conceptual model
Use the algorithm to solve addition or subtraction problems	Solve addition and subtraction word problems that require the use of algorithm and conceptual model to prove.	Students can use the algorithm correctly to solve addition and subtraction problems in the context of a word problem

PART 4: Goals of Instruction

Mathematical practice goals for students:

- MP 1. Make sense of problems and persevere in solving them.
- MP 2. Reason abstractly and quantitatively.
- MP 3. Construct viable arguments and critique the reasoning of others.
- MP 4. Model with mathematics.

Instructional goals related to our school research theme:

- Students can solve addition problems using visual representations based on place value
- Students can explain their strategies and mathematical reasoning
- Students can engage in mathematical discussions which require them to respond to, critique and ask questions of one another

Common Core State Standards for Mathematics
Key Related Prior Learning:

- 2.NBT.B.5 Fluently add and subtract within 100 using strategies based on place value, properties of operations, and/or the relationship between addition and subtraction.
- 2.NBT.B.6 Add up to four 2-digit numbers using strategies based on place value and properties of operations.
- 2.NBT.B.7 Add and subtract within 1000, using concrete models or drawings and strategies based on place value, properties of operations, and/or the relationship between addition and subtraction; relate the strategy to a written method. Understand that in adding or subtracting 3-digit numbers, one adds or subtracts hundreds and hundreds,

tens and tens, ones and ones; and sometimes it is necessary to compose or decompose tens or hundreds.

- 2.NBT.B.8 Mentally add 10 or 100 to a given number 100900, and mentally subtract 10 or 100 from a given number 100900.

Learning in This Unit:

- 3.NBT.A.2 Fluently add and subtract within 1000 using strategies and algorithms based on place value, properties of operations, and/or the relationship between addition and subtraction.

Future Learning:

- 4.NBT.B.4 Fluently add and subtract multi-digit whole numbers using the standard algorithm.

PART 5: Background and Rationale

Background: Many students have a superficial understanding of place value. We want to push 5 their conceptual understanding of place value so they develop a strong number sense and deeper understanding of number structure. This will ultimately enable them to solve more complex mathematical problems.

Below are a few examples of what students are able to do and where their thinking is currently:

- Students are able to say the name of the place value (e.g., "This is the tens place") Students are able to identify the value of a given digit (e.g., "The digit 4 in the number 45 represents four tens")
- Students are able to decompose numbers (e.g., 741 = 700 + 40 +1)
- Students (some) are able to use decomposing as a mental math strategy, i.e., 76 – 34 = 7 – 3, 6 – 4 = 42
- Students are able to represent numbers with base ten blocks

Below are some examples of what students are currently struggling with:

- Students struggle to show multiple representations of a number
- Students struggle to subtract numbers where regrouping is needed (e.g., 429 – 284 =) Students struggle to explain *why* regrouping is needed (e.g., Why do we need to regroup with 429 – 284 =)

- Students do not know how to represent numbers using drawings (e.g., 1 square = 100, 1 vertical line = 10, 1 small circle = 1)
- Students cannot regroup using drawings, i.e., the conceptual understanding of regrouping or ungrouping is missing
- Students cannot use base ten blocks to trade the value for regrouping or ungrouping, i.e., having 13 ones means we trade ten ones for one ten (in the context of a + or – problem)
- Students are not operating conceptually from a base ten model. Most students continue to add or subtract ones instead of tens in all strategies including number line or place value vertical stacking
- Students do not recognise 10 or multiples of 10 as friendly numbers and therefore do not use the strategies built around 10

Rationale: Prior to the research lesson, we wanted to ensure that students have had opportunity to manipulate with base ten blocks to make numbers to 1000, and be able to represent a number in multiple ways. We found, however, that students still were not able to grasp the reason for why these models were useful. This meant that we needed to design a lesson that allows us to bridge the gap between 2nd and 3rd grade. The diagrams that we decided to use allow students to draw upon their prior learning to make sense of place value, and why adding like place values is important. This will help students start to make the connection between the diagrams and the algorithm, and leads to understanding why we need to align place values when we write problems vertically.

PART 6: Research Lesson

Flow of the Research Lesson

Learning Activities and Anticipated Student Responses	Teacher's Support/ Questioning	Points of Evaluation
1. Introduction and Posing the Task Part 1 (5 min) Independent work time: Students are given the diagram with 356 cats. "How many cats are there?"		Students are able to determine the number of cats, using a counting or grouping strategy.
2. Anticipated Student Responses • counting on by 1's • skip counting by 2's or 5's • counting by 10's and ones • counting groups of 20's, or other large groups of cats, but misinterpreting what		

(*Continued*)

Learning Activities and Anticipated Student Responses	Teacher's Support/ Questioning	Points of Evaluation
number it represents (i.e., thinking that 20 groups of 10 is 2,000) • multiplying 20 × 20, and subtracting the cats that are in the empty space • seeing that ten 10's equals 100 and making groups of 100, then 10's and 1's		
3. Neriage Part 1: "Kneading" Discussion to Compare Solutions and Draw Out Key Mathematics (10 min) Strategies to highlight during discussion, in order of presentation: • Strategy #1 counting by 1's, 2's, 5's • Strategy #2 counting by tens and ones • Strategy #3 counting by 20's, then ones • Strategy #4 seeing groups of 100's, tens and ones	• Did anyone make a mistake? • How did you keep track of your numbers? • How long did it take? • Where is the 6 in this picture? Where is the 5? Where is the 3? • Can anyone try making a group of 100? • What strategy is most consistent with the way we organise or say numbers? Why don't we say "35 tens?"	Students see and hear various ways of counting 356. Students can see the 100's in the diagram.
4. Posing the Task Part 2 (5 min) Independent work time: Students are given a new diagram with 432 cats. "How many cats are there in this diagram?"	"To avoid mistakes, you may want to look for 10 groups of 10".	Students use the strategy of finding 100's, then 10's and 1's.
5. Neriage Part 2: "Kneading" Discussion to Compare Solutions and Draw Out Key Mathematics (10 min) Select a few students to share out their strategies for counting, particularly those	• Which strategy did you use? Why? • Which strategy can we use that can ensure that we are not going to make a mistake? • Which strategy is most efficient? Which strategy is most reliable?	More students understand the strategy of looking for 100's.

(*Continued*)

Learning Activities and Anticipated Student Responses	Teacher's Support/ Questioning	Points of Evaluation
who used the strategy of looking for 100's.	• Reinforce the under-standing of place value by asking: Where is the 4 in this picture? Where is the 3? Where is the 2? • Don't anticipate that students will avoid using 100's, but if they do, ask: Can anyone try making a group of 100?"	
6. Posing the Task Part 3 (5 min) "How many cats do we have altogether?" • Independent work time • Share with an elbow partner your strategy for adding		Students use the strategy of finding 100's, then 10's and 1's.
7. Neriage Part 3: "Kneading" Discussion to Compare Solutions and Draw Out Key Mathematics (10 min) Select a few students to share their strategies for adding, particularly those who used the strategy of adding by place value.	• How did you add? Why did you add like that? • Scribe thought bubbles to show what students are thinking when adding (*see Board Plan below*) • Ask other students: Can you understand why s/he did it that way? • To attend to precision: "Which 8 do you mean?" (The sum is 788.)	Students apply the strategy of adding 100's, 10's and 1's, to adding two sets of numbers.
8. Summing up (10 min) Individual Student Written Reflection	Writing Prompt: Write a letter to your family. What do you want to tell them about today's math lesson?	Students write that the strategy of looking for 100's is most efficient and useful when adding 3-digit numbers.

Board Plan

Strategy #1: counting on by 1's, 2's or 5's	Strategy #3: counting by 20's	Strategies for finding 432, if needed	Strategies for adding the two sets of numbers

Strategy #1:
counting on by 1's, 2's or 5's

Strategy #3:
counting by 20's

Strategies for
finding 432, if
needed

Strategies for
adding the two
sets of numbers

For example:

*I have to add 3
and 4 because
there are 300 cats
in the first number
and 400 cats in the
second number.
So far there are
700 cats.*

3 + 4 = 7

Strategy #2:
counting by 10's,
then 1's

Strategy #4:
finding 100's,
then 10's and 1's

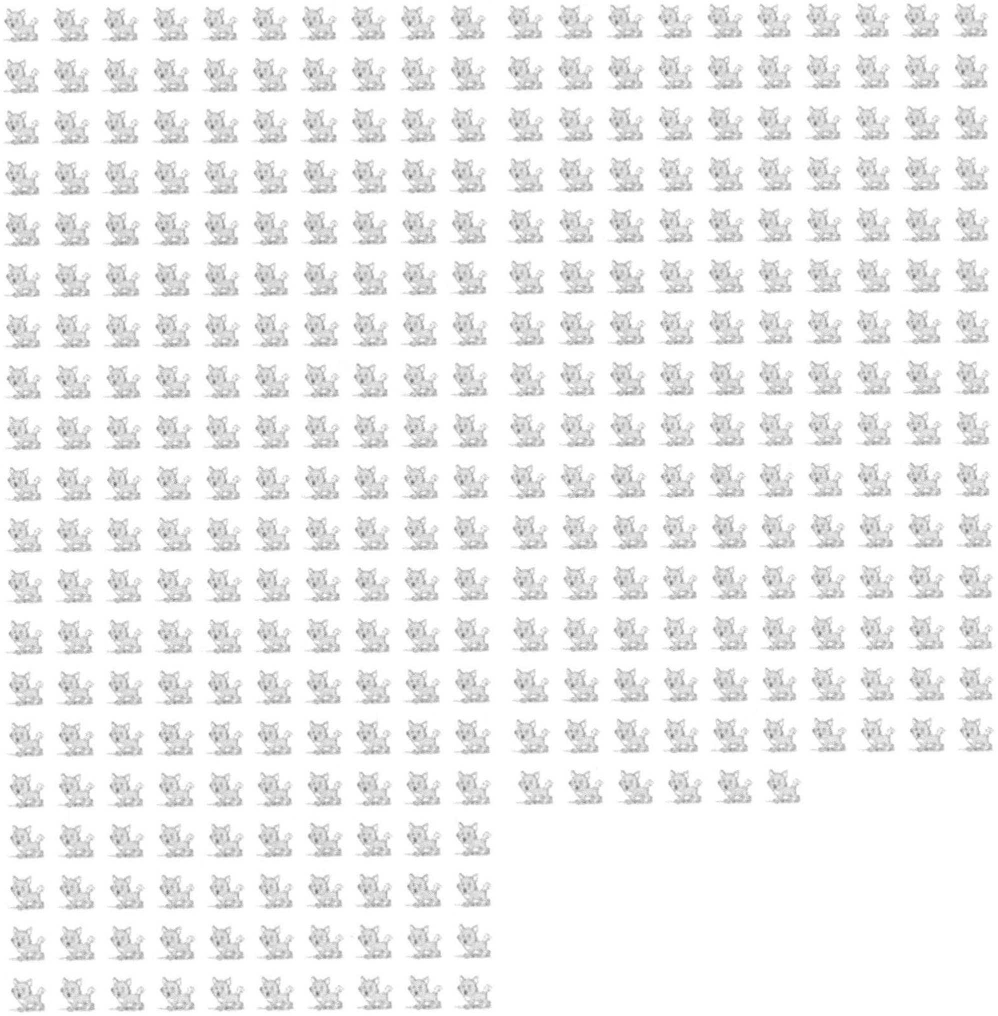

Appendix 2. Cross-Site Public Research Lesson

14 December 2017; 8:00 am–3:30 pm
School M

Experiential Norms	Today's Expectations
*Keep equity at the centre *Speak your truth AND respect differences of opinion *Be mindful of patterns of participation. Be mindful of power dynamics and share space. *Expect and accept non-closure *Ground our work & discussions in the lives and experiences of students and families	*If you are here with us, you are engaged with us *Step out of room if you need to use phone, email, multi-task, etc. *If you are joining for the lesson, you are committing to being fully present for the full lesson (no coming/going; no cell phones; no distractions)

General Outcomes for Math Lesson Study	Today's Outcomes
Deepen our understanding of how we teach through problem-solving within the SFUSD core curriculum Deepen our toolkit of best practices for supporting students that have been historically underserved and thus have gaps in their mathematics understanding and learning Deepen our understanding of how we strategically engage and re-engage students with knowledge and/or skill gaps in the SFUSD math classroom	Learn the history and rationale of Teaching Through Problem-Solving Learn about SFUSD's work with TTP and Lesson Study and its impact on teaching practice, school culture, adult PD, and teacher leadership Explore a K-8 vertical progression of the concepts related to today's research lesson (division with remainders) Experience and consider implications for a full public research lesson Share learnings, insights and implications for practice in small, role-alike groups

Planning Team:
(names omitted)

Agenda

Time	Agenda Item
8:00-8:30 (30)	**Breakfast & Pre-Work: Nora** • <u>Sign-in</u> and nametags • Pick up handouts • Check out a headset • Grab food (breakfast burritos) • Prepare for the day by reading the lesson plan for today's research lesson

8:30-8:45 (15)	**Opening Moves: Nora**
	• Introduction of facilitators and expert commentator
	• School shout out...which schools are in the room today?
	• Guest shout out...where are guests coming from?
	• Purpose for today's experience
	• Review outcomes & norms (see above)
	• Logistical information:
	  ○ 2-hour parking around school (move cars as needed)
	  ○ Lunch is on your own. We recommend these nearby restaurants:
	    ■ Estella's Sandwiches (Sandwiches, Salads), Le Cafe du Soleil (Sandwiches, Salads), Metro Cafe, Cafe International (Sandwiches, Salads), Perilla (Vietnamese), House of Thai (Thai), Indian Oven (Indian) – all places within 3 blocks on or near Haight Street
	• Roles for the day:
	  ○ Facilitators: Math & QTEA teams
	  ○ Process Observers:

8:45-9:10 (25)	**Rationale for Teaching Through Problem-Solving (TTP)** Dr. Takahashi (DePaul): • History of international shift toward Teaching Through Problem Solving • Overview and rationale for problem-based math in SFUSD and globally Noam Szoke (Math): • Design of the SFUSD math curriculum • What does it mean to *use* the SFUSD math core curriculum? (doc)
9:10-9:35 (25)	**Lesson Study in SFUSD** *Central Administrators:* (names omitted) • What is lesson study? • History of lesson study in SFUSD

(*Continued*)

	• How lesson study is supporting math instruction and pedagogy • How lesson study is impacting the curriculum in SFUSD *Teachers:* (names omitted) • Impact of lesson study on teacher practice • Site impact of move to whole-school lesson study from a teacher perspective (instruction, pedagogy, teacher leadership, shifts in school culture and school PD) *Principals:* (names omitted) • Site impact of lesson study and the move to whole-school lesson study from a school leader perspective (instruction, pedagogy, teacher leadership, shifts in school culture and school PD)
9:35-10:05 (30)	**K-8 Vertical Progression (division with remainders): Alyssa Foss** • K-8 progression of concepts for upcoming research lesson • Big ideas and developmental skills at each grade level • Examples from the SFUSD curriculum
10:05-10:25 (20)	**Q&A: Nora**
10:25-10:35 (10)	**Break**
10:35-11:15 (40)	**Pre-Lesson Protocol (fishbowl): Fishbowl Participants** • Overview and context for the research lesson • Lesson rationale • New learning • Clarifying questions (inner circle) • Clarifying questions (outer circle)
11:15-12:15 (60)	**Research Lesson: 4th Grade Math Class**
12:15-1:15 (60)	**Lunch Break** • Please refrain from discussing the lesson or the teacher moves, since the teacher has not yet had a chance to reflect and share learnings
1:15-2:00 (45)	**Post-Lesson Protocol (fishbowl): Fishbowl Participants** • Teacher reflection • Evidence share and analysis • Discussion and next steps
2:00-2:30 (30)	**Expert Commentary: Dr. Takahashi**
2:30-3:15 (45)	**Small Group Break-Outs** *Groups and Facilitators:* *(Guests choose which group is most relevant to join)* • *K/1:* • *2/3:* • *4/5:*

(*Continued*)

	• *6–12:* • *Admin/Central:* ***Discussion Prompts:*** • What are your initial reactions and questions? • What did you learn that is relevant to your practice? • What are implications for your practice? What are implications for your school, department or district? • What is a next step that you will try?

3:15-3:30
(15)
	Closing Moves: (name omitted)
	• Feedback Form
	• Debrief/Process Check
	• Announcements
	   ○ We have **many upcoming public research lessons** at participating lesson study schools (for math/TTP and for all content areas)
	   ○ We will be offering two spring **Deeper Dives** on TTP and math lesson study (March 19 & April 16, 4–7 pm)
	• Celebrations

4:00 onwards!	**Optional Happy Hour at (Restaurant Name)** • Post-research lesson celebrations are standard practice in Japan - the teacher that taught should never buy their own beverages:) • This is a great chance for teachers and administrators to connect across sites, roles, and districts

Thank you for joining us today!

Feel free to contact Nora Houseman (Supervisor in the Office of Professional Learning and Leadership) for more information, with questions, or to get involved in lesson study work in SFUSD. HousemanN@sfusd.edu; 415-265-6960

Appendix 3. Public Research Lesson Protocol: Lesson Study 2017–2018

Facilitator Script

<table>
<tr><td>

NORMS (insert school norms or use these)

- Keep equity at the centre
- Be part of the solution
- Be engaged and present
- Be mindful of patterns of participation (step up/step back)
- Respect differences of opinions and learn from each other while moving forward

</td></tr>
</table>

PROTOCOL FOR PRE-LESSON DISCUSSION

Time: Approximately 50 minutes before the research lesson
Roles: Facilitator, timekeeper, note-taker, process-checker, lesson observers
Outcomes:
- Participants clarify the rationale, big ideas, and goals of the research lesson
- Participants agree on observation data to record in alignment with lesson objectives, intended student learning outcomes, research question, and theory of action

Time	Component
5 min	**WELCOME AND INTRODUCTIONS** Welcome! I am … (name, explain your role as facilitator, etc.). Thrilled to be here … WAVE (intros): Name, role, preferred gender pronouns, possibly quick ice-breaker prompt Introduce or assign note-taker(s), time-keeper(s) and process-checker(s) Review norms Give brief overview of the LS agenda for the day Any clarifying questions?
10 min	**READ AND REVIEW LESSON PLAN** Feel free to write up and mark up the lesson plan as you read
10 min	**BACKGROUND AND CONTEXT:** Framing- Emphasise that the lesson belongs to the whole lesson study team, not just the teacher teaching. Ask group to address their questions to the whole team, not just the teacher of the lesson. Planning team shares: • What is your **research question** and **theory of action**? Why did your team choose this focus? Why is this focus important to student learning and/or student experience at this site? • What is the **context and rationale** for this research lesson? Why is it important and relevant for students? How is it connected to the **research question** and **theory of action**? • What are your specific **student learning objectives** and **intended student learning outcomes**? What are you hoping or expecting students to **do or say**? • What is the **new student learning** in this lesson? • How will you **assess student learning**? • How will you **assess progress** toward your **theory of action**?

(*Continued*)

10 min	**CLARIFYING QUESTIONS** Explain the difference between clarifying questions and probing questions. Ensure participants understand this is not the time to dissect the lesson design or Research Question/Theory of Action, but rather to seek clarity as to the intent of the lesson design and the meaning of the Research Question/Theory of Action.
5 min	**COLLECTING EVIDENCE:** • Planning team explains what evidence they would like participants to collect, in alignment with lesson objectives, intended student learning outcomes, research question, and theory of action • Planning team shares note-taking/evidence-collection template and how to use it • Planning team assigns individuals or groups of students for each observer to observe (or assigns observers to other duties – such as observing teacher moves, patterns of participation amongst students, types of questions asked, etc.)
5 min	**DISCUSS IMPORTANCE OF LESSON OBSERVATION GUIDELINES:** Emphasise that teaching publically is very vulnerable, and we want to ensure respectful and supportive presence and behaviour anytime we are in another teacher's public lesson. Review expectations for observing the lesson (see table). Ask the teacher if observers can ask questions of students during and/or after the lesson. Emphasise there will be no talking and no interference during the lesson (flies on the wall!). **Guidelines for Observing the Research Lesson** 1 Respect the classroom atmosphere. Silence phones, refrain from side conversations, and arrive on time and stay for the entire lesson. 2 Do not help students or interfere with the natural flow of the lesson; for example, be careful not to block students' view when they need to see the board or the teacher. 3 Collect data requested by the lesson planning team, or focus on the "points to notice" laid out in their instructional plan. Prepare by reading the lesson plan thoroughly. 4 Focusing on the same student or skill(or pair of students/skills) over the entire lesson is likely to yield the best picture of whether and how the students developed understanding. 5 If the lesson study team concurs, it is all right to ask clarifying questions of a student after the lesson is concluded.
5 min	**CLOSING WAVE:** • What do you want to get out of today?
	*5 minutes to transition to classroom for the lesson
	OBSERVE RESEARCH LESSON!!!

PROTOCOL FOR POST-LESSON DISCUSSION

Time: Approximately 90 minutes (depending on size of the group)
Roles: Facilitator, timekeeper, notetaker, process-checker, lesson observers
Outcomes:
- Share evidence collected
- Discuss implications for teaching and learning based on student learning evidence collected
- Hear and discuss expert commentary
- Agree on enhancements to the lesson and strategic next steps for the team

Time	Component
5 min	**REVIEW & SELECT EVIDENCE TO SHARE:** We will now take about 5 minutes to review our notes then each observer will have 2 minutes each to <u>share selected evidence directly related to the Research Question/Theory of Action</u>. This is the time to consider what evidence is most useful to share, as we will not share everything we observed. Evidence should be what students did or what students said – descriptive and non-evaluative statements – such as "3/4 students at the table were able to generate the algorithm" or "Joe stated, I tried multiplying but now I am lost". Strategically select key points of evidence you feel will best support and push this team, whether that is patterns, outliers, predicted responses, or unpredicted responses. Observers takes a few minutes to review their notes, consider the research question and theory of action, strategically select evidence to share, and prepare to share out whole group.
5 min	**INSTRUCTOR'S REFLECTION:** We will now give ____ 5 minutes to reflect on the lesson, specifically in relation to the research question and theory of action. This is the time to share insights or learnings that came from implementing the lesson, or any surprises or difficulties encountered in doing so. We have no expectation that ___ has had time to reflect and analyse, so this is just a chance to share initial reactions. The presenting teacher shares reflections on the lesson as it relates to: the research question/theory of action; surprises and/or difficulties encountered; anything that was learned in conducting the lesson.
15 min (2 min per person)	**EVIDENCE OF STUDENT LEARNING:** Observers will now share evidence of student learning. A reminder that we are not evaluating or celebrating students, the teacher, or the instruction, but rather sharing selected, concrete evidence from the lesson. (Adjust time based on size of group and monitor time per person - interject if needed.) Formal observers share **evidence** of **student learning**, specifically what students were able to do or say. How did or didn't students meet the learning goals of the lesson? What evidence of the research question and theory of action were observable? Evidence may include student work, verbatim record, etc.
25 min	**GROUP DISCUSSION/DEBRIEF:** We will now engage in a three part debrief. I will guide us through each component of the debrief if we do not naturally address all three components. Please be mindful of airtime given that this is an unstructured conversation and there are __ people in the room; thus each person has roughly __ min to speak.

(Continued)

	I **Student Learning & Thinking:** What have we learned about our students, the content, and instruction? Were the lesson goals and learning targets met? How did the lesson design enable student learning and illuminate student thinking? Was new learning embraced and did students engage in productive struggle? Were students engaged and hooked? What might we have done differently? II **Research Question & Theory of Action:** What have we learned about our research question and our theory of action? What implications does this have on our next steps? Do we need to revise our theory of action? III **Next Steps:** What are our strategic next steps as a team?
20 min	**EXPERT COMMENTARY**
10 min	**Q&A/FURTHER CONVERSATION** We will now have 10 minutes to ask questions of the expert commentator and/or to engage in further discussion, given the expert commentary.
5 min	**DEBRIEF OF DAY / PROCESS CHECK:** We will now have 5 minutes to debrief and reflect upon the process today. We will first hear from our process-checker on observations and noticings – in particular our ability to adhere to our norms. We will then open the process-check to any reflections or debriefs that anyone would like to add.
5 min	**CELEBRATIONS** Lead celebrations Make plan for clean-up Thank you!
	Head out for dinner/beverages to celebrate!!!

Appendix A. Materials to support *Kyouzai Kenkyuu and Neriage*

Websites

Collaborative Lesson Research – UK: https://www.collaborative-lesson-research.uk/
The website contains information about Lesson Study including guides to get you started, and has packages to support kyouzai kenkyuu in specific topic areas.

IMPULS: http://www.impuls-tgu.org/en/
This website contains a wide range of research proposals (some with accompanying videos of the research lessons).

Lesson Study Alliance: https://www.lsalliance.org/
The website contains information about Lesson Study including guides and proformas to get you started. It also has a database of Lesson Study research proposals. Blog posts can also support with your research as part of kyouzai kenkyuu.

The Lesson Study Group at Mills College: https://lessonresearch.net/
The website contains information about Lesson Study and Teaching Through Problem-Solving including guides and proformas to get you started and courses to enhance your knowledge and understanding. It also provides access to Lesson Study research proposals and videos of research lessons.

Books
To support with facilitating the whole-class discussion:

Smith, M. S., & Stein, M. K. (2018). *Five Practices for Orchestrating Productive Mathematical Discussion*. SAGE Publications.
Takahashi, A. (2021). *Teaching Mathematics Through Problem-Solving: A Pedagogical Approach from Japan*. Routledge. https://doi.org/10.4324/9781003015475

To support kyouzai kenkyuu

Brownell, J. O., Chen, J.-Q., & Ginet, L. (2014). *Big Ideas of Early Mathematics: What Teachers of Young Children Need to Know*. Pearson.
Carpenter, T. P., Fennema, E., Franke, M. L., Levi, L., & Empson, S. B. (2015). *Children's Mathematics: Cognitively Guided Instruction*. Heinemann.
Fujii, T., & Majima, H. (Eds.). (2020). *New Mathematics for Elementary School*. TOKYO SHOSEKI.
Ma, L. (2020). *Knowing and Teaching Elementary Mathematics: Teachers' Understanding of Fundamental Mathematics in China and the United States* (3rd ed.). Routledge.
Takahashi, A. (2021). *Teaching Mathematics Through Problem-Solving: A Pedagogical Approach from Japan*. Routledge. https://doi.org/10.4324/9781003015475
Takahashi, A., McDougal, T., Friedkin, S., & Watanabe, T. (Eds.). (2022). *Educators' Learning from Lesson Study: Mathematics for Ages 5–13*. Routledge.

Part 3

Pathways to getting started in Collaborative Lesson Research

3.1 Two major pathways to getting started in collaborative lesson research; learn by designing research lessons and learn by observing research lessons

Akihiko Takahashi

Since Lesson Study was introduced by researchers (Lewis & Tsuchida, 1998; Stigler & Hiebert, 1999; Yoshida, 1999), researchers and educators worldwide have tried to use Lesson Study as an innovative teacher professional development approach for their teachers and schools. Because Lesson Study was a new approach and no one in their school systems know about it, they had to read research articles that introduce to readers outside Japan based on case studies conducted in schools to understand how Japanese teachers conduct Lesson Study (e.g., Fernandez & Yoshida, 2004; Fujii, 2016; Lewis & Tsuchida, 1998; Takahashi & McDougal, 2014; Yoshida, 1999). After they read some of the research articles, researchers and educators who decided to try it by themselves invited their teachers and school administrators to work with them on a new professional development approach. Handbooks and articles for practitioners written by leading researchers and practitioners are often used to support teachers in implementing Lesson Study for schools outside Japan (e.g., Lewis, 2002; Lewis & Hurd, 2011; Takahashi & McDougal, 2016; Takahashi & Yoshida, 2004; Weeks & Stepanek, 2001). Lesson Study artifacts, including lesson plans and research lesson videos produced by pioneer projects outside Japan, are also used as resources as examples of adaptation.

3.1.1 Two ways in engaging lesson study

One of the unique characteristics of Lesson Study (LS) is the use of live classroom observation as its core activity. Typically, a team of teachers carefully design a lesson to assess issues in teaching and learning to seek ways to overcome the issues to improve student learning. They invite other teachers and educators who are not part of the lesson planning team to observe the research lesson and conduct a post-lesson discussion to exchange what they observed and discuss critical ideas for improving teaching and learning. It is very rare to conduct the post-lesson discussion only among the team who design the research lesson in Japan. In Lesson Study, all the teachers of the school or even teachers from other schools are usually invited to observe and engage in the post-lesson discussion (e.g., Takahashi & Yoshida, 2004; Yoshida, 1999).

Thus, there are two ways to engage in Lesson Study. One way is to engage in Lesson Study as a member of the lesson planning team or the teacher who teaches the research lesson. They spend several weeks preparing the research lesson proposal, known as a lesson plan before the research lesson (Murata & Takahashi, 2002). The team conducts an intensive study about the topic that they design to teach and carefully anticipates how the students may react to the task and the key questions the design team comes up with. The team often conducts a mock-up lesson to discuss details of their plan including the way of

DOI: 10.4324/9781003375272-10

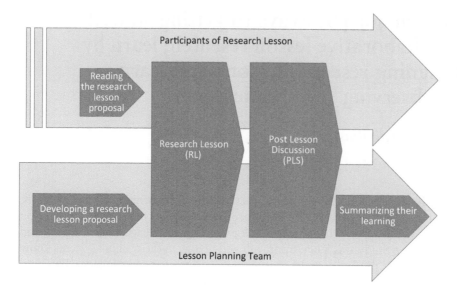

Figure 3.1.1 Two ways in engaging Lesson Study.

presenting the major tasks and how the teacher utilizes visual aids including the board writing to facilitate the discussion. Experienced teachers also prepare how to answer questions that the participants of the research lesson may ask the team during the post-lesson discussion.

Another way is to engage it as research lesson participants who are involved not in the lesson planning team. They often do not know how they decided to investigate the topic by designing the lesson before coming to the research lesson and first learn the team's ideas by reading their research lesson proposal just before the research lesson. In contrast with the participants who are part of the planning team, the research lesson participants do not necessarily have in-depth knowledge and expectations of the research lesson. They tend to bring a wider perspective to observe a research lesson and engage in the post-lesson discussion. Figure 3.1.1 shows these two different ways of engaging in Lesson Study.

Although both parties observe the same research lesson, they are expected to bring slightly different ways of observing the lesson. The lesson planning team's major interest is how the lesson they spent several weeks designing addresses the issue in teaching and learning. They may have specific students' reactions to the lesson design they may expect to observe. In other words, the planning team's major interest is testing their hypotheses, which is how the teaching based on the research lesson supports their students learn to accomplish the objectives of the lesson by addressing issues that they planned to overcome. Thus, the team members' observations and data collections tend to be focused on the issues they plan to address.

For the participants of the research lesson, observing a research lesson designed by other teachers provides an opportunity to learn how other teachers design and teach a lesson. One of the advantages of Lesson Study is for teachers not only to learn by reading carefully designed research lesson proposals but also to observe the research lessons based on the proposal. Moreover, they have opportunities to discuss the team's lesson design and the impacts on the student learning with the team who designed the research lesson, including the teacher who teaches the research lesson, after the research lesson observation.

Different from the lesson design team, the participants of a research lesson may observe the research lesson from more of a variety of viewpoints depending on their interests. Some of them are interested in learning how the particular topic of the research lesson can be taught. Some novice teachers may be interested in learning pedagogical ideas that the team decided to employ. Some teacher leaders may want to know more about how the school's research theme is addressed in the research lesson. Depending upon the participants' prior experience and interests, their focus on the research lesson observation may vary.

Therefore, Japanese teachers and educators value the post-lesson discussion as a place where a variety of observations and interpretations are shared and critical issues in improving teaching and learning are discussed.

Many lesson study efforts outside Japan did not include observers other than members of the planning team, except perhaps for a researcher leading the project. There may be various reasons for this. Many teachers associate having observers in their room with being formally evaluated and are therefore shy about inviting others into their classroom. Teachers typically lack experience with carefully observing lessons and providing critical feedback, and therefore the team might feel that it will not be valuable to invite others. And, there are often significant logistical challenges involved in freeing teachers from their own classroom duties to observe a research lesson. Whatever the reason, failing to include outside observers means missing an important opportunity to learn from the diverse – and fresh – perspectives of observers who were not part of the planning team. More observers can potentially collect more data about the impact of the lesson on students. And not inviting outside observers also means depriving others of the rare but valuable opportunity to learn: from observing the lesson, participating in the discussion, and hearing the final comments by the outside expert (see more on this idea in Chapter 3.2).

3.1.2 How teachers get started in engaging in lesson study?

Novice teachers in Japan typically start Lesson Study by observing research lessons as participants. It is rare for Japanese teachers to start engaging in Lesson Study by planning research lessons without having any opportunities to participate in research lessons as participants. Typical novice teachers in Japan often participate in research lessons (RL) and post lesson discussions (PLD) that are conducted in the schools they belong to as a part of their schools' professional development and conducted at other schools as a part of the district professional development opportunities or a part of public research open house before they plan and/or teach a research lesson. In other words, Japanese teachers experience a part of the Lesson Study cycle as participants of RL and PLD before joining a complete Lesson Study cycle by themselves.

There are various opportunities for teachers to join RLs and PLDs as observers. Local school districts usually organize RLs for their teachers as a part of monthly professional development, and some schools invite teachers from other schools to join their research open houses with RLs. and observe research lessons, post-lesson discussions, and final comments (Murata & Takahashi, 2002; Takahashi, 2006). Thus, Japanese teachers have more opportunities to observe RLs designed and taught by other teachers and engage in PLDs as LS participants than conduct RLs as a part of lesson planning team members or the teacher who teaches research a lesson. From the author's experiences of supporting Lesson Study in Japan, it is safely assumed that typical elementary school teachers in Japan have nearly a handful of opportunities to observe RLs every year. On the other hand, opportunities for being part of the lesson planning team may occur only once a year. Opportunities for teaching research lessons for a typical classroom teacher in Japan would be much fewer than being a part of a planning team.

One of the advantages of Japanese teachers having more opportunities for observing other teachers' research lessons is the fact that they can see a variety of examples of carefully designed lessons. A typical research lesson proposal for a research lesson, different from a lesson plan for everyday teaching, includes the research theme of the Lesson Study, the rationale of the lesson design including the results from the groundwork, *Kyouzai Kenkyuu*, and anticipated student responses, and a plan for providing visual aids, e.g., *Bansho* to engage in discussions. Reading the team's research lesson proposal prior to the actual research lesson observation helps them understand not only how the teacher of the research lesson plan to teach the lesson but also the team's thought processes in coming up with the ideas to address issues in teaching and learning. Because research lesson proposals include the critical issue around teaching the topic that the research lesson is designed to address and the rationale behind its design, they help teachers, particularly novice teachers learn how teachers can learn to improve teaching and learning by going through Lesson Study. It may be hard for novice teachers to learn how to provide an authentic learning experience for students only by reading books. Live research lessons can provide teachers to see exemplary lessons based on practicing teachers' efforts in addressing issues in teaching and learning. Of course, not all the research lessons successfully demonstrate good practice for other teachers to use, the post-lesson discussions provide opportunities to propose how the lesson can be improved.

Another benefit of participating in research lessons is learning how to analyze teaching in terms of student learning. Through research lesson observation and post-lesson discussion, the participants can witness the following four critical skills that Hiebert et al. (2007) argue as basics for becoming reflective practitioners.

Skill 1: Specify the Learning Goal(s) for the Instructional Episode
Skill 2: Conduct Empirical Observations of Teaching and Learning
Skill 3: Construct Hypotheses About the Effects of Teaching on Students' Learning
Skill 4: Use Analysis to Propose Improvements in Teaching

During the post-lesson discussion, the participants often discuss how the research lesson impacted student learning and what they learned from the design of the lesson, and the teaching they witnessed. Teachers, particularly novice teachers, can learn other teachers' expertise related to the above four critical skills.

3.1.3 Challenges in getting started lesson study outside Japan

In most cases outside Japan, teachers get started with Lesson Study by reading books and articles to learn what Japanese teachers do and recruit enthusiastic teachers to form a lesson planning team. Then, start preparing a research lesson by following available resources to design a lesson that they will be teaching as a research lesson. As we discuss in the previous section, it is very rare for Japanese teachers to start designing research lessons without experiencing research lessons and post-lesson discussions. Some of the pioneers of the Lesson Study project teachers and researchers show how challenging it is to jump into Lesson Study without observing other teachers' Lesson Study work (Takahashi, 2011).

When you initiate CLR, it is strongly recommended to provide participants to experience Lesson Study as an observer of the research lesson and engage in a post-lesson discussion before they engage in planning lessons. In case, there are no live research lessons available in your area, having them experience research lesson observation and post-lesson discussion using videos of authentic research lessons and post-lesson discussion may be an alternative.

References

Fernandez, C., & Yoshida, M. (2004). *Lesson Study: A Japanese approach to improving mathematics teaching and learning*. Routledge.

Fujii, T. (2016). Designing and adapting tasks in lesson planning: A critical process of Lesson Study *ZDM Mathematics Education, 48*(4), 411–423. 10.1007/s11858-016-0770-3

Hiebert, J., Morris, A. K., Berk, D., & Jansen, A. (2007). Preparing teachers to learn from teaching. *Journal of Teacher Education, 58*(1), 47–61. 10.1177/0022487106295726

Lewis, C. (2002). *Lesson Study: A handbook of teacher-led instructional change*. Research for Better Schools.

Lewis, C., & Hurd, J. (2011). *Lesson Study step by step: How teacher learning communities improve instruction*. Heinemann.

Lewis, C., & Tsuchida, I. (1998). A lesson is like a swiftly flowing river. *American Educator*(Winter 1998), 12–51.

Murata, A., & Takahashi, A. (2002). *Vehicle to connect theory, research, and practice: How teacher thinking changes in district-level Lesson Study in Japan*. Proceedings of the Annual Meeting [of the] North American Chapter of the International Group for the Psychology of Mathematics Education (24th, Athens, GA, October 26-29, 2002). Volumes 1–4 ERIC/CSMEE Publications.

Stigler, J., & Hiebert, J. (1999). *The teaching gap: Best ideas from the world's teachers for improving education in the classroom*. Free Press. http://www.loc.gov/catdir/bios/simon051/99027270.html

Takahashi, A. (2006,Number 8). Types of elementary mathematics Lesson Study in Japan: Analysis of features and characteristics. *Journal of Japan Society of Mathematical Education, LXXXVIII*, 15–21.

Takahashi, A. (2011). Jumping into Lesson Study—Inservice mathematics teacher education. In L. C. Hart, A. Alston, & A. Murata (Eds.), *Lesson Study research and practice in mathematics education* (pp. 79–82). Springer.

Takahashi, A., & McDougal, T. (2014). Implementing a new national curriculum: A Japanese public school's two-year Lesson-Study project. In A. R. McDuffie & K. S. Karp (Eds.), *Annual Perspectives in Mathematics Education (APME) 2014: Using research to improve instruction* (pp. 13–21). National Council of Teachers of Mathematics. http://books.google.com/books?id=nHiEngEACAAJ

Takahashi, A., & McDougal, T. (2016, July). Collaborative lesson research: Maximizing the impact of Lesson Study. *ZDM Mathematics Education, 48*(4), 513–526. 10.1007/s11858-015-0752-x

Takahashi, A., & Yoshida, M. (2004, May). How can we start Lesson Study?: Ideas for establishing Lesson Study communities. *Teaching Children Mathematics, 10*(9), 436–443.

Weeks, D. J., & Stepanek, J. (2001, Spring). Lesson Study: Teachers learning together. *Northwest Teacher, 2*(2). http://www.nwrel.org/msec/nwteacher/spring2001/index.html

Yoshida, M. (1999). *Lesson Study: A case study of a Japanese approach to improving instruction through school-based teacher development* [Dissertation, University of Chicago]. Chicago.

3.2 Learning to analyse lessons from observing research lessons

Thomas McDougal

When one thinks about learning through Lesson Study, one reasonably thinks first about what is learned by the team that plans the research lesson. But much of the power of Lesson Study as a systemic form of professional development comes from the learning opportunities that research lessons create for outside observers. And perhaps the most far-reaching outcome of observing research lessons is that one can become more proficient at learning from one's own teaching, and thus better equipped to continue improving throughout one's career.

Heibert and colleagues (Heibert *et al.*, 2007) propose a collection of competencies that teachers need to acquire in order to learn from studying teaching. Their analysis focuses on the problem of preparing preservice teachers, but their analysis is relevant also for helping in-service teachers learn from observing lessons – their own lessons and those of others.

The overall goal is for teachers to be able to accurately assess how a lesson impacted the students, and make suitable changes when a lesson falls short of achieving its goals.

Two competencies are needed to do this. The first competency is "pedagogical content knowledge" (Shulman, 1986).

> This is the kind of subject matter knowledge needed to unpack the content learning goals for students, to understand students' thinking about the subject, to simplify the complex ideas of the subject in ways that sustain the integrity of the subject, to represent ideas in accessible ways for students, to post key questions and problems, and so on.
>
> (Hiebert *et al.*, 2007, p.49)

The second kind of competence is about the ability to analyse lessons to develop "hypotheses about cause-effect relationships between teaching and learning". They break this competence into four skills:

> (a) setting learning goals for students, (b) assessing whether learning goals are being achieved during the lesson, (c) specify hypotheses for why the lesson did or did not work well, and (d) using the hypotheses to revise the lesson. (*Ibid.*)

Let's look at how we can develop these competencies and skills while observing a research lesson.

Reading the research proposal

The first step in learning from a research lesson is to carefully read the research proposal prepared by the planning team. While this document is sometimes referred to casually as a

DOI: 10.4324/9781003375272-11

lesson plan, it is much more than that, as the example in Chapter 2 illustrates. The document should describe the research that the team did regarding the topic of the lesson, likely including, for example, relevant portions of the standards, a comparison of approaches to the topic found in various textbooks and elsewhere, and typical student misunderstandings. It may also include what the team has learned from their own experience about challenges in teaching the topic. With all of this information, the document provides an opportunity for the reader to extend their pedagogical content knowledge, as described above.

Carefully reading the research proposal is also important for giving back to the planning team, an obligation of all observers. A research lesson is *research*, an experiment testing certain ideas about how to improve student growth. Observers need to know what the team's research questions are in order to be prepared to collect relevant data.

In CLR, a research lesson will address two research questions. This first is specific to the teaching and learning of specific content, something like "Will this lesson help students understand X?" The second relates to some long-term educational goal, often a school-wide goal, which may or may not be content-specific. This long-term goal is called the *research theme*. One school, for example, has a research theme aimed at developing students as autonomous learners through lessons designed as teaching through problem-solving. Another has a broader research theme about cultivating a joy of learning. So the second research question would be something like, "If we teach our lessons in such-and-such way, will students experience the joy of learning?"

To understand the research questions, the first place to look is the learning goals of the lesson. Are they clear? precise? meaningful? Learning goals may be expressed in terms of what students will be able to do, or in terms of some cognitive changes the team hopes to create (see McDougal, 2016). Observers can develop their own capacity to set clear learning goals for lessons by reading goals that have been carefully crafted by the planning team.

In addition, the team will usually articulate a hypothesis about how certain decisions about the lesson design will affect the students. They may identify specific evidence – "points of evaluation" – they want observers to look for. Reading the proposal, we may also develop theories or questions about how the lesson will work, and generate our own ideas about evidence we will want to collect. The example of a research proposal in Chapter 2 describes the team's theory of action about how using an inquiry approach will develop students' conceptual understanding, and gives very concrete suggestions for what they would like observers to look for during the lesson. The right-hand column of the lesson flow section also describes specifically what they expect will indicate student understanding of the content.

The Teaching for Robust Understanding (TRU) Framework (e.g., Schoenfeld, 2013) can provide a useful structure to help guide analysis of the lesson plan. Schoenfeld argues that instruction is effective when it addresses each of five dimensions well: the content; cognitive demand; equitable access to content; agency, ownership, and identity; and formative assessment (see Table 3.2.1). Considering how well the lesson plan addresses these five dimensions can help one prepare to observe the lesson itself with a focus on the most critical aspects of teaching and learning.

The research lesson proposal is critical for helping observers understand why the lesson planning team decided to teach the lesson as described, and why the team invited outside educators to observe it. By thoroughly studying the proposal, observers will be prepared to collect data relevant to the team's research questions and to contribute to a high-quality post-lesson discussion. Thus, a well-prepared research lesson proposal is important for maximising the learning opportunities for everyone participating in CLR.

Table 3.2.1 The Teaching for Robust Understanding Framework (https://truframework.org)

The Five Dimensions of Powerful Classrooms

The Content	Cognitive Demand	Equitable Access to Content	Agency, Ownership, and Identity	Formative Assessment
The extent to which classroom activity structures provide opportunities for students to become knowledgeable, flexible, and resourceful disciplinary thinkers. Discussions are focused and coherent, providing opportunities to learn disciplinary ideas, techniques, and perspectives, make connections, and develop productive disciplinary habits of mind.	The extent to which students have opportunities to grapple with and make sense of important disciplinary ideas and their use. Students learn best when they are challenged in ways that provide support for growth, with task difficulty ranging from moderate to demanding. The level of challenge should be conducive to what has been called "productive struggle".	The extent to which classroom activity structures invite and support the active engagement of all of the students in the classroom with the core disciplinary content being addressed by the class. Classrooms in which a small number of students get most of the "air time" are not equitable, no matter how rich the content: all students need to be involved in meaningful ways.	The extent to which students are provided opportunities to "walk the walk and talk the talk" – to contribute to conversations about disciplinary ideas, to build on others' ideas and have others build on theirs – in ways that contribute to their development of agency (the willingness to engage), their ownership over the content, and the development of positive identities as thinkers and learners.	The extent to which classroom activities elicit student thinking and subsequent interactions respond to those ideas, building on productive beginnings and addressing emerging misunderstandings. Powerful instruction "meets students where they are" and gives them opportunities to deepen their understanding.

Observing the lesson

Observing a research lesson is an especially good opportunity to improve one's ability to see whether a lesson's goals are being achieved. At a research lesson, one is free of the responsibility of conducting the lesson and also, if one is an outside observer, free of any emotional attachment to the outcome that would skew one's perceptions. Heibert *et al.* (2007) note that this skill entails three subskills:

(a) appreciating that evidence about students' learning is essential ... ; (b) recognizing what counts as evidence that students are achieving the learning goals; and (c) knowing how to collect evidence ... (p. 52)

As mentioned above, the lesson plan itself will usually provide helpful suggestions regarding relevant evidence, and we will come back to the topic of evidence when we look at the post-lesson discussion. For the lesson itself, let us start with the last subskill, knowing how to collect evidence. On this point, we have a few suggestions.

Our primary responsibility is to collect data about the impact of the lesson on the students. The best vantage point for this purpose is usually along the sides of the classroom, which affords a good view of students' faces. We also will want to stand most of the time, so that we can observe multiple students and peer over their shoulders at what they write, and occasionally kneel down, so we can hear what they say. A clipboard allows us to take notes while standing or kneeling. Also essential is to have one or more copies of a seating chart, to be able to tie observations to specific students. If a seating chart is not available, you can quickly make one with codes for different seating positions that can later be mapped back to students (see Figure 3.2.1).

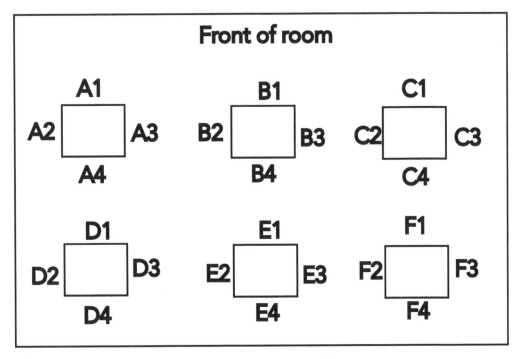

Figure 3.2.1 A sample coded seating chart. With such a chart, notes can refer to specific students by code.

Once the lesson begins, there are various strategies for observing, each with advantages and disadvantages. One is to focus on a limited number of students and carefully track their evolution throughout the lesson. Using this strategy, for example, one might be able to identify elements of the lesson that lead students to a key insight. Another strategy is to quickly survey the entire class at various times during the lesson, to get a sense of the prevalence of certain ways of thinking. This strategy might reveal, for example, that a particular misconception is widespread, or that many students are confused about the problem, or, conversely, that many students finish the task early and are sitting idle.

There are also a number of different strategies for taking notes and collecting data. One is to make notes directly in the research proposal, in the section describing the lesson flow. This approach makes it easy to compare what was planned or expected with what actually happens. A disadvantage, of course, is that there is limited space in which to write. It can help if the lesson plan is printed single-sided, with the back sides blank for additional notes.

Other strategies are to use multiple copies of a seating chart to record observations over time, or to use a phone camera to take pictures of student work, although it is sometimes hard to remember which photo came from which student, and sometimes the ease of taking photos leads one to being less attuned to what students are saying and doing.

It can be valuable to have time information along with your notes. Time is the most precious commodity in teaching, and having information about when key events occur can help everyone think about how to use time most effectively. For example, it is unfortunately common for introductory or warm-up activities to occupy an outsized portion of the lesson period. Having time information also makes it easier for different observers to coordinate their observations and develop hypotheses about the impacts of certain events on students.

An iPad app, LessonNote™, was developed by Lesson Study Alliance specifically to support lesson observation and is currently available for free (see Figure 3.2.2). Data input is built off a seating chart: tapping on an icon in the seating chart – representing either a student, teacher, group, or display (e.g., a whiteboard) – opens an area in which one can write notes, copy student work, or take photos. To record observations about multiple students quickly, one can create a note containing the seating chart. And, one can mark transitions between different lesson modalities: whole-class instruction or discussion, group work, and individual work. All notes and modality transitions are time-stamped, and notes identify which icon in the seating chart (e.g., which student) they are associated with.

Regardless of the approach one chooses to take, the obligation to focus on the students creates an almost perfect opportunity to develop an important component of our ability to assess whether learning goals are being achieved: our ability to see what is actually happening. We are free of the normal duties of teaching and therefore able to pay close attention to whichever students we choose, including those who may escape notice by the teacher; and as outside observers we have no emotional stake that might skew our perceptions. A Japanese educator once said, "What's the most important benefit of lesson study? You develop the eyes to see children". (Itoh, in Lewis & Hurd, 2011)

Discussing the lesson

The post-lesson discussion provides an opportunity to help inexperienced observers understand the importance of collecting evidence of student learning. Heibert *et al.* (2007) note that "[i]t is tempting to assess teaching effectiveness based on what the teacher does rather than on how the students respond". (p. 52, citing Morris (2006) and Santagata *et al.* (2007)) If an observer makes a claim based on a teacher move, a good moderator will

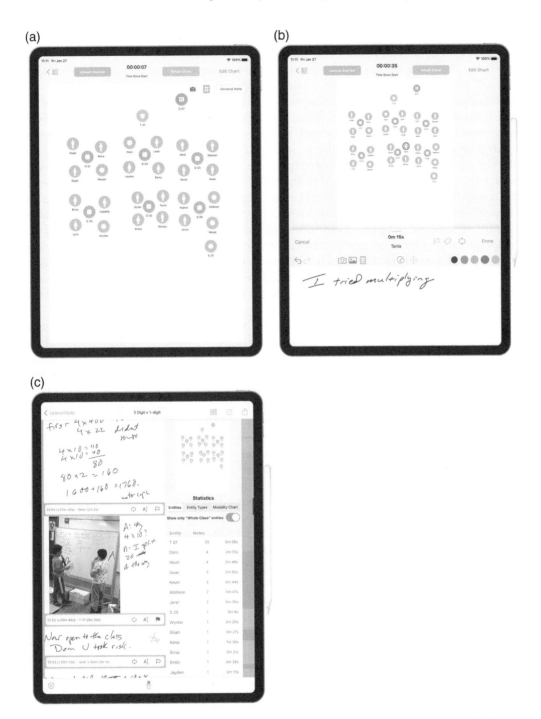

Figure 3.2.2 Screenshots from LessonNote™ showing (a) the seating chart interface; (b) the note-taking area; and (c) the notes review screen.

respond by asking observers how that move impacted students (see chapter 3.5 for more about the moderator role). Inexperienced observers get to hear more experienced colleagues cite specific student actions and reactions. As we listen to what the others observed, and to what the *koshi*, or final commentator, observed, we might sometimes think, "Next time I will look for that", where "next time" might well be our own classrooms.

Another pitfall for inexperienced observers is to conclude that the lesson was successful on the basis of a few vocal students. When they hear contrary data from another observer who surveyed the ideas of many students, they can learn to pay attention also to students who are not so vocal to get a broader picture of student thinking.

But the goal of a post-lesson discussion is not merely to report what was observed, but to interpret the data to determine whether the learning goals were achieved, and to answer other research questions posed by the planning team. This is an opportunity to practice both assessing whether learning goals were achieved and specifying hypotheses for why they were or were not achieved. Feedback comes in the form of the hypotheses offered by others, especially by the final commentator. When a lesson ends without getting to the main learning goal, for example, inexperienced observers are often ready to make excuses, like "This topic just needs more time". But other observers might point to an absence of change in student thinking across multiple tasks and argue that fewer, more carefully crafted tasks could have led more quickly to the goal.

This leads to the fourth competency proposed by Hiebert *et al.*: using a hypothesis to revise a lesson. The goal of CLR is to improve teaching across the board by testing ideas and analysing results in individual research lessons. Therefore, revising the lesson is outside the scope of CLR. Nevertheless, it is usually by considering how this lesson could be improved that we articulate ideas for making other lessons better. Inevitably, one walks away from a research lesson thinking, "How would I do that lesson?" And, in fact, teachers who will be teaching the same topic in their own classroom will frequently try a revised version of the lesson themselves.

At the end of the post-lesson discussion, there is usually a mini-lecture by a *koshi*, an invited expert, often referred to as "final comments", in which she or he may discuss the content of the lesson, share observations from the lesson different from those already discussed along with an analysis, and offer suggestions for future work. (See the discussion of the *koshi* in chapter 3.5 of this volume.) This provides observers with a final opportunity to expand their pedagogical content knowledge, to acquire ideas about how to better observe a research lesson, to see how an expert analyses student learning and about what that expert deems as evidence, and to hear the expert's ideas about how a lesson could be revised – all of the competencies Hiebert *et al.* posit as important for learning from studying teaching.

Conclusion

Using the framework proposed by Heibert *et al.*, we see how observing a research lesson and participating in the post-lesson discussion is an almost perfect opportunity for teachers to become better at learning from teaching. We can acquire pedagogical content knowledge; we can learn how to set clear learning goals for students; we can learn to better observe students for evidence of whether the learning goals have been achieved; we can generate hypotheses about why the lesson goals were achieved or not and check those hypotheses against the hypotheses of the invited expert; and we can think and hear others' ideas about how the lesson could be revised. This is why CLR can be such a powerful learning experience not only for those who develop the lesson but also for those lucky enough to observe it.

References

Heibert, J., Morris, A. K., Berk, D., & Jansen, A. (2007, January/February). Preparing teachers to learn from teaching. *Journal of Teachers Education*, *58*(1), 2007. American Association of Colleges for Teacher Education.

Lewis, C. C., & Hurd, J. (2011). *Lesson Study step by step: How Teacher learning communities improve instruction*. Heinemann.

McDougal, T. (2016). Learning Goals Should Describe Cognitive Change. Blog post. Retrieved 8 January 2023 from https://www.lsalliance.org/2016/05/learning-goals-describe-cognitive-change/

Morris, A. K. (2006). Assessing pre-service teachers' skills for analyzing teaching. *Journal of Mathematics Teacher Education*, *9*(5), 471–505.

Santagata, R., Zannoni, C., & Stigler, J.W. (2007). The role of lesson analysis in pre-service teacher education: An empirical investigation of teacher learning from a virtual video-based field experience. *Journal of Mathematics Teacher Education*, *10*(2), 123–140.

Schoenfeld, A. H. (2013). Classroom observations in theory and practice. *ZDM, The International Journal of Mathematics Education*, *45*, 607–621. DOI: 10.1007/s11858-012-0483-1

Shulman, L. S. (1986). Those Who Understand: Knowledge growth in teaching. *Educational Researcher*, *15*, 4–14. 10.3102/0013189x015002004

3.3 Learning to analyse teaching through the observation of Japanese research lessons

Jacqueline Mann

Background

In the United Kingdom, teachers' first experience of Lesson Study has frequently occurred when planning a research lesson. This may be led by those with experience in conducting and observing research lessons or may be initiated by those with little hands-on experience who have heard about the benefits. This is a contrast to Japan where teachers new to Lesson Study will predominantly observe research lessons multiple times before participating in a planning team. When it is possible to observe a research lesson prior to conducting your own Lesson Study cycle this is wholeheartedly recommended.

Through our work on Lesson Study, we were able to observe research lessons in practice during two visits to Japan. Each week-long trip consisted of a schedule of visits to a variety of elementary, middle and high schools as well as a visit to a textbook publisher and Tokyo Gakugei University. Research lessons and post-lesson discussions were observed live, with simultaneous translations provided to headsets worn by the research group.

Here we look at the process of observing a research lesson using examples from our visits to Japan and the insights it provided to us as UK educators.

Before a research lesson

A research proposal will usually be received before arriving at a research lesson. The contents of the proposal will vary but a detailed research proposal in Japan will typically contain:

- The research question(s)
- Information about the class (year group, class size etc.)
- An overview of the unit of study and where the lesson sits within this
- A detailed lesson plan for the research lesson itself
- The expected board layout

When Japanese teachers and educators refer to a research proposal they are describing more than just a lesson plan for the observed lesson. The detail here describes a typical research proposal.

The research questions

The idea of a research lesson is to research a particular aspect of student learning, this may be specific to the mathematical concepts or incorporate a wider idea. During our trip we

DOI: 10.4324/9781003375272-12

witnessed aspects around mathematical concepts, such as, to understand the size of remainders and to be able to calculate them when dividing decimal numbers by whole numbers. Alternatively, research questions were around mathematical behaviours, for example, to improve students' ability to generate new ideas through comparing and contrasting solutions or a wider focus, such as developing dispositions for learning toward harmonious living. In Japan, schools conduct lesson study in all subjects, there will often be a whole school research question that all subjects work towards as well as a research question chosen for that particular lesson.

An overview of the unit of study

Japan has a very clear mathematics curriculum and schools choose from a specified list of approved textbooks that follow this curriculum. The Japanese mathematics curriculum is not only coherent, but any changes are carefully considered, researched, and gradually introduced. During a visit to a textbook publisher, we learned about the development of the textbooks; new editions are carefully considered and members of committees include teachers, educators and researchers. New editions take around four years to go from a first draft to publishing and the main content changes are often relatively small. In fact, some textbook problems in the latest edition of the textbooks are based on those used in the 1950s. Lesson Study is influential in the design of the textbooks with new problems (or changes to problems) coming from research lessons that have been observed by committee members.

The stability and coherence of the National Curriculum and textbooks support the process of Lesson Study. Teachers can be confident in students' prior learning and the way in which these concepts have been taught. They can also benefit from the accumulated knowledge of their colleagues who may have taught these same or similar problems many times previously. For instance, when teaching the area of a trapezium, teachers will know that students will have been introduced to models of cutting and rearranging shapes such as parallelograms and triangles as well as to the idea of doubling shapes. These ideas allow students to manipulate the trapezium to develop methods for calculating the area. A student's conceptual understanding is carefully constructed using prior knowledge to ensure concepts are sequenced and linked.

The research proposal will contain the current unit of study and which lesson is being used for the research lesson. This allows observers to understand what knowledge the students should have prior to the lesson and where the learning will lead after the lesson. Many research lessons will be based upon one of sometimes several pivotal problem-solving lessons within each unit, where students study a single problem in greater depth to highlight key conceptual understanding. Interestingly, as seen in Figure 3.3.1, there is a much greater focus on students thinking for themselves, rather than a focus on the teacher explaining with repeated reference to "think about".

A detailed lesson plan

Details for the observed lesson are also contained within the proposal. The plan for the observed lesson contains a description of each part of the lesson, the problems to be used and expected student activities. It includes teacher questions and detailed anticipated student responses as can be seen in Figure 3.3.2. These lessons will have been carefully planned over the course of several meetings, consisting of several hours devoted to a single

2.   Unit Lesson Plan

Hr	Aim	Learning Activities	Instructional Techniques & Evaluation Benchmarks
1	Multiplying Decimals p. 51-61 (5 hrs)		
1	Prologue		
	○ Show the figure on p54. Lead a discussion reviewing the place value when the decimal is multiplied times 10, times 100, times 1/10, and times 1/100, as well as the relationship between the multiplicand and the product in multiplication problems while raising students' interest and attention in the new material covering multiplication of decimals when the multiplier and divisor are whole numbers. (approx 10 mins)		
	○ Understand the meaning of the calculation for decimal × whole number and be able to perform them.	· Set up the equation and consider the reasons its construction. · Consider the calculation method for 0.3 × 6. · Summarize the calculation method for 0.3 × 6. · Practice calculations.	Prior learning <multiplying whole numbers 3 × 6> ■ Show attempts at thinking about the meaning of the calculation decimal × whole number and the way to solve it by relating it to previously learned whole number multiplication. 【interest】
2	○ Understand how to perform calculation by multiplying a decimal to the tenths place by a single-digit whole number and be able to calculate it.	· Think about how to calculate 3.6 × 7. · Think about how to write the multiplication algorithm to calculate 3.6 × 7. · Summarize the algorithm for 3.6 × 7. · Practice calculations.	Prior learning <Algorithm for multiplying whole numbers> ■ Thinks about and explains how to multiply decimals with a figure in the tenths place by a whole number in the ones place using figures or equations based on previously covered multiplication algorithm for performing multiplication of whole numbers. 【Thinking】 ■ Can multiply a decimal number to the tenths place by a single-digit whole number. 【Skill】
3	○ Understand the multiplication algorithm for multiplying a decimal to the tenths place by a single- or double-digit whole number (including when the multiplicand is a pure decimal number or the product ends in 0) and be able to calculate it.	Think about how to write out multiplication algorithms to solve 0.2 × 4, 0.8 × 5, 7.5 × 4 (including when the multiplicand is a pure decimal number and when the last number in the product is 0). · Practice calculations. · Think about how to write out and solve 1.8×34. · Summarize the method for working through 1.8 × 34. · Tackle computational and story problems of the types above.	Prior Learning <Multiplication of twodigit whole numbers> · Can use the multiplication algorithm to multiply a decimal to the tenths place by a single- or double-digit whole number (including when the multiplicand is a repeating decimal number or the product ends in 0). 【Skill】 · Understand the algorithm for multiplying a decimal number to the tenths place by a one- or two-digit number (including when the multiplicand is a pure decimal number

Figure 3.3.1 An excerpt from a unit plan: "Let's Think about Multiplying and Dividing Decimal Numbers" Arakawa Dairoku Nippori Elementary School – Grade 4.

lesson. The Japanese refer to this process as *Kyouzai Kenkyuu*, which is often translated as "the study of teaching materials", this aspect is highly important but has often been missed when Lesson Study is practiced outside of Japan (Takahashi & McDougal, 2016), see Chapter 4.2 for further discussion on this aspect.

Teaching Through Problem Solving (TTPS) lessons are centred around promoting student understanding through a focus on teaching through problem-solving. Lessons are carefully constructed so that students can develop understanding through prior knowledge. This pedagogical approach has been developed over many years in Japan and early movement towards this can be traced back to the late 1950s (Takahashi, 2021).

The expected board layout

The lesson proposal often contains an image of the expected board layout. Laying out the lesson so that the thinking for the entire lesson is visible throughout the lesson is an important factor. In Japan, this is known as Bansho and has high pedagogical regard. Japanese teachers will try not to erase anything during a lesson so that students can more easily compare and contrast their thinking. As a result, teachers can move back and forth with ease between student solutions during the neriage phase, a powerful practice to witness. Figure 3.3.3 illustrates the idea of Bansho, this lesson was observed during our visit and written up as an example of the ways in which a carefully planned board can support student discussions (Baldry et al., 2022).

(3) Progression

Process	Instruction (Major lines of questioning & anticipated student reactions)	☆ Approach to the research topic ◉ Support & points of note ■ Assessment
From problem to Task	**1. Read the problem and understand what is being asked.** T Review last lesson (confirmation) "Let's look back on what we did yesterday." T "Alright, let's look at today's problem." Story Problem: You are going to make white chocolates. You have 46.7g of bar chocolate. Melt the chocolate and divide it out into white chocolates that weigh 3g each. How many 3g white chocolates can you make, and how many grams of white chocolate will you have? T "What's different here from what we learned last time?" C "Division of decimal numbers by whole numbers is the same, but today, we are working with remainders. T We are dividing into 3g pieces, so we are going to have a remainder leftover, aren't we? "Today's goal is here: Goal: Let's think about the size of the remainder in division of decimal numbers."	☆ Encourage students to recall that in the division of decimals up to the previous lesson, the number divided exactly without a remainder. Set up the new topic. ◉ Help students clearly grasp the task of thinking about the size of the remainder in a division problem dividing a decimal number. ◉ Ensure students understand that because we are diving up chocolates at 3g each the decimal is the remaining chocolate. ◉In this lesson, we focus on a different situation than previous lessons: division resulting in a remainder.
Solve on your own	**2. Calculate using the long division algorithm.** T Let's use long division to figure out how many 3g chocolates we can make and how much leftover chocolate we will be left with, in grams. How man grams leftover will get get? C1 46.7÷3＝15 R17 C2 46.7÷3＝15 R1.7	☆◉ Have students look at the size of the remainder they've come up with using the previously learned content as a foundation. ☆◉ Have students give evidence for their thinking from previously learning with regard to the size of the remainder they've come up with.
Interaction	**3. Present the quotient and remainder (R) and check them.** T How many chocolates (quotient) and how much leftover in grams (remainder) did you come up with? C1 The quotient is 15 and the remainder is 1.7. (We'll get 15 pieces and 1.7g leftover) C2 The quotient is 15 and the remainder is 17. (We'll get 15 pieces and 17g leftover.) T Why do you think so? C1 We're making each piece of 3g of chocolate, and so if we had 17g leftover, we would be able to make 5 more pieces. That's why the leftover can't be 17g; it has to be 1.7g. C2 In the division problem 46.7÷3, we are using 0.1 as our base unit, and so the figure 17 means 17 units of 0.1. Therefore, the remainder is 1.7. C3 The whole number (integer) part of 46.7 is 43. When we divide it by 3, we get 15 remainder 1. The remainder is 1 and a decimal of 0.7, and so the total makes 1.7.	◉In talking about the size of the remainder, have students use the order for long division and the meaning of the story problem as their foundation and build their logical argument. ◉When necessary, use real-world examples like liquid quantities or length to show division in action. ■ Students can explain the remainder as a given number of parts of the decimal place being used as the base unit (presentation, notebook). 【Mathematical reasoning】 ☆ Have students recall division of

Figure 3.3.2 An excerpt from a research lesson: "To understand the size of remainders and be able to calculate them when dividing decimal numbers by whole numbers", Arakawa Dairoku Nippori Elementary School – Grade 4.

Figure 3.3.3 The board plan for an observed lesson- "Solving for corner angles shaped like the Japanese Hiragana character Ku (types of angles within parallel lines), Takehaya Junior High School, attached to Tokyo Gakugei University – grade 8.

The detail contained in a Japanese lesson proposal provides observers with a clear picture of the lesson to be observed and where the learning is situated before entering the lesson. Making use of this information will enable you to gain more from the process and support you in being a valuable contributor during the post-lesson discussion.

During a research lesson

When observing a research lesson it is important to remember that the focus is on the student learning. Research lessons should be viewed as an opportunity to observe how students learn and should be approached in a non-judgemental way. As the lesson proposal contains the key elements of the lesson, much of the observer's time can be used in focusing on the students rather than on the teacher. What are the students doing while the teacher is presenting the problem and how are they reacting to the problem? When the students start to work on the problem, often independently at first, what do they do and how do they get started?

Two key considerations are where to stand when the teacher is speaking and who to observe when the students are actively working. Many experienced Japanese teachers and educators will stand at the front edge of a class as this allows them to see the whole class while the teacher is speaking. When standing at the back, it is harder to see the students' faces and may lead to a heavier focus on the teacher. Second, decisions need to be made about who to focus on during the student activity. When the students begin their independent work or discussions, observers are typically free to walk around the room (but not to interact with the students). Do you want to see what every student is doing, do you focus on a single student or do you try to observe a group? Do you want a wider picture of the entire lesson or a more detailed focus? What and who you choose to focus on will be influenced by your reason for observing the research lesson. Are you new to Lesson Study and want to gain insight to the process, are you interested in how teachers use a particular pedagogical technique, or do you have another reason?

What should be recorded?

A research lesson focuses upon student learning; therefore, data collected from a lesson should concentrate on this. Accurate quotes and observations are useful for the post-lesson discussion. For instance, rather than an interpretation "student x calculated the missing angle using alternate angles" record what was actually seen "student x drew an auxiliary line through angle y and wrote angle ABC on the diagram". Did the anticipated solutions appear? Were these as expected, or did they differ in some way? Quotes from students are also helpful, for the lead teacher quotes of student discussions are particularly valuable as they will have been walking around helping and observing students and may not have picked up on comments made by other students.

One of the greatest privileges of observing a research lesson is the chance to listen. It is expected that observers will not interact in any way with students during a lesson. To listen to students discuss and puzzle out answers, argue, explain their reasoning and reach conclusions independent of the teacher is an opportunity we do not often have. During a research lesson, take accurate records of what you see and hear as you will want to share these as precisely as possible during the post-lesson discussion. Don't try to observe everything, a tighter focus aligned to your current needs will generally be more beneficial.

After a research lesson

After the lesson, teachers and educators will gather for a post-lesson discussion. This often follows a set and fairly formal structure. A chairperson will invite the planning team and lead teacher to speak first. They will speak about the lesson referring back to the research questions, the lesson plan and the aims of the lesson, giving their opinions based on what they have observed. The advantage of planning as a team is that there is a group responsibility for the lesson. This helps ensure a non-judgemental focus on student learning rather than what the individual lead teacher did.

The chairperson will then open up to questions and comments from other observers. Observers are encouraged to share their observations, questions and comments. These are based on what they have seen and the thoughts the lesson may have provoked. Your observations and notes will be valued by the planning team, particularly those that help decide if the research questions were answered. Questions are more commonly centred around how rather than what. Rather than asking "What did students learn?" you will more commonly hear questions such as "How do we know that students learnt x?". This supports the non-judgemental nature of the post-lesson discussion through ensuring the focus remains on the students rather than the teacher.

In a larger public Lesson Study, there will usually be a talk from an invited Koshi after the post-lesson discussion. In Japan, lesson study is the predominant form of CPD. It is intended that all teachers from novice to expert can gain from attending a research lesson. The Koshi is usually a highly regarded professor or educator and teachers will travel vast distances when a particular Koshi is known to be speaking.

The Koshi will speak about the lesson, what they observed and how they felt this met the objectives of the research questions. They will then link this to a partially pre-prepared talk that elevates the knowledge of the audience. An expert Koshi is able to weave together elements of pre-prepared developmental aspects with live examples witnessed in the lesson. Bringing the learning into the context just witnessed.

Conclusion

Attending a research lesson is an opportunity to develop many of the aspects valued by teachers and educators and it can be seen why it is the predominant form of CPD in Japan. There are many gains from attending a live research lesson prior to starting your own journey into Lesson Study, such as:

- An understanding of the bigger picture of Lesson Study, the why, when, and how
- Observing a model for Lesson Study
- Appreciation of the level of detail and planning for a research proposal
- The opportunity to observe and consider student learning in detail
- Hearing a variety of thoughts and insights into a single lesson
- Improved mathematical content knowledge
- Improved pedagogical knowledge
- Improved observational skills
- Improved reflective capacities

When attending a research lesson these skills are developed contextually. From inexperienced to experienced, whether in Lesson Study or teaching, research lessons offer a multitude of learning opportunities, before, during and after the lesson. Although live research lessons are preferred, do not be overly concerned if these opportunities are not immediately available in your early journey into Lesson Study.

References

Baldry, F., Mann, J., Horsman, R., Koiwa, D., & Foster, C. (2022). The use of carefully planned board work to support the productive discussion of multiple student responses in a Japanese problem-solving lesson. *Journal of Mathematics Teacher Education.* 10.1007/s10857-021-09511-6

Takahashi, A. (2021). Teaching Mathematics Through Problem-Solving: A Pedagogical Approach from Japan. Retrieved 8 May 2021, from Routledge & CRC Press website: https://www.routledge.com/Teaching-Mathematics-Through-Problem-Solving-A-Pedagogical-Approach-from/Takahashi/p/book/9780367858827

Takahashi, A., & McDougal, T. (2016). Collaborative lesson research: Maximizing the impact of lesson study. *ZDM, 48*(4), 513–526. 10.1007/s11858-015-0752-x

3.4 Learning to analyse teaching in terms of student learning

Sarah Leakey

In Chapter 3.1, two pathways are discussed for getting started with CLR: as a member of the lesson planning team or as an observer of the research lesson. A key turning point that accelerated my understanding of Lesson Study in general but also how to analyse teaching in terms of student learning was participating in a series of online modules led by the International Math-teacher Professionalization Using Lesson Study (IMPULS) group in collaboration with the Collaborative Lesson Research UK (CLR-UK) group. The course explored teaching through problem-solving (TTP): a pedagogical approach used in Japan which is elaborated on in Chapter 5.3. It consisted of four modules (each lasting approximately one week) on the following topics:

- Module 1: Per unit quantity and speed
- Module 2: Congruent triangles and quadrilaterals
- Module 3: Division with remainders
- Module 4: Division of fractions

The online modules fell somewhere in between the two pathways. As an observer would, we watched a recorded research lesson and post-lesson discussion (recorded in Japan and translated into English). However, we also spent much time researching curriculum materials and anticipating student responses; activities that are more typical of a planning team. Chapter 1.2 highlights the requirement for adapting Lesson Study when used outside Japan; using online modules such as these, although not used in Japan, may be a useful adaptation to getting started with CLR in areas where Lesson Study is not yet established. The section that follows focuses predominately on Module 1.

3.4.1 Before observing a research lesson

We engaged in a similar practice to *kyouzai kenkyuu* (described in Chapters 1.1 and 3.5) and explored curriculum coherence and sequencing as well as the mathematics relevant to the unit associated with the research lesson. This helped us to consider student learning in terms of the prerequisites for the research lesson and the foundations that are being built for future learning (see Figure 3.4.1).

Within the broader unit of work, the idea of "per unit quantity" is introduced using the concept of crowdedness (see Figure 3.4.2 and Table 3.4.1) followed by population density which sets students up to learn about rates such as speed which was the focus of the research lesson (see Box 3.4.1). This detailed analysis highlighted the importance of paying close attention to task design and presentation to maximise student learning in relation to

DOI: 10.4324/9781003375272-13

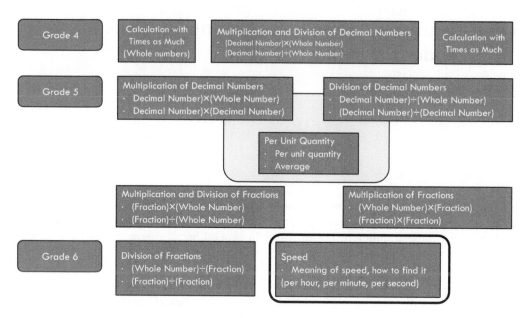

Figure 3.4.1 An overview of the curriculum sequence related to "Per Unit Quantity" and "Speed", provided by Dr. Takahashi during Module 1.

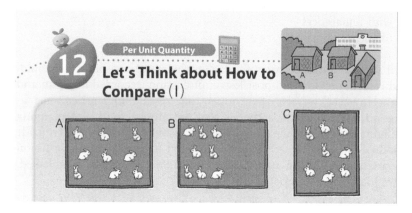

Figure 3.4.2 Extracts from the "Per Unit Quantity" lesson about crowdedness from *New Mathematics for Elementary School 5B* (Fujii & Majima, 2020, p. 29).

Table 3.4.1 Extracts from the "Per Unit Quantity" lesson about crowdedness from *New Mathematics for Elementary School 5B* (Fujii & Majima, 2020, p. 29)

Cage	Area (m²)	Number of rabbits
A	6	9
B	6	8
C	5	8

the intended goal(s) of the lesson. (Further information about lesson design can be found in Chapter 5.2.) Key features that stood out to me are discussed next.

1 The importance of visual presentation

In the crowdedness problem, students attempt to use the visual image to determine the order of cages A, B and C according to how crowded they are. Cages A and B have the same amount of space but different numbers of rabbits; although a superficial look might give the impression that B is more crowded. Cage C is a different (unknown) size to Cages A and B, therefore, students do not have enough information, from the image alone, to compare Cages A and C.

2 The impact and relevance of delaying student access to key information required

After students have established they lack enough information to compare Cages A and C additional information is provided (see Table 3.4.1).

By withholding key information (the area of each cage) students' attention can be drawn to the new mathematics they are learning. To compare crowdedness two quantities are required: in this case area and number of rabbits. In contrast, comparison situations students experienced in the past, such as comparing children's heights, require just one quantity.

3 The importance of the numbers involved in the task

The numbers in the task are small making them relatively easy to work with. Additionally, their deliberate choice helps to draw out key aspects related to the mathematics under investigation. In this case, crowdedness could be easily established if one of the conditions was the same (Cage A and B have the same area and Cage B and C have the same number of rabbits). However, if both the area and number of rabbits are not the same (as in the case of Cage A and C), finding a unit quantity for either area or rabbits could help solve the problem.

As I engaged in subsequent IMPULS modules, as well as understanding how task design features (such as those just described above) could be applied to other areas of mathematics, I also began to better understand their more generalised impact on teaching and learning. For example, visual presentation and delaying student access to key information can promote student-generated questions and curiosity drawing students' attention to key features of the mathematics relevant to the goal(s) of the lesson. In the module on division with remainders, the use of a visual chart that showed four recreation games supported students to notice patterns and identify the relevance of the remainder to the problem. In the module on congruent quadrilaterals, students had prior experience of the conditions required to draw congruent triangles and were initially only given the four side lengths after hypothesising that this would be sufficient to draw the shape, as it had been with the triangles. This generated surprise when this information alone was insufficient and drove the students to understand why this did not work when it had previously. Making deliberate number choices, as in the crowdedness problem, can enhance students' focus on a new mathematical idea. In TTP lessons where understanding the choice of operation is not the key focus, but instead, students are extending their understanding of a particular concept, relatively simple numbers may be inserted into a problem to enable them to quickly establish the operation required. More complex numbers then replace these and provide an opportunity to grapple with the lesson goal(s). This was the case in the module on division of fractions whereby the operation, division, was quickly established by the students allowing the main part of the lesson to focus on a more complex calculation and the meaning of the quotient which was a fraction.

Box 3.4.1   Extracts from the "Who is the fastest? (Speed)" research proposal from the planning team at Sugekari Elementary School (IMPULS, 2013)

Goals of the research lesson

- Students are able to think about how to compare the speed of running and explain it by paying attention to the two quantities involved, the distance a person ran and the amount of time a person ran.
- Students are able to recognize the merit of finding per unit quantity and utilise it willingly.

Problem
Let's think about the order of speed of these three children.

First table presented

Child	Time (seconds)
A	6
B	6
C	5

Second table presented
(After students have had an opportunity to attempt to solve the problem using just the information from the first table.)

Child	Distance (m)	Time (seconds)
A	40	6
B	30	6
C	30	5

Having completed this earlier groundwork, it became much easier to anticipate student responses for the crowdedness problem (see Figure 3.4.3) and the research lesson (see Figure 3.4.4). Generally speaking, this anticipation allows you to tune in to the (mis)understandings that students have and consider how to facilitate a whole-class discussion (discussed in Chapter 3.5) to enable students to achieve the goal(s) of the lesson. Additionally, when a student employs a response not anticipated it stands out. For me, this helps highlight insights into the students' (mis)understandings that I had not considered and sheds light on my own ideas about teaching and learning relevant to a particular area of mathematics.

A final task before watching the research lesson was to ensure we had read the planning team's research proposal (described in more detail in Chapters 1.1 and 3.5) so we knew what to expect in the lesson and understood the rationale behind the teaching choices they had made.

Problem : Investigate how to order cages A, B, and C according to how crowded they are.

Anticipated Strategies :

→ A and B have the same area.
A is <u>more crowded</u> than B because there are <u>more rabbits</u> in the <u>same amount</u> of <u>space</u>.

→ B and C have the same number of rabbits.
C is <u>more crowded</u> than B because it has <u>less space</u> for the <u>same number</u> of <u>rabbits.</u>

→ Comparing A and C

① Using <u>a common multiple</u>

la) Make the number of rabbits the same.			1b) Make the area the same.		
Cage	Area(m²)	No. of rabbits	Cage	Area (m²)	No. of rabbits
A	6 × 8 = 48	9 × 8 = 72	A	6 × 5 = 30	9 × 5 = 45
C	5 × 9 = 45	8 × 9 = 72	C	5 × 6 = 30	8 × 6 = 48

C is <u>more crowded</u> than A because it has <u>less space</u> for the <u>same no. of rabbits.</u>

C is <u>more crowded</u> than A because it has <u>more rabbits</u> for the <u>same amount of space.</u>

② Finding <u>the amount of space per rabbit</u>

Cage	Area(m²)	No. of rabbits	Calculation
A	6	9	6 ÷ 9 = 0.6̇6̇ → 0.6̇6̇ m² per rabbit.
C	5	8	5 ÷ 8 = 0.625 → 0.625 m² per rabbit

C is <u>more crowded</u> than A because it has <u>less space per rabbit.</u>

③ Finding <u>the number of rabbits per m²</u>

Cage	Area (m²)	No. of rabbits	Calculation
A	6	9	9 ÷ 6 = 1.5 → 1.5 rabbits per m²
C	5	8	8 ÷ 5 = 1.6 → 1.6 rabbits per m²

C is <u>more crowded</u> than A because it has <u>more rabbits per m².</u>

Figure 3.4.3 My anticipated strategies for the crowdedness problem after engaging in *kyouzai kenkyuu.*

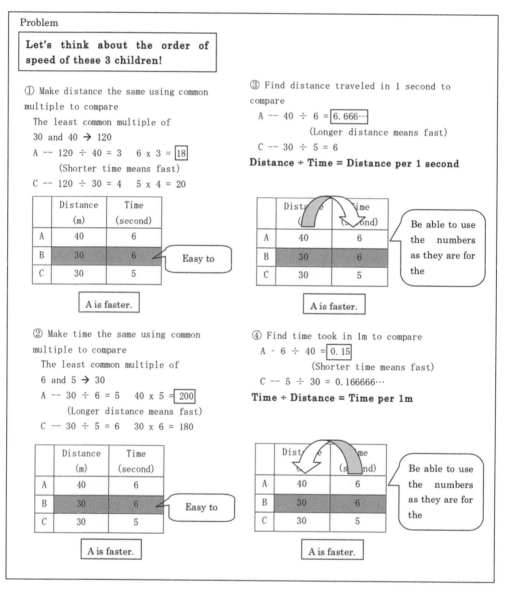

Problem

Let's think about the order of speed of these 3 children!

① Make distance the same using common multiple to compare
  The least common multiple of
  30 and 40 → 120
  A -- 120 ÷ 40 = 3   6 x 3 = ☐18
       (Shorter time means fast)
  C -- 120 ÷ 30 = 4   5 x 4 = 20

	Distance (m)	Time (second)
A	40	6
B	30	6
C	30	5

Easy to

A is faster.

② Make time the same using common multiple to compare
  The least common multiple of
  6 and 5 → 30
  A -- 30 ÷ 6 = 5   40 x 5 = ☐200
       (Longer distance means fast)
  C -- 30 ÷ 5 = 6   30 x 6 = 180

	Distance (m)	Time (second)
A	40	6
B	30	6
C	30	5

Easy to

A is faster.

③ Find distance traveled in 1 second to compare
  A -- 40 ÷ 6 = ☐6.666···
       (Longer distance means fast)
  C -- 30 ÷ 5 = 6
  Distance ÷ Time = Distance per 1 second

	Distance ( )	Time (nd)
A	40	6
B	30	6
C	30	5

Be able to use the numbers as they are for the

A is faster.

④ Find time took in 1m to compare
  A - 6 ÷ 40 = ☐0.15
       (Shorter time means fast)
  C -- 5 ÷ 30 = 0.166666···
  Time ÷ Distance = Time per 1m

	Dist ( )	me (s nd)
A	40	6
B	30	6
C	30	5

Be able to use the numbers as they are for the

A is faster.

Figure 3.4.4 Anticipated strategies and board plan from the "Who is the fastest? (Speed)" research proposal from the planning team at Sugekari Elementary School (IMPULS, 2013).

3.4.2 While observing a research lesson

A research proposal contains "points of evaluation" (see Figure 3.4.5) that the planning team want observers to gather data on. This will help them address issues, related to teaching and learning, that they have identified. I find the tight focus of Lesson Study research lessons helps to keep the emphasis on student learning (rather than on the teacher) and is grounded in more strategic observations about what students said and did and the subsequent impact of this. A detailed account of the essence of observation as part of CLR can be found in Chapter 3.2.

1 0. Viewpoints for looking at the lesson

① When the students are solving the problem on their own and discussing solution methods, did the teaching methods, such as providing hints with question sentence format, asking students to explain each other with partner, and asking *hatumon* to students' responses help the students to deepen their thinking as well as engaging them learning autonomously.

② Did the student discussion help to achieve the goal of discussion, "**search more effective ideas**."

③ Other points that observes noticed during the lesson. (e.g., How main goal/task was established during the lesson?).

Figure 3.4.5 Points of evaluation from the "Who is the fastest? (Speed)" research proposal from the planning team at Sugekari Elementary School (IMPULS, 2013).

A key aspect of TTP lessons that makes them particularly effective for use alongside Lesson Study and enables observers to address these "points of evaluation" is that student thinking is visible. This is achieved in three main ways:

- Students record their thinking in their notebooks. This might include their own strategies, a friend's strategy, a lesson summary, and a reflection.
- The whole-class discussion (*Neriage*). This accounts for the longest part of the lesson where students share, compare and contrast different ideas. The type of *Neriage* can be adjusted depending on the goal(s) of the lesson (Takahashi, 2021).
- The use of carefully planned boardwork (*bansho*). This is used to show the "story" of the lesson so students can more easily make sense of and refer back to one another's strategies and ideas.

When reflecting on the speed lesson a number of people in our CLR-UK discussions made similar observations with respect to the first point (see Figure 3.4.5) about helping students deepen their thinking. I have exemplified these observations using extracts from the lesson.

1 Students were encouraged to understand other students' strategies and explain these in their own words.

    T: *Who can explain his idea?*
    Anyone who didn't use this idea, can you explain?
    I want to ask anyone who didn't write this number 120, but when you saw RA's idea, you had a lightbulb moment.
    S: *This 120 metres came from the least common multiple of 40 metres and 30 metres because this person ran 40 metres in 6 seconds. RA thought how many seconds would it take to run 120 metres. He did the same thing for this person – 30 metres in 5 seconds. RA thought about how many seconds it would take to run 120 metres.*

2 Assumptions were not made about what the students did or did not know so if a student gave a partial or vague response questions were asked to encourage them to be clearer rather than the teacher filling in the gaps for them. Sometimes this was done by "playing the fool".

T: *What is this 120?*
S: *It is the distances for A and C put together.*
T: *You said, put distances for A and C together – 40 plus 30? 40 plus 30, but that's 70. What did you mean by putting them together?*
S: *I meant I made the conditions the same.*
T: *What did RA make the same?*
Ss: *Distance*

3 Students responding solely with a numerical answer were prompted to explain how this number related to the problem. This was very evident in Module 3 (division with remainders) and Module 4 (division of fractions). In the division of fractions lesson, the problem was:

We are making 1/5 kg hamburger patties using 3 ½ kg of ground meat. How many hamburger patties can we make, and how much ground meat will be left over?

Lots of students had obtained an answer of 7½ but when asked what the ½ was, there was confusion as to whether this was ½ of a burger patty or ½ of a kilogram of mince.

The type of *Neriage* used in the division of fractions lesson is described by Takahashi (2021) as being used to address misconceptions through debate by using a task designed to provoke both correct and incorrect solutions. It had quite a different structure from the type of *Neriage* used in the speed lesson which was intended to help students develop a new idea by discussing various approaches in order from simplest to most sophisticated.

From personal experience conducting and observing TTP lessons with teachers and students in Scotland who are not familiar with this pedagogical approach, it can initially be challenging for both the student and the teacher. For teachers, the difficulty often lies in the initial choice of task, anticipating strategies and facilitating the whole-class discussion beyond just a "show and tell" of different ideas (see Chapter 5.3 for further insights into these issues). For students, responses to being given a problem they must solve independently can vary and generally include the following:

• Not attempting the problem as they are accustomed to being told what to do first.
• Most students use the same, pre-taught, strategy.
• The class use such a wide array of strategies that the teacher has difficulty managing the whole-class discussion.

Using Lesson Study alongside a range of quality websites, books and articles (see Appendix A for suggestions) can help teachers develop these aspects which will in turn impact their students' learning.

3.4.3 After watching the research lesson

The post-lesson discussions (described in more detail in Chapters 1.1 and 3.5), which frequently stimulated lively debate, provided an opportunity to gain new or alternative perspectives. This allowed me to reflect on the impact TTP lessons have on student learning compared to transmission approaches more typically used in the United Kingdom, where students are often shown how to solve a problem first and then repeat what they have been shown as a way of "practising". In contrast, in TTP lessons the students tackle the

Table 3.4.2 Describing Per Unit Quantity

Measure	Per Unit Quantity 1	Per Unit Quantity 2
Crowdedness: *Rabbits*	rabbits per unit area (rabbits per m^2)	area per rabbit (m^2 per rabbit)
Crowdedness: *Population density*	people per unit area (people per km^2)	area per person (km^2 per person)
Speed	distance per unit time (km per hour)	time per unit distance (hours per km)

problems for themselves, generating varied responses, before a teacher-facilitated whole-class discussion. In the crowdedness lesson, the anticipated strategies (see Figure 3.4.3) were as follows:

- finding a common multiple
- finding the area per rabbit
- finding the number of rabbits per square metre

Thinking and reasoning mathematically, rather than just getting an answer to a question, is fundamental to TTP lessons. As the sequence of lessons progressed, task design was adjusted to highlight the effectiveness of some strategies over others even though they all resulted in the correct "answer". Contexts that involve larger numbers (such as population density) are used to help students see why using the common multiple strategy is not always effective or reliable. Introducing situations that involve comparing more than two things provides a purpose for finding an efficient strategy that works no matter what the comparisons are. In terms of understanding the rationale behind a particular convention, another example is related to *what* the per unit quantity is. There are always two options as illustrated in Table 3.4.2.

In the United Kingdom, many students are explicitly taught the typical convention in "Per Unit Quantity 1". If students happen to calculate in the format of "Per Unit Quantity 2" they may be unsure how to interpret their answer. In a TTP lesson, the varied strategies produced allow the relative advantages and disadvantages of these to be discussed helping students to better understand why the typical conventions used are those in the "Per Unit Quantity 1" column. When this convention is used the *larger* number relates to being more crowded or a faster speed whereas when the "Per Unit Quantity 2" calculation is used a *smaller* number relates to being more crowded or a faster speed. Through comparison and discussion, students begin to realise that conventions such as distance per unit time make more sense than time per unit distance because it is more logical that a *larger* number would relate to being *more* crowded or *faster*.

3.4.4 Concluding remarks

The IMPULS modules and accompanying CLR-UK discussions were invaluable to support my own understanding and use of both Lesson Study and TTP. Engaging in multiple modules enhanced my understanding of how ideas, such as the three task design features mentioned in Section 3.4.1 (visual presentation, delaying access to information and deliberate number choice), could be applied more broadly to other areas of mathematics to improve teaching and learning.

Observing student learning in research lessons and comparing my own anticipated student responses with those in the research proposals and subsequent student responses in lessons has had multiple benefits including

- improving the nature and quality of my own anticipated responses
- making more deliberate choices about which responses to select in a whole-class discussion; how and why they would be shared and how this supports the goal(s) of the lesson.

This has been supported by access to knowledgeable others, engagement in *kyouzai kenkyuu* and the discussions that our team had as we developed our shared understanding.

While there is nothing quite like watching a live research lesson, a recorded lesson has other benefits such as access regardless of location; and the ability to re-watch the lesson to check something or see it from a different perspective after engaging in a wider group discussion. The materials suggested in Appendix A, which include websites where recorded research lessons can be located, could be used to support groups to set up their own version of what we did as a way of getting started with Lesson Study.

References

Fujii, T., & Majima, H. (Eds.). (2020). *New mathematics for elementary school*. Tokyo Shoseki Co., Ltd.

International Math-Teacher Professionalization Using Lesson Study (2013). *Grade 6 mathematics lesson plan: Who is the fastest? (Speed)*. http://www.impuls-tgu.org/en/library/measurement/page-118.html

Takahashi, A. (2021). *Teaching mathematics through problem-solving: A pedagogical approach from Japan*. Routledge. 10.4324/9781003015475

Appendix A. Materials to support *Kyouzai Kenkyuu and Neriage*

Websites

Collaborative Lesson Research – UK: https://www.collaborative-lesson-research.uk/
The website contains information about Lesson Study including guides to get you started, and has packages to support kyouzai kenkyuu in specific topic areas.

IMPULS: http://www.impuls-tgu.org/en/
This website contains a wide range of research proposals (some with accompanying videos of the research lessons).

Lesson Study Alliance: https://www.lsalliance.org/
The website contains information about Lesson Study including guides and proformas to get you started. It also has a database of Lesson Study research proposals. Blog posts can also support with your research as part of kyouzai kenkyuu.

The Lesson Study Group at Mills College: https://lessonresearch.net/
The website contains information about Lesson Study and Teaching Through Problem-Solving including guides and proformas to get you started and courses to enhance your knowledge and understanding. It also provides access to Lesson Study research proposals and videos of research lessons.

Books

To support with facilitating the whole-class discussion:
Smith, M. S., & Stein, M. K. (2018). *Five practices for orchestrating productive mathematical discussions*. Sage Publications.

Takahashi, A. (2021). *Teaching mathematics through problem-solving: A pedagogical approach from Japan*. Routledge. https://doi.org/10.4324/9781003015475

To support kyouzai kenkyuu
Brownell, J. O., Chen, J.-Q., & Ginet, L. (2014). *Big ideas of early mathematics: What teachers of young children need to know*. Pearson.

Carpenter, T. P., Fennema, E., Franke, M. L., Levi, L., & Empson, S. B. (2015). *Children's mathematics: Cognitively Guided Instruction*. Heinemann.

Fujii, T., & Majima, H. (Eds.). (2020). *New mathematics for elementary school*. Tokyo Shoseki.

Ma, L. (2020). *Knowing and teaching elementary mathematics: Teachers' understanding of fundamental mathematics in China and the United States* (3rd ed.). Routledge.

Takahashi, A. (2021). *Teaching mathematics through problem-solving: A pedagogical approach from Japan*. Routledge. https://doi.org/10.4324/9781003015475

Takahashi, A., McDougal, T., Friedkin, S., & Watanabe, T. (Eds.). (2022). *Educators' learning from lesson study: Mathematics for ages 5–13*. Routledge.

3.5 Planning, preparing, and conducting a research lesson

A step-by-step guide

Joshua Lerner and Thomas McDougal

For Japanese teachers, Lesson Study is "like air": it is a practice that pervades all aspects of teaching and learning in school and is thus made invisible (Fujii, 2016). Indeed, Lesson Study in Japan has evolved for over a century, as educators have incrementally and organically adapted its form through their practice. For those who do Collaborative Lesson Research (CLR) around the globe, however, the process can be daunting to begin and even harder to maintain. To practice CLR in a context where it is not "like air" – and sometimes where it is not known at all – requires a firm understanding of not only its structure, but the rationale behind each of the steps in the process and how they work together to create a beautiful whole.

In this chapter, we take a "how-to" approach in describing how a school might engage in CLR over the course of one academic year. We begin with a description of what the work should look like at the start of the year, including creating a research theme and creating a schedule of research lessons. Second, we give a step-by-step guide for how to plan a research lesson and provide an example of an exemplary research lesson proposal. Third, we describe a protocol for holding the research lesson and post-lesson discussion. Finally, we give suggestions for how to reflect and report your new learning for the benefit of your school and the wider education community.

In the descriptions that follow, we draw upon our own experience as CLR practitioners and facilitators in Chicago as well as the work of leading thinkers, writers, and researchers both nationally and internationally. Many of the ideas here have been iterated from the invaluable work conducted by Catherine Lewis and Akihiko Takahashi and can be investigated further through handbooks (e.g., Lewis, 2002; Lewis & Hurd, 2011), as well as websites such as LessonResearch.net and LSAlliance.org. Thus, rather than serving as a substitute for these sources, this chapter can be considered another useful tool in the decades-long effort to grow CLR around the world.

3.5.1 Beginning of the school year

One research lesson can be a nice experience for those involved, but the power of CLR emerges with multiple research lessons, in which ideas learned from one lesson transfer to the next one. Toward that end, it is a good idea at the start of the school year to consider the scope of your work and create a schedule of planning meetings and research lessons for the year. If your school has one planning team, we recommend conducting at least one research lesson in the first term and another in the second. If there are enough teachers to form multiple planning teams, each team can hold one research lesson, perhaps one in the first term, one in the winter, and one in the spring. Members of the planning team for

DOI: 10.4324/9781003375272-14

one research lesson can participate in the other research lessons as observers. Teachers who are not on a planning team can also be invited to the research lessons, thus broadening schoolwide learning and increasing interest and investment in CLR for subsequent years.

Write a research theme

The purpose of CLR is to overcome persistent issues in teaching and learning at your school through teacher collaboration. The first step in the process, then, is to decide on a common issue to address in order to establish a shared vision of school improvement. This is the *research theme*, and it will drive everything you do with CLR in your school over the course of a not-insubstantial period.

The research theme has two parts. The first part asks teachers to consider long-term desired outcomes *for their students*. Consider the following prompts as a way of shaping the research theme: "Ideally, what qualities will students have when they graduate from our school? What are the actual qualities of our students now?" (Lewis & Hurd, 2011, p. 44). By identifying the gaps between the long-term goal and the current reality of the students, a research theme can be formed. For example, at Peirce School of International Studies in Chicago, teachers across grade levels noticed that students were overly concerned with arriving at the correct answer in mathematics class, and this led them to be self-conscious and less willing to share their ideas. The team's theme expressed the desire for students to become more "collaborative, trusting, and encouraging".

The second part of the research theme involves an entry point for achieving the desired outcome. In other words, if the first part is the *what* of the research theme, this second part is the *how*. For example, at Peirce, the teachers decided that, in order to increase collaboration and trust among students broadly, it was best to focus on improving their own practice of facilitating mathematics discussions. This included practices such as giving students a chance to share work in their journals first with peers before presenting to the class, building routines in which students could ask each other questions, and regularly celebrating examples of how errors lead to new learning. These practices became a focus of the CLR work conducted at the school in 2018 and 2019.

A good research theme is short enough to be memorable and specific enough to be observable in lessons. In our own practice, we have found that longer research themes lead to a less focused understanding of what we are trying to achieve as a team or school. Here are a few clearly written research themes used successfully by schools in Japan and the United States:

- For students to value friendship, develop their own perspectives and way of thinking and enjoy learning ... [by] ... work[ing] together in ways that enable them to recognise one another's ideas as they engage in observations, experiments, and activities (https://lessonresearch.net/study-step/develop-research-theme/)
- Nurture students' mathematical agency and identity through the design of lessons that engage students in problem solving and productive talk (Lewis et al., 2022)
- To improve students' ability to give a viable argument and critique the reasoning of others by teaching students to use journals to record their own ideas and the ideas of others, and using the whiteboard strategically to support student journal writing and classroom discussion.[1]
- To help students become better able to engage with problem solving and mathematical modelling. (From the research project, "Lessons for Mathematical Problem Solving"[2])

To write a research theme, a member of your planning team should first facilitate a discussion with everyone participating in CLR at your school. Talk through the two parts outlined above and what they look like among your students. After team members have agreed on a working draft, invite a single group member to write one or two clear, concise sentences to sum up your theme. Finalise and approve the statement as a team.

Above all, encourage your team to savour this initial step. Rarely do we engage in professional development that begins with such a powerful question that comes from teachers themselves: Who do we want our students to be, and how can we help them get there? What makes us feel pride and joy as educators? In doing so, you will be motivated and excited to delve into designing your research lessons.

3.5.2 Planning for a research lesson

When one team is ready to begin planning a research lesson, it will be important to agree on a schedule of meetings. You can expect to devote 8 to 12 hours to the process. We have seen this accomplished in different ways. If feasible, your team may want to schedule a series of two-hour meetings over the course of four to six weeks. Another option is to meet for longer chunks of time, such as two or three half-day planning meetings.

How you choose to split up the planning time will be influenced by your school context and its parameters. Keep in mind, however, that it is difficult to generate excitement and investment in CLR if it is considered auxiliary or something that is only worked on during out-of-school hours. Therefore, we highly recommend finding ways to build planning time into the work day itself, by being creative with school schedules or providing classroom cover for participating teachers.

Choosing the topic of your research lesson

The first time they do a research lesson, teachers are sometimes tempted to choose a topic for which they already have a solid, reliable lesson. They may feel that their research lesson should be a "model lesson", one about which they already feel confident. But the purpose of CLR is research: to learn something new about how to improve teaching and learning. Use your time wisely, and choose a topic that merits the extra effort you are going to put into investigating it and planning the lesson.

It is also a good idea to choose a topic that is addressed at or near the beginning of a unit. If the lesson falls late in a unit, then observers (including your team) may be unable to determine to what extent the student responses are a result of that lesson or of previous lessons. Important insights from a foundational lesson, on the other hand, can have a sustained impact throughout the rest of the unit.

Kyouzai Kenkyuu – *investigating materials for teaching*

Once you have chosen your topic, it is tempting to dive straight into designing a lesson, but you want to ensure that the lesson you design will be a good fit for your students and for the mathematics you want them to learn whilst also ensuring a focus on the research theme and standards. Standards may specify what students should learn in each grade, but they do not specify ordering, pacing, and instructional strategy. Textbooks, on the other hand, provide both sequencing, pacing, and instructional ideas, and therefore it is usually a good idea to base your unit plan and lesson plan on existing textbooks. But, textbooks are generally designed by their authors for inexperienced teachers and "average" students.

Since this is unlikely to describe your situation – after all, what is an "average" student? – some adaptations are likely to be necessary. To make those adaptations wisely, some groundwork is necessary (Takahashi, 2021).

The Japanese term for this groundwork is *kyouzai kenkyuu* (Watanabe et al., 2008). This translates as "research (or study) of instructional materials"; we use the Japanese term in CLR because the English translation fails to capture the full meaning of it. As discussed in chapter 1.1, *kyouzai kenkyuu* considers the mathematics, the students, and the teacher – all three components of the instructional triangle (National Research Council, 2001).

The mathematics

For the topic you have chosen, your research should strive to answer the following questions:

- What is the full depth of the mathematics students need to know to understand the topic?
- What approaches do different textbooks take? What contexts do they use? What is the rationale behind the authors' decisions? What are the relative advantages and disadvantages of each approach?
- What is the intended learning trajectory related to the topic, from prior through later grades, in the textbooks and in the standards?
- What are common student misconceptions around the topic?

Resources to help you with these questions include standards documents, different curricula (especially the teacher's guides), and journal articles, among others.

The students

To create a lesson well-designed for your students, consider the mathematics from the students' point of view. First is the question of what the students already know and do not know related to the topic. This is answered partly by examining the sequencing of ideas within the curriculum, but you may also want to do some formative assessment, through observations, worksheets, homework, etc. When you choose a task for the lesson, you and your colleagues should solve it first. Consider and discuss different ways students might solve it, whether the task presents the right level of challenge, and whether the task is well-suited to the desired learning goal. The task or problem you give should focus the students toward the new mathematical content you want them to learn. It may not be necessary that all students are able to solve the problem you give them, but all students should be able to access it to some degree.

The teacher

As teachers, you have your own instructional vision which will shape your lesson. The most important part of that vision is your learning goals for the lesson. Although some teachers write learning goals in behavioural terms – "Students will be able to …" – their ability to do something mathematical depends on what they know or understand (McDougal, 2016). Students could know how to do something because they know a certain procedure, or because they understand the underlying mathematical structures and made connections to previous knowledge.

For example, a typical behavioural goal for a lesson might be, "Students are able to calculate the area of a parallelogram". It might seem straightforward to design a lesson for this goal. But if we think about the cognitive (and affective) changes that might lead to this new capability, we might come up with many different ideas, such as these two:

a   Students know the formula A = b × h for the area of a parallelogram, and they know that the height is the perpendicular distance between the bases.
b   Students realise that they can transform a parallelogram into a rectangle with equivalent area by cutting and rearranging part of it, and that the rectangle has dimensions equal to the length of a base of the parallelogram and the height of the parallelogram (measured perpendicular to the base). The area of that rectangle, and therefore of the parallelogram, is therefore given by A = b × h. Students are excited that they can use their previous learning to determine the area of a new shape, and are eager to try other shapes.

One can imagine how these two learning goals are likely to lead to very different lessons. Therefore, articulating your learning goals in terms of the cognitive (and possibly affective) changes you hope to cause is a crucial step in designing your lesson.

For Japanese teachers, *kyouzai kenkyuu* is a part of everyday lesson planning, though of course everyday *kyouzai kenkyuu* is less intensive than what you do as part of CLR. Minimally, everyday *kyouzai kenkyuu* means examining the tasks and pedagogical ideas in the textbook, considering whether they are a good fit for the current students, and anticipating how the students are likely to respond. Doing intensive *kyouzai kenkyuu* in CLR could be considered as training for everyday *kyouzai kenkyuu*. Not only will it improve your research lesson, it will lead to better daily lessons as well.

Write a research lesson proposal

By this point, your team has written a research theme and studied the standards and curriculum materials associated with your given topic. It is now time to write a research lesson proposal. The research lesson proposal serves multiple purposes. In writing this proposal, your team will:

* communicate your long-term vision for students through the research theme
* give a synopsis of key findings from your study of the content (*kyouzai kenkyuu*)
* describe the progression of learning within the given unit of study from the curriculum
* showcase your detailed lesson plan for the chosen research lesson, including a rationale for why particular instructional choices were made
* guide your colleagues by suggesting what to look for and consider when they observe the research lesson

While the above description provides an overview of the central components of a research lesson proposal, your team will want to use an agreed-upon template such as the one we have found useful at https://lessonresearch.net/study-step/access-tlp/. It is helpful if everyone in the team examines each section carefully to prepare for your upcoming work together.

Spotlight on the design of the research lesson

For decades, Lesson Study has been used by educators in Japan to develop their practice of a particular style of teaching mathematics, known as Teaching through Problem Solving

(TTP) (e.g., Becker & Miwa, 1987; Schoenfeld, 1985; Stacey, 2005; Takahashi, 2021). As a framework for teacher research, CLR can actually be used to study and test other pedagogical ideas in math, or indeed in any subject. We have seen powerful research lessons taught to investigate topics in science, civics, literature, physical education, and more. But since many outside of Japan use CLR to investigate TTP, we offer some suggestions in this section for how to plan for this style of teaching.[3] Specifically, we will "zoom in" on some key lesson design features, including the creation of a *neriage map*, and the use of a recommended format for writing your plan.

Writing a "neriage map"

TTP lessons tend to follow a certain structure: the presentation of a problem, time for students to attempt to solve it, a thorough class discussion about the ideas generated by students, and a summary and reflection on the new mathematics that was learned (see Table 3.5.1).

The heart of the lesson is the engaging and collaborative mathematical discussion among the class. *Neriage* is the Japanese term for the facilitation of this discussion. In Japanese, the word *neriage* means kneading or polishing up – a metaphor for using discussion to refine student ideas into a new and powerful mathematical understanding (Shimizu, 1999). It is a complex teaching skill, one that takes careful planning and lots of classroom experience to improve. Fortunately, your team can use CLR to develop your *neriage* practice.

Once your team has a good understanding of the desired learning goal and the problem you will use – perhaps a problem/lesson from your textbook or an alternative resource you have found – you can begin sketching a *neriage map* to anticipate the overall flow of ideas in the lesson (Takahashi, 2021). As seen in Figure 3.5.1, a *neriage map* shows all the key features of a TTP lesson, including: the presentation of the problem; a key mathematical idea that students should be considering to frame their work; the sequencing of class discussion based on anticipated student ideas; and a likely summary of new learning. In this

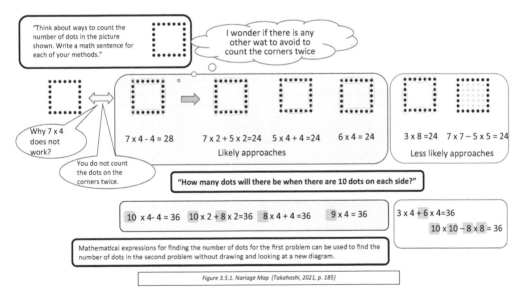

Figure 3.5.1 Neriage map (Takahashi, 2021, p. 185).

lesson, the planning team has considered a possible flow of ideas to help students understand how expressions can be generalised to represent dots arranged to form a square, even when the side length of the square changes.

By writing a *neriage map* for your own research lesson, your team will have a powerful, shared vision for a possible flow of mathematical ideas during the lesson. Your team now must consider the "nuts and bolts" of how you will bring this exciting lesson to life. Below we recommend a format for guiding your planning.

A recommended format for your plan

For decades, CLR teams have used a common template for designing TTP lessons. Study the template in Table 3.5.1 below. In the left column, the team has a designated space to plan for each of the phases of a TTP lesson. Rather than writing a script or dialogue between teacher and students, consider just noting the key moves the teacher will make to move the lesson along its intended path. In the right column, plan some strategic accommodations or suggestions that the teacher can make to support certain students at key moments in the lesson. Use the descriptions within the table as well as the example found in Appendix A to guide your planning.

The recommended length of time for each section in this template is based on a lesson approximately 50 minutes in length. Your team may want to adjust this depending on the grade level and topic of the lesson. Always plan for an efficient and engaging introduction and posing of the problem. You want students motivated and excited to begin working on the lesson's central task. Then, when they have time to solve the problem, it is not necessary to wait for each student to finish their work. Rather, give only enough time so that all students can attempt one or two useful methods. These ideas can then be used to generate a productive discussion.

Finally, notice how the greatest amount of time is reserved for comparing and discussing. Your team may choose to adjust the length of the discussion depending on the age or experience of your students. There is no denying, however, that this section is the most important of the lesson and deserves the most careful attention and time for development. After all, the purpose of all of the preceding sections is to get students ready to share their experiences during this section (Takahashi, 2021).

Table 3.5.1 Template for a typical TTP lesson (Takahashi, 2021, p. 186)

Flow of the lesson, anticipated student responses	*Support from the teacher*
1. Introduction (3–5 min) Get students ready and motivated for today's problem.	
2. Pose the problem (5–7 min) Plan how the problem will be worded and/or presented to students.	
3. Solve the problem (7–10 min) Write a list of the anticipated student responses	

4. Compare and discuss (15–25 min)
  Plan the questions and structure you will use for the discussion
  of ideas first outlined in your *neriage* map.	

5. Summarise (5–10 min) Write the wording of an anticipated summary of new learning.	

Tips for facilitation

At first, the creation of a research lesson proposal can seem like a daunting task. In Table 3.5.2, we offer a few concrete processes, taken from our work in Chicago, to help your team plan your process, stay on track, and ultimately generate a successful proposal.

Consult a knowledgeable other

Almost every team will benefit from feedback on their ideas at some point during their planning. A *knowledgeable other* (KO) is an outsider with deep knowledge of the content who can help the team expand their understanding of the mathematics, either directly or by steering them toward valuable resources. The KO should also be able to push the team's pedagogical thinking. At the same time, the KO needs to be careful that the team retains ownership of ideas in the lesson.

There are a few questions that commonly help teams improve their lesson design:

- What is the students' reason for doing this task, other than that the teacher is asking them to do it?
- Why is this the best task for your learning goal?
- What will indicate to you that the class is ready to learn from the discussion?
- How will you make student thinking visible?
- After this lesson, what would a student ideally say he or she learned?

Write a board plan and conduct a mock lesson

After your team has created a rough draft of the research lesson proposal, it is time to do two final activities to prepare for your research lesson: planning boardwork and conducting a mock lesson. As you will see in this chapter, these activities are interrelated. Taken together, these two steps give team members insight into how students might experience their upcoming lesson, ultimately helping the team work out the kinks and finalise their plan.

Table 3.5.2 Productive CLR processes

Productive Processes when Writing the Research Lesson Proposal
The team is led by a facilitator, such as a teacher leader or instructional coach, who plans agendas, focuses the team on short-term goals, and helps everyone stay on track.
Each planning session includes an agenda specifying which sections of the research lesson proposal the team hopes to complete (see Appendix B for agenda templates).
Team members create meeting norms at the outset to establish a culture of respect, accountability, and teamwork.
The team maintains time limits for each section and moves through the planning process without getting stuck on fine details. Knowing that there is usually time later to fine tune previous decisions, the team might use a shared signal to indicate it's time to keep moving (a personal favourite is "ELMO", which, said lovingly, means "Enough, let's move on!")
As the team proceeds through each section of the planning process, a note-taker captures important ideas in the document, to be cleaned up and finalised later by individual team members.
Team members keep their eyes on the big picture. They regularly recognise and celebrate their hard work, knowing that their research lesson proposal will ultimately advance learning not just for themselves but for their colleagues as well.

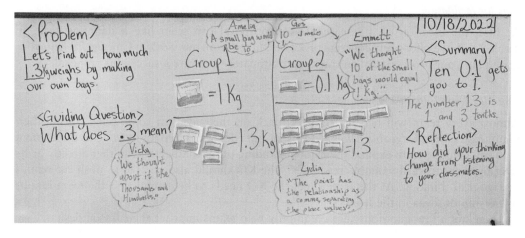

Figure 3.5.2 The boardwork for a research lesson on the meaning of decimal numbers.

Boardwork *(bansho)*

Japanese teachers use the term *bansho* to describe the skill of writing on the board throughout a lesson (see Figure 3.5.2). Yoshida (2005) has described exemplary *bansho* as fulfilling the following aims: to present a clear progression of the lesson from beginning to end; to reflect important student ideas and the ways in which they are compared and discussed by the class; and to foster student note-taking skills by presenting information in a clear and logical manner. Veteran teacher Aubrey Perlee has framed the careful planning of boardwork as providing a "roadmap" for teachers during a lesson. With a reference or sketch of the planned boardwork nearby, the teacher can use it as a reference as she guides student discussion (Takahashi et al., 2022).

To create a *bansho* plan, you may first want to sketch out your ideas on a single piece of paper, determining what section of the board will be dedicated to presenting the problem, showcasing student ideas, the class summary, and so on. As you do this, you will draw upon the flow of ideas you first outlined in your *neriage* map while also taking into account your knowledge of your own students and what you can expect from them during the lesson. Further, the *bansho* plan is meant to organise exactly how your students will see the ideas presented visually on the board. This includes the overall organisation of the board, the size of your writing, and even the use of colour to present different types of ideas visually. A best practice, therefore, is to write the final plan for your boardwork in the classroom where the lesson will be taught and then take a picture as a reference. A perfect opportunity to do this comes when your team carries out a mock lesson.

Conducting a mock lesson

Before the actual research lesson, the team should do a dry run-through of the lesson, with the instructor teaching the lesson and the others acting as students. We call this a "mock lesson". The goal of a mock lesson is to fix up any loose ends from the original plan. As the teacher progresses through the lesson, other members of the team see the lesson from a student's perspective and may give feedback, such as, "Should we write down the problem on the board before or after we discuss the scenario with the class?" or "Will we invite students to write down all chosen solutions on the board before the discussion, or will the class discuss each solution method as it is presented?" The group can stop at any time to finalise these instructional decisions, making notes in the lesson plan document to indicate the new changes (Takahashi, 2021).

Once the research proposal is ready, make it available to anyone who will be attending the lesson so that they can be prepared to observe the lesson strategically.

3.5.3 The day of the research lesson

The day of the research lesson is a significant milestone, a high point after weeks of hard work and dedication. Here is the schedule for a typical research lesson day:

- Pre-lesson meeting (30–45 minutes)
- Research lesson (50 minutes)
- Post-lesson discussion (60–90 minutes)
- Team reflection (30–60 minutes)
- Celebration after school (variable)

Planning the logistics of the research lesson day begins in the weeks leading up to the day itself. One thing your team will want to make sure to do ahead of time is invite colleagues to your research lesson to observe and participate in the discussion. Having fresh eyes observing the lesson will make for a richer discussion. Consider inviting teachers from your building who are interested in the topic or who teach adjacent grade levels. Another recommended practice is to develop a broader Lesson Study community by inviting teachers from nearby and/or partner schools.

There are also finer details to consider in the run-up to the day itself. You will want to have an instructional leader, usually the same person who has been facilitating the planning meetings, who can organise the day's logistics, including: coordinating classroom coverage, reserving a meeting space, providing snacks or refreshments, and even scheduling a celebratory gathering to take place afterward. However you delegate these responsibilities, it is essential that these details are planned for in advance, so on this important day all participating teachers can focus on learning as much as they can from the research lesson and discussion.

Hold a pre-lesson meeting

The first event of the day is the pre-lesson meeting. Gathering around a large conference table or in a circle is ideal. Begin with introductions and norms for your work together. Although you hope that everyone will have read through the research proposal, it may still be wise, if time allows, to give all invited guests a few minutes to review it. The team will then give an overview of the lesson, making sure to specify the learning goal, and perhaps review what students have learned thus far in the unit. Observers may ask clarifying questions about the plan itself – not probing questions – and then discuss what they hope to pay close attention to during the lesson. The teacher and planning team should leave a few minutes early to greet their class, while the rest of the participants go over guidelines for successful observation. Provide copies of a seating chart so that observers who don't know the students can identify who is who when taking notes. Some observers may want multiple seating charts on which to record notes at different times during the lesson. See Chapter 3.2 for additional tips about observing a research lesson.

Table 3.5.3 (Adapted from Lewis & Hurd, 2011)

Observing the Research Lesson

Respect the classroom atmosphere. For example, silence phones, refrain from side conversations, arrive on time, and stay for the entire lesson.

Do not help students or otherwise interfere with the natural flow of the lesson. For example, be careful not to block students' view when they need to see the board or the teacher.

Collect data requested by the planning team. The request to observe specific features of the lesson, or particular students, may come from the team during the pre-lesson meeting or might be written directly into the "Evaluation" section of the research lesson proposal.

Conduct the research lesson

Table 3.5.3 gives an overview of observation guidelines. Following these norms will help observers collect good data from the lesson, essential for a successful post-lesson discussion. This is no small thing. In our work in Chicago, we often recall how, when a single teacher is working with a class of students, it is so challenging to attend to what each child is doing. But with the help of 5 to 10 observers, the teacher and team will have a more complete picture of what their students understand. Meanwhile, observers will develop their skill of "professional noticing" or, as a principal in Japan once so elegantly observed, "the eyes to see children" (Lewis & Hurd, 2011).

Finally, we give a suggestion for entering and exiting the classroom where the research lesson is taking place. The students will be excited and perhaps a little nervous to see teachers from their school who have come to join them. You can put them at ease in an instant with a big smile and an enthusiastic wave hello. This warm greeting between students and staff at the start of a research lesson makes visible the community of learning that you are working to develop. Finally, when the lesson is over, it is nice to applaud the students.

Engage in the post-lesson discussion

The post-lesson discussion is the climax of CLR. The research, the planning, and the lesson itself lead to this session, in which teacher learning should be maximised and solidified. The goal of the post-lesson discussion is to learn as much as possible about mathematics, about students, about how the lesson design and execution impacted the students, and, most important, about how future lessons can be improved.

The post-lesson discussion should have a moderator, who bears the responsibility of making sure that the discussion is as fruitful as possible. The moderator should be someone with significant experience with Lesson Study, solid understanding of the content of the lesson, and a good eye for observing students. This person should not be a member of the planning team, but could (and often does) work at the school.

To encourage discussion, arrange seating so that people easily can see each other, with the members of the team together at one end and the moderator nearby. We recommend the following protocol. First, the moderator welcomes everyone to the discussion and, on behalf of all the participants, and thanks the planning team and, especially, the teacher for having provided this opportunity for everyone to learn. The group may applaud the teacher. Second, depending on the level of experience of the group, the moderator may want to remind participants of the purposes of the discussion: to help the planning team answer their research questions and to learn as much as possible about student thinking and lesson design. Then the moderator outlines the process:

1 remarks by the teacher;
2 observations and discussion, starting with some (but not necessarily all) of the planning team and then opening up to all participants; and
3 remarks by the invited final commentator.

Remind participants that the discussion should be grounded in data.

To start the discussion, the moderator invites the teacher of the lesson to share observations from the lesson, analysis of those observations, and to discuss any significant deviations from the plan. Invite the teacher to raise any issues that she or he would especially like the group to discuss, or specific data the teacher would like to get from observers. Avoid inviting the teacher to comment on "how the lesson went", as this invites vague platitudes ("I think it went well") that are usually not productive.

The first 10 minutes or so of the discussion is usually best spent generating additional questions or issues that participants want to discuss. Some or all of the planning team might start, depending on how many of them there are, then the floor can be opened to the other observers. A good prompt will encourage participants to reference something they observed during the lesson as a reason for their choice of question or issue. The moderator should take notes, with an eye toward developing a list of topics to focus the discussion.

As soon as the moderator has a good list, choose an issue and focus on it for as long as the discussion is productive. In addition to the issues raised by the participants, refer also to any evaluation questions that the team included in the lesson plan. We recommend starting with more concrete, narrowly focused prompts, such as "What did we see students doing with the manipulatives?" or "How did students initially approach the problem?" These should be followed up with prompts to analyse the data, such as "How do we think the manipulatives shaped student thinking?" or "Why do we think students approached it this way?" Bigger issues, such as whether the goals of the lesson were accomplished or not – and why – are best delayed until participants have had some time to hear each other's observations in the context of narrower questions and to think about the implications. Although the moderator should try to honour the issues and questions raised by the team and participants, the moderator has the responsibility to use judgment about what is most important for improving teaching and learning. This may include raising issues not mentioned by the group.

Disagreements make for a more productive – and more lively – discussion, and the moderator should highlight them. "So-and-so is suggesting that the problem was too easy for the students. Do you agree?" "So-and-so disagrees with you. What's your response?" As discussion on each topic winds down, bring closure by summarising the conclusions (or lack thereof) before moving on to the next one.

The quality of the research lesson proposal, as well as the experience level of the participants, will make the moderator's job easier or harder. A good proposal will have clearly stated learning objectives, clearly stated (and observable) research questions, and will identify critical points in the lesson, all of which make good foci for discussion. Experienced Lesson Study participants will collect abundant concrete data to support focused discussion, and will not hesitate to raise important issues of concern. Less-experienced participants are likely to speak in generalities without supporting data and are usually less willing to speak critically of the lesson. In such a case, the moderator will need to push, tactfully. "So-and-so says that the lesson went well. What data could we use to support that statement?" "How did the students' thinking evolve? How can we tell?"

To help the group focus on data, it can help to provide hard copies of student work, or photos thereof, along with photos of the board work if the discussion takes place elsewhere than the classroom. Photos can be collected into an electronic document and shared online.

Finally, the moderator should formally close the discussion, thank everyone for their contributions, and invite the final commentator to give remarks.

Maximise learning with the koshi, or final commentator

In Japan, a post-lesson discussion nearly always concludes with about 20 to 40 minutes of remarks by an invited expert: a *koshi*, or final commentator. While this is not always the case with Lesson Study in other countries, we believe that having a final commentator often turns a merely pleasant experience into a powerful learning experience. Indeed, we have seen research lessons that were clearly unsuccessful in terms of student learning rescued by final comments that left participants excited by how much *they* had learned. This is why a final commentator is a required component of CLR.

The role of final commentator has been little studied. In the only study of the role that we know of, Takahashi (2014a) interviewed and analysed the final comments of three educators who were highly popular in the Tokyo area as final commentators for school-based Lesson Study. According to the three educators studied by Takahashi, the final commentator is responsible for:

- bringing new knowledge from research and the curriculum, including the textbook and relevant standards, and connecting it to observations from the lesson;
- showing the connection between theory and practice, such as highlighting evidence from the lesson relevant for assessing progress toward the school's research theme and making suggestions for future work;
- helping others learn how to reflect on teaching and learning.

Based on our experience outside Japan, we add the following goals:

- motivating the team and school faculty to continue their Lesson Study efforts; and
- suggesting a direction for future work.

These last two are especially important in contexts where Lesson Study is not a firmly established part of the school culture, and where an extra push might be important for keeping it going.

Considering these five goals, certain desirable criteria for a final commentator emerge. Ideally, this person has the following:

- Deep knowledge of the content.
- Knowledge about content-specific pedagogy, including recent research.
- A broad perspective gained from teaching experience and observation of other research lessons.
- Understanding of the school context and research theme.
- Skill at observing students and using data from a lesson to support arguments about pedagogy and student learning.
- Tact.

As one might appreciate, persons possessing all of these are not easily found, and this list might be intimidating to anyone called upon to play the role. The educators interviewed by Takahashi found it hard to imagine how one might become skilled at providing final comments without observing many, many research lessons and hearing final comments given by other experienced educators. But we offer here a structure for organising final comments that can help make the task manageable for both experienced and inexperienced final commentators. We call it "the 5-cards structure for preparing final comments", or simply "the 5-cards method".

The 5-cards structure for preparing final comments

The 5-cards method was developed by Akihiko Takahashi, based on his research analysing experienced final commentators in Japan (2014a). It has been used by several educators in Chicago who have served as final commentators, and they have found it helpful for organising their thoughts for final comments. It is based on the five goals of final comments listed above. The idea is to group thoughts about a lesson into five categories, often physically instantiated as five large note cards or sheets of paper. The five categories are shown in Table 3.5.4.

Comments regarding the first two, Curriculum Study and Lesson Design, should mostly be prepared ahead of time by reviewing a draft of the lesson research proposal – which the team should send to the final commentator about a week before the lesson. Other comments are prepared during the post-lesson discussion, which is one reason the final commentator usually does not participate in the post-lesson discussion.

When delivering final comments, remarks usually roughly follow this ordering, with Curriculum Study and Next Steps each delivered in their entirety. Comments for the other three categories may be intertwined, however, as one makes connections whenever possible to observed facts and between the research theme and the design of the lesson.

As an example of comments based on **curriculum study**, a final commentator for a lesson about area talked about the four stages of learning about different kinds of measurement and reviewed how the curriculum works through those stages with area. The commentator also noted how, unlike quantities previously studied by students (length, mass, liquid

Table 3.5.4 The 5-card structure for preparing final comments (Takahashi, 2014a)

Curriculum study	Lesson design	Observed facts from the lesson	The school research theme	Next steps
• Highlight the essential ideas of the topic of the lesson and the unit. • Review the learning progression of the topic in connection to the prior and future grades. • Discuss known issues in teaching and learning the topic, including research findings, if any.	• Highlight critical features of the lesson/unit designed by the team and what we can learn from them. • Offer suggestions to improve the research lesson proposal.	• Share observations of critical issues in the research lesson, such as notable student learning (or lack thereof) and impacts of the lesson. • Share what you learned by watching the research lesson as a professional educator.	• Note observed progress related to the school research theme • Offer suggestions for the next team's research lesson with respect to the school's research theme	• Praise the team's efforts • Offer concrete ideas for the teacher of the lesson and other teachers to move ahead based on comments from the other 4 categories.

capacity), there is no tool for directly measuring area, and therefore it must be calculated, either by counting squares or calculating based on measured lengths.

As an example of comments on **lesson design**, a final commentator for a lesson about decimal multiplication asked participants to consider whether all three tasks in the lesson were necessary to achieve the goals of the lesson. Using **observed facts**, she noted that students solved the first two tasks easily without learning anything new, and argued that jumping straight to the third task would have saved valuable time and would have gotten to the new learning more directly.

Regarding one school's **research theme** around problem solving and productive struggle, a commentator praised the team for having the courage to present students with a problem without previously telling them how to solve it. He noted, however, that many students very quickly solved the problem incorrectly (**observed facts**) and then waited a long time before the discussion began. He suggested (**next steps**) that teachers might in future lessons give students a very short time to work, then stop to discuss why an incorrect method was incorrect, and then let students attack the problem again. This, he argued, would help students struggle more productively.

Choosing the final commentator

The choice of final commentator is normally made by the lesson planning team, consulting with the school leadership. It should be someone whose opinion will be respected. There is one restriction we consider important: the final commentator should come from outside the school. This is because they need to be able to speak frankly (if always tactfully) about what they see in the design of the lesson and, most important, what they observe during the lesson.

The final commentator may be a university educator, a district curriculum specialist, an administrator, or a teacher – ideally one with experience teaching at multiple grade levels. If you invite someone who has not previously participated in Lesson Study, make sure that the person understands what you hope they will contribute. You may suggest that he or she read this section. And, again, please send him or her a draft of your lesson plan well in advance!

3.5.4 After the research lesson

After the post-lesson discussion and final comments, it will be important for your team to identify some key takeaways for your teaching practice and then report this new learning to your colleagues more broadly.

Gather for a formal reflection session

The first step in this process is when your team gathers to reflect on the research lesson, post-lesson discussion, and final comments. Whenever possible, make sure to build in time for this reflection meeting as part of the day's events. One team member should facilitate, asking everyone to report one or two key insights from their experience. This can be specific to the content taught in the research lesson or might be a more generalisable point about pedagogy or student learning. The facilitator's job is then to synthesise these notes into two or three coherent and practical points and summarise them clearly in the reflection section of the research lesson document. The addition of this reflection turns the document from a research lesson *proposal* into a research lesson *report*.

A useful example of powerful reflection comes from veteran educator Brigid Brown, reporting the results from a grade 3 research lesson on quotative division (Takahashi et al., 2022). Team members across multiple grades saw, as a result of the research lesson, the usefulness of labelling equations based on what each part represents within a story context. This insight then drove a shared and sustained development of this practice in the future. At Peirce School in Chicago, an insight from a recent grade 5 research lesson had implications for all grade levels. Members of the team committed to moving away from providing "just in case" support when introducing a new problem to their students. As such, teachers redoubled their effort to allow students to productively struggle through new problems in their classrooms.

Sharing what is learned

Of course, CLR is not just about helping the planning team members develop their own practice, but rather improving teaching and learning across the school more broadly (Takahashi & McDougal, 2016). Toward this end, your team will want to establish some systematic ways to share new learning with your colleagues. Some examples include:

- One-page newsletters after each research lesson
- Bulletin board in a prominent place at school
- Presentation at staff workshop
- End-of-year reports synthesising learning from multiple research lessons, shared with school staff and participating teachers from other schools (see Figure 3.5.3)

School-wide CLR and beyond

School-wide Lesson Study is practiced widely in Japan, and a few successful cases of school-wide CLR exist outside of Japan as well (Lewis et al., 2022). In school-wide CLR, teachers collaborate as a faculty, with multiple teams planning research lessons each year, all driven by a unified research theme. Even if you are just beginning your CLR journey, it can be inspirational to consider such a future for your school.

As your school moves toward implementing school-wide CLR, new structures are needed to align work across teams. One way to do this is to establish a CLR steering committee (Takahashi & McDougal, 2014). Ideally, the committee should include members across grade levels who are participating on various teams along with an instructional leader to facilitate and align the work. At Peirce School of International Studies, the steering committee met monthly in the 2019–2020 school year to:

- Update and finalise the school-wide research theme
- Establish a calendar of research lessons (in this case, for grades 1, 3, 5, and 7)
- Report back new learning from each research lesson
- Work together to communicate results to the broader staff, through informal conversations with team members, a bulletin board displayed in the school lobby, and a midyear newsletter.

CLR is a form of teacher research. As such, the opportunities for sharing results extend far beyond your school. There is a growing public library of research lesson reports (i.e., proposals with post-lesson reflections) housed at https://LSAlliance.org. Members of CLR teams and instructional leaders have participated on panels at local professional development initiatives,

RESEARCH LESSONS AND REFLECTIONS FROM SEMESTER 2

8th Grade: Systems of equations

Teachers from 7th and 8th planned a lesson to introduce systems of equations to 8th grade students. We reflected on the problem, where x = number of lawns mowed, and y = dollar amount earned. In other words, y was always dependent on x. <u>Moving forward, we might want to consider choosing a scenario in which the variables are independent of one another.</u> Students can then manipulate both values and realize that only the values that work for both equations successfully solve the system.

Kindergarten: Numbers greater than ten

Teachers from K, 1st, and 2nd planned a lesson to introduce students to numbers beyond ten. In this lesson, students explained to their classmates how they counted 14 apples. Students learned that the number 14 can be thought of as *10 and 4 more*. <u>We learned that it is helpful to give students only 10 blocks when matching blocks to objects. When they run out of blocks, they can see the remaining amount -- 4 more!</u>

3rd Grade: Division with remainders

Teachers from 3rd, 4th, and 5th prepared a 3rd grade lesson for the Chicago Lesson Study Conference. The goal was for students to learn that the remainder should never be larger than the divisor. <u>We reflected on the importance of returning to the context of the problem throughout the lesson to help students see the "why" behind a rule or procedure.</u> We were proud of the class discussion, especially the strong participation of our female students.

Figure 3.5.3 Excerpt from an end-of-semester report shared at Peirce School of International Studies, Chicago, Illinois.

presented at national mathematics conferences, and published articles describing the changes they have made in their classroom practices. These practitioners first began by learning about CLR from a colleague or resource and then trying it out as a member of a planning team at their school. The goal of sharing results is to spread professional knowledge and to improve teaching and learning broadly. But the potential for this learning starts with you and your colleagues: sitting together as a team, uniting in a shared purpose, and beginning the work.

Notes

1 https://www.lsalliance.org/clr-a-powerful-form-of-lesson-study/
2 https://www.nottingham.ac.uk/research/groups/crme/projects/lemaps/index.aspx
3 For a more about designing TTP lessons, see … Takahashi, A. (2021). *Teaching Mathematics Through Problem-Solving: A Pedagogical Approach from Japan* (1st ed.). Routledge.
4 The relatively short time allocated here to *kyouzai kenkyuu* reflects partly the level of experience at Peirce and their access to high quality materials for their primary curriculum. Other teams may spend 2–3 hours on this.

References

Becker, J. P., & Miwa, T. (1987). *Proceedings of the U.S.-Japan Seminar on Mathematical Problem Solving* (Honolulu, Hawaii, July 14–18, 1986) [COLLECTED WORKS - Conference Proceedings] (INT-8514988).

Fujii, T. (2016). Designing and adapting tasks in lesson planning: A critical process of Lesson Study [journal article]. *ZDM*, 1–13. 10.1007/s11858-016-0770-3

Lewis, C. (2002). *Lesson Study: A handbook of teacher-led instructional change.* Research for Better Schools, Inc.

Lewis, C., & Hurd, J. (2011). *Lesson Study step by step: How teacher learning communities improve instruction.* Heinemann.

Lewis, C. C., Takahashi, A., Friedkin, S., Liebert, S., & Houseman, N. (2022). Sustained, Effective School-wide Lesson Study: How Do We Get There? *Vietnam Journal of Education*, 45–57.

McDougal, T. (2016). Learning goals should describe cognitive change. *Lesson Study Alliance blog.* https://www.lsalliance.org/2016/05/learning-goals-describe-cognitive-change/

National Research Council (2001). *Adding it up: Helping children learn mathematics.* National Academy Press.

Schoenfeld, A. H. (1985). *Mathematical problem solving.* Academic Press Inc. https://www.google.com/books/edition/_/0cbSBQAAQBAJ?hl=en&gbpv=1&bsq=resources

Shimizu, Y. (1999). Aspects of Mathematics Teacher Education in Japan: Focusing on Teachers' Role. *Journal of Mathematics Teacher Education*, 2(1), 107–116.

Stacey, K. (2005, 2005/01/01/). The place of problem solving in contemporary mathematics curriculum documents. *The Journal of Mathematical Behavior*, 24(3), 341–350. 10.1016/j.jmathb.2005.09.004

Takahashi, A. (2014a). The Role of the Knowledgeable Other in Lesson Study: Examining the Final Comments of Experienced Lesson Study Practitioners. *Mathematics Teacher Education and Development*, 16(1), 4–21. https://mted.merga.net.au/index.php/mted/article/view/204

Takahashi, A. (2021). *Teaching Mathematics Through Problem-Solving: A Pedagogical Approach from Japan* (1st ed.). Routledge.

Takahashi, A., & McDougal, T. (2014). Implementing a New National Curriculum: A Japanese Public School's Two-Year Lesson-Study Project. In A. R. McDuffie & K. S. Karp (Eds.), *Annual Perspectives in Mathematics Education (APME) 2014: Using Research to Improve Instruction* (pp. 13–21). National Council of Teachers of Mathematics. http://books.google.com/books?id=nHiEngEACAAJ

Takahashi, A., McDougal, T., Friedkin, S., & Watanabe, T. (Eds.). (2022). *Educators' Learning from Lesson Study: Mathematics for Ages 5–13.* Routledge.

Watanabe, T., Takahashi, A., & Yoshida, M. (2008). Kyozaikenkyu: A critical step for conducting effective lesson study and beyond. In F. Arbaugh & P. M. Taylor (Eds.), *Inquiry into Mathematics Teacher Education, Association of Mathematics Teacher Educators (AMTE) Monograph Series* (Vol. 5, pp. 131–142).

Yoshida, M. (2005). Using lesson study to develop effective blackboard practice. In P. Wang-Iverson & M. Yoshida (Eds.), *Building our understanding of lesson study* (pp. 93–100). Research for Better Schools.

Appendix A: "What Does the .3 Mean?" Introducing Decimals in the Context of Base Ten

Note: This is an abridged version of the research proposal. To access the full proposal, which includes a post-lesson reflection, go to the Lesson Research Reports database hosted by Lesson Study Alliance at

https://LSAlliance.org/LRdatabase.html

Team Members

Berenice Heinlein, Gabriella Moncher, Tonya Harbottle, Jeffrey Rossiter, Joshua Lerner, Andrea Calhoun

Lesson Date:	Instructor:	Grade Level:
10/18/22	Berenice Heinlein	4th

1 Title of Lesson

What does the .3 mean?

...

8 Goals of the Research Lesson

Content Goal: Students will understand that, in decimal numbers, ten smaller, equal units combine to make a new whole. (Note: learning the terminology "tenths" will come in Lesson 2.) Students become curious and excited to learn more about these new types of numbers. **Language Goal:** Students begin to work with sentence structures indicating equality and/or comparison, as part of the unit language target (see above).

9 Lesson Flow

Learning task and activities, anticipated student responses, key questions or comparisons that will build insights	Teacher Support
Introduction [3–5 min.] Show a photo of a decimal number in the tenths place (food container) • Have you seen numbers like this before? • Where else have you seen numbers like this? Show a few pictures of decimal numbers. Make a slide of a few images with decimals • How are they different from other numbers we've studied before?	Prior to lesson: Meeting with students who are newcomers so that they understand the context. Use big colour images on the ViewSonic. Vocabulary words from previous units in English and Spanish.
Posing the Task Today we're going to investigate these types of numbers. I have made a bag of sand. When I measure the weight, the scale shows 1.3 kg. Let's find out how much 1.3 kg weighs by reproducing it using sandbags. Guiding Question: How can we determine the value of .3 in the number 1.3? (What does the .3 mean?) Problem: "Let's find out how much 1.3 kg weighs by recreating our own bags". Introduce the various sized bags that the students will receive (1 kg and 0.1 kg) and explain that students will have access to these in order to recreate an amount that weighs 1.3 kg. Each group will get to measure twice and must discuss how they want to group these various bags for each measurement.	Plug in the ELMO to broadcast the readout of the scale. Review that "kilogram" is a unit of weight. Invite some students to hold the bag and "feel" how much 1.3 kg weighs. This will also reinforce to EL students that we are talking about "weight" Model the process so students know what to expect.
Anticipated Student Responses Students in groups get a chance to make a bag and test it once. "Choose something to measure so that you get more information to help you solve this problem. Write down the reading from the scale". After the first measurement, discuss as a small group: What did the scale say for your bag? How will you use this new information to make a 1.3 kg bag?	Show students a model for how to keep track of their trials in their notebooks. **Trial:** **Bags:** **Weight:** Students write their reasoning after their second measurement.

(Continued)

Learning task and activities, anticipated student responses, key questions or comparisons that will build insights	Teacher Support
Groups get a second attempt based on the initial scale reading and the discussion. Response 1: 1 big bag and 3 small bags weigh 1.3 kg. Response 2: 13 small bags weigh 1.3 kg. So, 1 small bag is 0.1 kg. Response 3: A trial amount and an adjustment (Example: 8 small bags weigh 0.8 kg and then they add more, finding that 11 small bags weigh 1.1 kg)	
Comparing and Discussing, including Teacher Key Questions Were you able to make 1.3 kg bag? What helped? What did you learn from your first attempt that helped you? Show response 1 and have students explain their thinking. If no students come up with Response 2, have students come up who tried some other idea (response 3). What changes do you think they could make? We probably need more small bags. Then ask the guiding question: How can we make 1.3 kg using just small bags? Mathematical questions: • How much does one small bag weigh? • How was the combination of bags that you used reflected on the reading on the scale? • What is the relationship between the weight of the big bag and the small bag?	Show the trials for the showcased responses with the scale reading on the board for the whole class to see as part of the discussion. Use drawings of bags to show what students tried. Use "One point three" as a way of saying a 1.3 scale reading for this lesson, and say, for today, we are going to say these numbers in this way. Students restate one another's ideas and translate when someone shares their ideas in Spanish to support ELs.
Summing Up Rough ideas: Ten smaller bags equals one big bag. Ten 0.1's gets you to 1. In this case, the large bag is 1 kg. The small bag is 1 tenth kilogram and we found 1 and 3 tenths kilograms. Possible reflection: How did your thinking change from listening to classmates' ideas?	Check in with Spanish-speaking students during this time.

Appendix B: Sample Agenda for a Lesson Study Planning Meeting

Lesson Study
Half-Day Planning Meeting #1
Tuesday, May 2

Purpose: To kick off Lesson Study again at Peirce since the pandemic began and to enjoy our time together working as a team of awesome teachers and learners.

Outcomes:

- Have a concrete understanding of Lesson Study and its role at Peirce over the years
- Pick a math topic that is meaningful to us and learn more about its content progression
- Write down a rough draft of the unit goals and the unit sequence
- Set a date for the research lesson and next two planning meeting dates

Plan:

8:15   Check in

8:30   History of Lesson Study at Peirce
        Reflections on the process
        Review of Peirce's research theme

8:45   Shared agreements

8:50   Picking a topic
        Start to gather resources

9:10   Break

9:15   *Kyouzai kenkyuu*[4]
        Goal is to investigate the unit/sequence we might use + other curricula, articles, books
        Keep track of insights and questions in a shared document

10:15   Break

10:20   Goals of the unit
        Rough outline of unit plan/sequence

10:50   Housekeeping – scheduling, timesheets, goals for our next meeting

11:15   Break – go team!

Part 4

Capacity building for Conducting Collaborative Lesson Research

4.1 Building capacity for a team to conduct CLR

Bob Sawyer

Schools that have engaged in Collaborative Lesson Research (CLR) recognise that it is a powerful form of school improvement and which, in previous chapters, has been exemplified in a number of different ways. At the same time, they have also acknowledged that there are a number of challenges in accessing the full potential of CLR, one of which is the challenge of building and sustaining the capacity required to realise the benefits of the process. This chapter describes the main features of capacity building for a school wishing to develop CLR either as a system integral to the school's ongoing improvement programme or as an initial research proposal that has been designed to respond to a particular issue identified from the school's self-evaluation processes.

I begin with a discussion on the essential conditions for implementing CLR in a school and I identify the challenges that arise when insufficient attention is given to one or more of them. I go on to discuss the practical strategies that schools have used to implement and sustain the development of CLR.

Finally, I present a number of important messages from headteachers in relation to their experiences when building capacity.

4.1.1 Essential conditions for implementing CLR

Capacity building entails leaders investing in the development of individual and collaborative efficacy of a whole group or system to accomplish significant improvements (Fullan, 2008, p.13). The successful implementation of CLR into a school professional learning community requires the same level of commitment which in my experience requires attention to a number of key features that are discussed below.

The first of these is conviction. In practice, this means that all those leading on CLR hold the view that CLR is an effective and important tool in supporting the professional learning of teachers. Developing a culture in a school in which teachers are recognised as learners as well as the pupils involves the development of strategies that enable the teachers to learn in the workplace. Examples of these strategies are given in the next section.

It is also important that the key components of the CLR process are understood both in terms of their purpose and content and particularly by the teachers who will be involved in the process. In some schools, this was achieved through briefings at development meetings and by reading judicious articles, for example, see Lewis and Hurd's (2011) book, "*Lesson Study Step by Step*". At the same time, however, it is important to not only talk and learn about CLR but to actually get on and do it!

Without sufficient resources, which initially many schools identify as time, experience indicates that those engaged in CLR will first of all experience frustration that quickly leads

DOI: 10.4324/9781003375272-16

Figure 4.1.1 Implementing CLR

to anxiety and a lack of enthusiasm. A simple but important strategy is to ensure that the CLR programme, however big or small is part of the school's calendar of events and that sufficient time is allocated to each of the components.

The skills required to implement CLR range from those that ensure the process is well organised and planned to the academic and technical skills of research and teaching. However, with regard to the latter, whilst it is important that these skills such as those required to teach the research lesson are sufficient to ensure that the CLR process is successful,[1] it is more important to understand that initially these skills may be underdeveloped and therefore will take time to become established and honed. This is an accommodation that should be built into the philosophy of CLR at the outset so that teachers understand that CLR is not about producing the perfect lesson.

4.1.2 Practical strategies for building capacity

Effective schools have a vision for what learning should look like and are able to clearly articulate this in terms of the attitudes and learning behaviours of their pupils. They also understand that it is the activity of teachers, the organisation of learning and the quality of teaching that have the biggest impact (Fleisch, 2011). Most importantly of all they see themselves as learning organisations. Schools that have developed the capacity to implement and sustain CLR have developed a leadership infrastructure that extends throughout different levels of the organisation.

The capacity to lead is best located in a team who can ensure that CLR has a position and identity in the school. As already stated the commitment to CLR must, in the first instance, be held at the highest level within the school and therefore the Headteacher or Principal will be an "advocate" of CLR. However, my experience of working with schools who have implemented CLR into their practice suggests that this alone is insufficient and that the CLR process needs to be embedded at several levels throughout the school that includes the participation and contribution of a wide range of personnel including early career teachers. Of course this is easier said than done and care needs to be taken to ensure that the resulting strategy is coherent and that it does not lead to confusion, duplication or fragmentation.

Some schools have attended to this issue by ensuring that all staff have a role to play in the CLR process and that their understanding develops by providing opportunities for them to lead on different aspects over time. For example, in one school every member of staff had an identified role in the CLR process. The roles identified were as follows:

- Research team lead
- Research team member
- CLR coordinator
- Observer
- Reader

In this structure, the CLR coordinator was an administrative role. A reader was every member of staff who was not going to be involved in observing the research lesson and the post-lesson discussion. These readers were asked to provide a "summary view" of the research lesson plan. The key points and questions from these summaries were presented at the beginning of the post-lesson discussion by the research team lead. Another school developed this role further. The post-lesson discussion was recorded (including the contribution from the "knowledgeable other") and teachers not directly involved in the process were provided with the opportunity to watch the recording and then provide a "statement of reflection" to their peers. Whilst this may sound very grand this was done by teachers presenting their view at a morning briefing or at a point in an already scheduled staff meeting or CPD session. These strategies reinforced the culture of a professional learning community where everyone was part of the CLR process.

This strategy of engaging all staff in the process in these and other ways not only creates capacity but creates a culture that signals that development in teaching and learning is part of the core purpose of being a teacher. It is important to note that this is not the only approach that has shown to be effective. Some schools have begun with a small-scale implementation involving staff from one- or two-year groups in a primary school or just part of a department in a secondary school. Importantly though where this approach has been successful clear plans were in place to involve other staff in subsequent cycles.

The implementation of school improvement initiatives can sometimes become vulnerable to changes in school circumstances and priorities. We know that when schools experience challenges from external evaluators or from changes in provision such as movements in staffing, the first casualties in responding to the issues can be those that concern the professional learning of teachers or those that relate to research and development. In order to create more stability, the capacity to implement and sustain can be safeguarded by locating the resource in structures as well as in personnel.

Some schools have done this by changing the way in which they carry out "essential" school activity. For example, one school decided to modify its performance management process by changing the way it monitored the quality of teaching and learning. The system for monitoring the quality of teaching in the United Kingdom normally uses a range of evaluation tools such as learning walks (observation of learning and teaching), scrutiny of pupils' books and pupil interviews together with an analysis of data. Surprisingly and perhaps remarkably is the frequency with which this is done with all teachers and more so as often the learning from this process is not captured and disseminated. Therefore, the school decided to streamline the monitoring process by significantly reducing the number of learning walks and redirecting the time towards engaging in CLR cycles. Initial concerns about a reduction in the quality of provision were unfounded as the school experienced no decrease in attainment outcomes. At the same time, this innovation released significant capacity for the leadership and implementation of CLR and also enhanced the status of teachers and the CLR process by creating a climate of trust and professional accountability.

The capacity to learn from CLR is one that is sometimes given insufficient attention which can result in a diminishing effect of CLR. In such circumstances, schools that first introduce CLR are naturally preoccupied with the establishment and running of the process but do not fully consider how the outcomes of the research will be shared and used. It is therefore important for schools to develop their strategy for disseminating learning. Some schools create the expectation that the learning from each cycle should be considered by the teacher and that the responsibility for incorporating this learning rests with them. This creates an environment where the professional learning of teachers is incremental and which can be used to feed into subsequent research cycles.

Other schools have taken the learning into school systems and used the evidence to support the continued professional learning for all staff. For example, one school, after three research cycles on the research theme of 'engagement in learning' concluded that pupils benefited from being told how they were going to learn in the lesson in addition to what they were going to learn. This then became part of the school's teacher handbook where the expectation was that all teachers would plan their lessons to indicate how the pupils would learn in a particular way. Crucially though, at the same time, this approach became part of the appraisal process and was developed as a target for every teacher. The school then allocated professional learning time to support teachers in developing their expertise in this area.

Both strategies can be effective. Research tells us that teacher's professional growth should be located in their own context and that improvements in practice occur when they take responsibility for their own learning and so engaging teachers in the CLR process in itself is of great value. Equally, as shown in the example above, the process can result in a step change in practice for the organisation and is one which is more likely to be successful due its development from research and enquiry.

4.1.3 Key messages from headteachers who have implemented CLR

1 Calendar dedicated time for CLR

Throughout this chapter, I have focused on the strategies and innovations used by leaders of CLR to develop and sustain the process in their schools and I have explained that without sufficient resources, the implementation of CLR would initially lead to frustration and then most commonly to an abandoning of the initiative.

From my experience, the first mistake that some schools make is by introducing CLR alongside everything else and without fully appreciating the additional capacity required. In such circumstances, the capacity required to develop and implement CLR generally comes from the enthusiasm and additional commitment of individual teachers, which we know from experience is not sustainable. As discussed above, the successful implementation of CLR is not just dependent on the capacity to "do" it is also dependent on the capacity to learn. Therefore, a useful question to ask at the beginning of the process is:

If we are going to implement CLR with the intention of creating a sustainable professional learning community, what are we going do or change in order to create the time and capacity to do so?

The answer to this question has in part been answered with some of the practical examples given above, however more dramatically, one Headteacher said: *"If you are going to do CLR then you should stop doing something else"*.

2 Be patient

Even when schools have identified a person to lead on CLR, established a research team and allocated a time resource to the person or team, the success of the programme and its longevity can be short-lived. In discussions with headteachers who have introduced CLR in their schools they indicate that one of the reasons why this can happen is due to the differing perceptions of school improvement. In the United Kingdom at least, the approach to school improvement is sometimes one in which an issue is identified, a school improvement plan is written, the plan is carried out which then leads to the assumption that the matter has been attended to. This approach is often effective in situations where there is a deficit in provision and there is a known and available solution. CLR is unlike the majority of school improvement programmes. It is not a deficit model and therefore schools have often been disappointed in the process when attempts have been made to use CLR in this way.

Due to its longitudinal nature, the improvements in learning and impact can take time to appear. The purpose of CLR is to respond to an issue to which the solution is not yet known and which may be dependent on the particular context of the school. Therefore, it is necessary to be patient and be confident that over time at least two things will happen:

- Learning and solutions will appear
- Teachers will grow in knowledge and expertise

3 Recognise the power and value of each component of CLR

In their systematic review of the effects Lesson Study, Cheung and Wong (2014) concluded that Lesson Study is a powerful tool to help teachers examine their practices and enhance student learning. In a number of chapters in this book it has been indicated that a planning team can expect to devote between 8 and 12 hours to the development of the research proposal or research lesson plan. There can be a temptation to associate the learning from the CLR process with just the outcomes of the research lesson and the post-lesson discussion. However, the time spent by the research team is considerable and therefore in addition to making a significant contribution to the CLR process the time allocated should also be recognised as a substantial investment in the professional learning of the teachers within the team. Some schools have recognised this by giving greater prominence to the research team in the first part of the post-lesson discussion. Others have explored the introduction of an additional component to the CLR process that involves the research team sharing their learning journey throughout the planning process. For example, in one school at the weekly briefing a member of the research team gave a brief update on the planning process and some of the issues that the team were working on.

4 Pay attention to detail

The effective implementation of CLR needs to be underpinned by detailed planning and good organisation. It may seem obvious but ensuring that the research planning team have a good environment to work in and that the research lesson and post-lesson discussion take place in the correct settings are important considerations.

5 Celebrate the outcomes and join other CLR communities

The outcomes and findings of the CLR process should be celebrated and communicated. As such, the documented findings should be shared with school stakeholders. For example, governors, managers and in some cases pupils and parents (particularly with pupils if the outcomes result in a change of approach).

Finally, schools should connect to the CLR international community to share their learning and obtain access to CLR resources including support from a Knowledgeable Other. Establishing early links with HE institutions who have expertise in Lesson Study and or CLR is very much recommended.

Note

1 By successful we mean that the outcomes from the research lesson produced learning relevant to the enquiry which is not necessarily the same as the lesson being judged as excellent according to some external criteria.

References

Cheung, W. M., & Wong, W. Y. (2014). Does Lesson Study work?: A systematic review on the effects of Lesson Study and learning study on teachers and students. *International Journal for Lesson and Learning Studies*.

Fleisch, B. (2011). Mona Mourshed, Chinezi Chijioke and Michael Barber: How the world's most improved school systems keep getting better.

Fullan, M. (2008). *The six secrets of change: What the best leaders do to help their organizations survive and thrive*. John Wiley & Sons.

Lewis, C., & Hurd, J. (2011) *Lesson study step by step. How teacher learning communities improve instruction*. Heinemann Portsmouth, NH.

4.2   Building capacity for *kyouzai kenkyuu*

Jacqueline Mann

Developing an understanding of the process of *kyouzai kenkyuu* cannot be attained in a single cycle of Lesson Study. It should be considered an ongoing and iterative process that becomes more nuanced with each cycle. Despite its importance in Japan, in-depth discussion is infrequent. I am going to describe a research lesson that stands out in my own development of understanding *kyouzai kenkyuu* to highlight my early experience of the process.

Approaching a lesson, task first

My participation in lesson study began through the Bowland Maths Lesson Study project.[1] The project involved using previously developed problem-solving tasks within the Lesson Study model and was supported by experts from Japan. This allowed a focus on developing understanding of key aspects of the process, such as understanding the structure of the Lesson Study cycle and developing a research lesson, without having to create a suitable task and lesson from scratch. There are many elements of Lesson Study and Collaborative Lesson Research that will resonate with participants; however, I was intrigued from the outset by the anticipation of student responses within the lesson plans that are typical in Japanese Lesson Study. Within teaching, we are often asked to predict and work with student misconceptions, but this struck me as different, as it was about working with a range of responses, correct and incorrect. Lesson Study is focussed on student learning and the anticipation of student responses *and* how, as teacher, to react to those is a crucial step along the journey to developing research lessons that embody the intent of Collaborative Lesson Research (CLR).

Approaching a research lesson with an agreed task allows the discussion to quickly get to the heart of student learning and how to facilitate this. I will refer to a particular research lesson carried out using a Bowland Maths task called "Splash Down"[2] to illustrate this. The task itself is part of a larger series of lessons called "You Reckon" that introduces the idea of plausible estimation and asks students to consider whether the school can collect enough rainwater from the roof to flush the school toilets.

I had the good fortune to work with the same colleague across a series of research lessons and we developed the practice of completing the task itself before looking at any teaching notes or guidance. This meant we were better able to approach the task from a student's perspective instead of possibly just considering the author's intent. This part of the process should not be underestimated when seeking out anticipated responses as the greatest variation possible is always desired. Planning a lesson using the student responses as a starting point ensures that a research lesson focuses on student learning, shifting the attention away

DOI: 10.4324/9781003375272-17

from what the teacher will do to focusing on how the students will respond to the problem situation provided to them. In the example of Splash Down, this approach allowed us to anticipate students' questions and needs for the task, for example, how big is the roof? How much rain will fall? And how would we provide this information? What mathematical concepts did the students need? Did they have an understanding of these? Would we provide everything when introducing the task or would we provide the information upon request? Would we provide accurate information or expect students to estimate values such as number of flushes per day? The interplay between the responses we anticipated, how we would respond to these needs and how this would impact the lesson allowed us to develop a lesson that had the student learning at the heart of it. What did we want the students to gain, both mathematically and in terms of improved problem-solving, and was our approach likely to achieve this?

At this stage, my understanding of the neriage element of Japanese Problem-Solving lessons (Takahashi, 2021) was limited and is the main difference between how I approached planning for lesson study research lessons then and how I have approached it more recently. For those new to the CLR process, choices need to be made about which elements of CLR are the "must haves" and which may be desirable but less essential (at that particular stage). Starting with a known or existing task or material can allow teachers to begin discussing anticipated methods and mathematical thinking of students without having to worry too much about task design. Having had the opportunity to focus on this aspect of lessons ensured I was in a stronger position when the opportunity arose to develop my understanding of *kyouzai kenkyuu*.

Approaching a lesson, objective first

The research lesson discussed here occurred due to the opportunity to work with a visiting Japanese Professor from the IMPULS[3] team at Tokyo Gakugei University. The nature of the visit was to look at statistics lessons in the United Kingdom prior to a proposed change in the Japanese curriculum. In Japan, curriculum changes are made gradually with careful research and consideration before that change is implemented.

This time the approach was different to my previous, and relatively limited, experience of lesson study and was a shift towards the CLR model of Lesson Study. We began by looking at the needs of the class (a class of 14- to 15-year-olds studying Statistics as a qualification in addition to mathematics) to identify a starting point for the lesson. It was decided that although the students could perform calculations to find a standard deviation, they did not have a deep enough understanding of the concept so we decided to search for, and decide upon, a task that would develop this.

A task, "hot shot"[4], from the resources developed for a course for post-16-year-olds studying mathematics at an intermediate level was decided upon due to it having many of the key features of the Teaching Through Problem-Solving approach (TTPS) approach – it was accessible to all and allowed for multiple approaches with the potential for added sophistication within these methods. The task contains an figure of nine targets each containing five shots. Students need to rank the competitors based on this figure.

Developing the task to facilitate students' conceptual understanding

When starting to attempt the task using our own and imagined student methods, we soon realised that the task, as it stood, was not completely suitable for the lesson objective.

Although variance and standard deviation could be used, students would not feel the need to use them. The task still had potential but needed adapting to fit our learning objectives. This was an important shift in our thinking: rather than deciding what objectives fit a chosen task, we were looking at what objectives we needed the task to fit and started adapting it to fit what we required.

The adjustments made were as follows:

- Ranking was unnecessary, so the best two competitors were considered
- The initial question would ask "who is the best competitor" to generate a greater variety of initial responses
- Nine targets were too many, we reduced this to six
- To have students consider the spread of the scores the competition rules were changed to count only the best three out of five shots

Planning for the neriage aspect of the lesson began very early in the overall planning process. For the students this should be the point in the lesson which deepens their understanding of the concept in focus, in this case variance and standard deviation. Solutions would be chosen by the teacher for comparison, and they need to be used to draw out the various ways of approaching the problem, ideally increasing in sophistication until the key concepts and misconceptions have been discussed and analysed. We wanted to show a need for variance and as a result, deepen the understanding of it.

Therefore, within the neriage:

- What solutions did we expect?
- Which solutions did we want to consider?
- What values would facilitate this?
- How could we ensure contrasting solutions would occur?

The interplay between what we wanted to happen in the neriage when comparing the solutions, the way the task and values would change to support this, and the reconsideration of anticipated responses is at the heart of *kyouzai kenkyuu* in the Japanese process but descriptions of it in the literature in practice are lacking. Here I describe in further detail the process that took place.

Adjusting the numbers

Within the task we wanted the best competitor to be clear for a particular method but for the second choice to require further analysis. This required that each calculation alone did not have two clear winners and the numbers were adjusted to fit this, see Table 4.2.1.

The table was produced in Excel with a formula for each calculation so that the impact of changes could be easily tracked. The tables would not to be shared with the students in the lesson. We knew that students would calculate the averages and measures of spread they were most familiar with first. However, the objective of this lesson was for students to gain a deeper understanding of variance and standard deviation. We had to think which values would help the students feel a need for a measure of variability as well as an understanding of what the results would mean in the context of the situation. The neriage element of a research lesson involves more than "show and tell": which solutions will be used and the order in which they will be used is carefully considered. The number of shots

Table 4.2.1 Table of initial values – Five shot values for each of the six competitors. Values were chosen that would give different combinations of competitors to create contrasting solutions and greater discussion during the neriage

	Shot 1	Shot 2	Shot 3	Shot 4	Shot 5	Total	Best three	Worst two	Mean (Total)	Median (Total)	Mode (Total)	Range (Total)
Archie	5	4	3	3	0	15	12	3	3	3	3	5
Betty	5	3	3	3	1	15	11	4	3	3	3	4
Callum	5	5	4	1	0	15	14	1	3	4	5	5
Daisy	5	4	3	2	1	15	12	3	3	3	–	4
Erin	5	5	2	2	1	15	12	3	3	2	5	4
Freya	4	4	4	4	4	20	12	8	4	4	4	0

	Shot 1	Shot 2	Shot 3	Shot 4	Shot 5	Mean (Best 3)	Median (Best 3)	Mode (Best 3)	Range (Best 3)	Difference between 3rd and 4th shots	Variance	Standard Deviation
Archie	5	4	3	3	0	4.0	4	–	2	0	3.5	1.87
Betty	5	3	3	3	1	3.7	3	3	2	0	2	1.41
Callum	5	5	4	1	0	4.7	5	5	1	3	5.5	2.35
Daisy	5	4	3	2	1	4.0	4	–	2	1	2.5	1.58
Erin	5	5	2	2	1	4.0	5	5	3	0	3.5	1.87
Freya	4	4	4	4	4	4.0	4	4	0	0	0	0.00

and values of those shots would depend on who was to be compared in the neriage. This was crucial in helping focus on what we needed the values to achieve and to continue trialling different values and versions to attain this. The next version of the task involved the students being given the results of ten practice shots with the rules for the actual competition remaining as the best three out of five shots, see Table 4.2.2.

A detailed discussion regarding the order of the sharing of solutions in the neriage, and what the students should see in the progression of the solutions shared, involved considering the anticipated solutions and trying to ensure enough variety would emerge for students to recognise the strengths and weaknesses of their own methods without having so many responses to cover that detail would be sacrificed. Each independent method should not give a clear solution on its own. We settled upon:

- A short consideration of totals/averages
- Developing into median and mode
- Frequency graphs to capture the "shape" of the distribution of the shots
- Variance/standard deviation

A key point when anticipating student responses was realising that giving the results of ten practice shots but keeping the competition rules as the best three out of five could cause the students to consider probability. In the current scenario the modal value was important as students would be focused on "which score is the competitor most likely to hit?". Therefore, we needed to change the competition rules to the best seven shots out of ten. Again, the importance of moving between the neriage and the task was evident in this case so that we could avoid having students looking at a different concept to the one intended.

Once the methods of solution and order of presentation had been decided, the values were further adapted to facilitate this:

- Ideas of no spread (Freya) and complete spread (Daisy) were kept
- Considering the total score and best 7 from 10 gave completely different possibilities
- The values were chosen so that no two competitors were clear winners (Table 4.2.3)

Developing teacher's pedagogical content knowledge

Although, at the end of the day, the focus of a research lesson is on student learning the development of the lesson also impacts teacher's own professional learning. We had a significant moment in developing our own understanding of the variance more deeply in the context of this task when we looked at measuring the variance from the centre of the target instead of from the mean. We realised that we had been looking at variance in a formulaic way rather than what it meant in this context. Variance is a measure of spread, typically taken as a spread from the mean. In this context though we wanted to look at the measure of spread from the bull's eye as we wanted students to identify who was most consistent in achieving a maximum score (Table 4.2.4).

This led us to simplify the neriage, we wanted to discuss the standard deviation earlier in the neriage so that more time could be spent focusing on this aspect. Now, to reduce the number of responses to be considered, instead of the best seven out of ten we would just have ten shots in the competition. Consideration was also given to elements such as the placement of the shots with Betty given a very small area for her shots to add to the discussion about what variance meant in the context of this task (Figure 4.2.1).

Table 4.2.2 Table of values, version 2 – Ten shot values for each competitor with results of anticipated calculations. Although ordered here, the actual values would be scattered on pictures of targets

	Shot 1	Shot 2	Shot 3	Shot 4	Shot 5	Shot 6	Shot 7	Shot 8	Shot 9	Shot 10	Total	Best three	Worst two	Mean (Total)	Median (Total)	Mode (Total)	Range (Total)
Archie	5	5	4	4	4	3	3	1	0	0	30	15	0	3	3.5	5	5
Betty	5	5	3	3	3	3	3	3	1	1	30	13	2	3	3	3	4
Callum	5	5	4	4	4	2	1	0	0	0	30	15	0	3	4	5,4	5
Daisy	5	5	4	3	3	2	2	2	1	1	30	14	2	3	3	–	4
Erin	5	5	5	5	2	2	2	2	1	1	30	15	2	3	2	5,2	4
Freya	3	3	3	3	3	3	3	3	3	3	30	9	6	3	3	3	0

	Shot 1	Shot 2	Shot 3	Shot 4	Shot 5	Shot 6	Shot 7	Shot 8	Shot 9	Shot 10	Mean (Best 3)	Median (Best 3)	Mode (Best 3)	Range (Best 3)	Difference between 3rd and 4th shots	Variance	Standard Deviation
Archie	5	5	4	4	4	3	3	1	0	0	5.0	5	5	0	1	4.00	2.00
Betty	5	5	3	3	3	3	3	3	1	1	4.3	5	5	2	0	1.78	1.33
Callum	5	5	4	4	4	2	1	0	0	0	5.0	5	5	0	1	4.22	2.05
Daisy	5	5	4	3	3	2	2	2	1	1	4.7	5	5	1	0	2.22	1.49
Erin	5	5	5	5	2	2	2	2	1	1	5.0	5	5	0	0	3.11	1.76
Freya	3	3	3	3	3	3	3	3	3	3	3.0	3	3	0	0	0.00	0.00

Table 4.2.3 Table of values version 3 – This table gave greater consideration to the rule change of best 7 out of 10 shots

	Shot 1	Shot 2	Shot 3	Shot 4	Shot 5	Shot 6	Shot 7	Shot 8	Shot 9	Shot 10	Total	Mean (Total)	Median (Total)	Mode (Total)	Range (Total)	Difference between 7th and 8th shots	Best 7
Archie	5	5	5	4	4	4	2	0	0	0	29	2.9	4	–	5	2	29
Betty	5	5	5	3	3	3	2	2	1	1	30	3	3	5,3	4	0	26
Callum	5	5	4	4	4	4	2	1	0	0	29	2.9	4	4	5	1	28
Daisy	5	5	4	5	3	3	2	2	1	1	30	3	3	–	4	0	26
Erin	5	5	5	5	4	4	0	0	0	0	28	2.8	4	5,0	5	0	28
Freya	3	3	3	3	3	3	3	3	3	3	30	3	3	3	0	0	31

	Shot 1	Shot 2	Shot 3	Shot 4	Shot 5	Shot 6	Shot 7	Shot 8	Shot 9	Shot 10	Mean (Best 7)	Median (Best 7)	Mode (Best 7)	Range (Best 7)	Variance (all)	Standard deviation (all)
Archie	5	5	5	4	4	4	2	0	0	0	9.7	4	5,4	3	4.77	2.18
Betty	5	5	5	3	3	3	2	2	1	1	8.7	3	5,3	3	2.44	1.56
Callum	5	5	4	4	4	4	2	1	0	0	9.3	4	4	3	3.88	1.97
Daisy	5	5	5	5	3	3	2	2	1	1	8.7	4	–	3	2.22	1.49
Erin	5	5	5	5	4	4	0	0	0	0	9.3	5	5	5	5.96	2.44
Freya	3	3	3	3	3	3	3	3	3	3	7.0	3	3	0	0.00	0.00

Table 4.2.4 The final table of values containing the calculations that were expected to be used in the lesson including the variance and standard deviation from the centre of the target

	Shot 1	Shot 2	Shot 3	Shot 4	Shot 5	Shot 6	Shot 7	Shot 8	Shot 9	Shot 10	Total	Mean (Total)	Median (Total)	Mode (Total)	Range (Total)	Shots in centre	Shots missed
Archie	5	4	4	4	4	3	2	2	2	0	30	3	3.5	4	5	1	1
Betty	4	4	3	3	3	3	3	3	3	2	31	3.1	3	3	2	0	0
Callum	5	5	4	4	4	3	3	2	0	0	30	3	3.5	4	5	2	2
Daisy	5	5	4	3	3	3	2	2	1	1	30	3	3	–	4	2	0
Erin	5	5	5	4	4	4	3	0	0	0	30	3	4	–	5	3	3
Freya	3	3	3	3	3	3	3	3	3	3	30	3	3	3	0	0	0

	Shot 1	Shot 2	Shot 3	Shot 4	Shot 5	Shot 6	Shot 7	Shot 8	Shot 9	Shot 10	Total of middle 8	Total of middle 6	Variance (all)	Standard Deviation (all)	Variance (from the centre)	Standard Deviation (from the centre)
Archie	5	4	4	4	4	3	2	2	2	0	25	19	2.22	1.49	6	2.45
Betty	4	4	3	3	3	3	3	3	3	2	25	18	0.32	0.57	3.9	1.97
Callum	5	5	4	4	4	3	3	2	0	0	25	20	3.33	1.83	7	2.65
Daisy	5	5	4	3	3	3	2	2	1	1	24	18	2.22	1.49	6	2.45
Erin	5	5	5	4	4	4	3	0	0	0	25	20	4.67	2.16	8.2	2.86
Freya	3	3	3	3	3	3	3	3	3	3	24	18	0.00	0.00	4	2.00

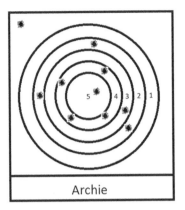

Figure 4.2.1 A figure of one of the targets with the competitor's ten shots. Similar figure were created for each of the competitors for the student worksheet.

Finally, we were able to ensure that the ranking for the variance from the centre was different from the ranking of the variance from the mean. Although the problem had changed multiple times this was seen in a positive light. The understanding gained by the planning team in terms of pedagogical content knowledge was highly valued.

The final plan for the neriage was updated to consider the questions that the teacher (T) would ask and the anticipated student (S) responses to this. See Box 4.2.5 for an extract of the plan.

Box 4.2.5   An extract from the lesson plan showing the anticipated student and teacher responses

Response 1 calculates the total of all the shots and/or the mean.

T: "Who does this give as the best competitors?"
S: "Betty is the best because she has the highest score. Then they all have the same total. We can't decide."
T: "How can we choose between them?"
S: "We need to look at the differences in the scores"
S: "Freya always scores 3 so we won't choose her"
S: "Callum scores more than Freya five times and less than her three times so Callum is better."
T: "So we need a way to look at the differences in the individual scores?"

Response 2 represents the data using a graph such as a frequency distribution.

T: "How does this representation help us? What does it show?"
S: "I can see which scores occurred the most"
S: "I can see that Alfie shots were very high scores or zero"
S: "I can see the shape of the shots"
S: "Daisy never scores zero but all the other shots are equally likely"
T: "Can we find a value that measures the differences in the shot scores?"

Response 3 calculates the variance and standard deviation from the mean.

T: "Why did you do this?" "Who are the best players and why?"
T: "Are Betty and Freya our best choices as they have the lowest standard deviation?"
T: "Erin has a large standard deviation? Is she a good or a bad choice?"
S: "I wanted to see how much the data varied?"
S: "Betty and Freya have the lowest standard deviation so they vary the least"
S: "Freya doesn't vary but her score is low each time. She will probably never be the worst competitor but she is also unlikely to win"
S: "Erin has a large standard deviation but that's because she has so many 5's."
S: "We want values above the mean but not below."
T: "If variance about the mean is not helpful how else could we do this?"

Response 4 calculates the variance and standard deviation from the centre of the target.

T: "Why did you do this?" "How is this different from the previous calculation"
T: "Who are the best players and why?"
S: "We want to know how close to the centre each shot lands so this calculation is better."
S: "Freya has the lowest standard deviation from the centre so she is our best choice."
S: "Freya only ever scores 3. We want a chance of scoring higher so Archie or Daisy are better choices. She also has a low standard deviation."
T: "Looking again at Betty, Erin and Freya is Betty still a good choice?"
S: "Erin is not a good choice because now we can see that her spread from the centre of the target is too big."

Conclusion

This was the first time that I felt I truly understood *kyouzai kenkyuu* in terms of the Japanese approach. Developing the lesson with a clear conceptual objective in mind enabled us to really drill down into not only what we wanted the students to understand but also developed our own understanding as teachers. However, this could not have been achieved easily within my first attempts at lesson study. As I have worked more within lesson study, moving into the CLR model it has become clear how important it is to start from where you are. Rather than trying to apply everything at once, consider what you want to achieve. Is there an area of mathematics you want to explore or is there a mathematical behaviour that needs improving? Do you want to build TTPS or do you have an existing teaching approach that you would prefer to use? Although a research lesson may only be used once, the knowledge and understanding developed throughout the process will be carried into your wider teaching repertoire allowing you to achieve greater depth with each new cycle.

Notes

1 https://www.bowlandmaths.org.uk/lessonstudy/
2 https://www.bowlandmaths.org.uk/materials/projects/online/you_reckon/You%20Reckon_Web/page_20.htm
3 http://www.impuls-tgu.org/en/
4 https://www.stem.org.uk/resources/elibrary/resource/75965/hot-shot-question-consistency

Reference

Takahashi, A. (2021). Teaching Mathematics Through Problem-Solving: A Pedagogical Approach from Japan. Retrieved 8 May 2021, from Routledge & CRC Press website: https://www.routledge.com/Teaching-Mathematics-Through-Problem-Solving-A-Pedagogical-Approach-from/Takahashi/p/book/9780367858827

4.3 Building capacity for providing expert commentary

Jeffrey Goodwin

Once a decision has been made to undertake a collaborative research lesson as part of Collaborative Lesson Research (CLR), a team will be assembled and the research question decided. The planning of the lesson will have taken place and decisions made about how the lesson research proposal will allow for the research question to be investigated. This will be finalised and one of the team will agree to teach the lesson to a selected class.

At this point, a decision will be made about the structure of the research lesson day. How will people be invited to observe the lesson? If the team is new to undertaking lesson research, it may be decided that only the planning team will attend; though, it can be very valuable to have other colleagues attending, as they will be able to add new perspectives and there will also be the opportunity for the value of the CLR process to be appreciated by a wider audience. The programme for the session will ideally include a pre-lesson discussion which sets the context of the lesson and allows the observers attending to consider the lesson plan and understand the rules for observing a research lesson. Then comes the research lesson itself. This will be followed by the post-lesson discussion with a moderator who will act as the chair and lead the discussion of what the observers noticed. There is one more decision to make, will you engage a *knowledgeable other*, in Japan called the Koshi (see Chapter 1.1 for discussion of this particular role), to make a final comment on the lesson? The term *knowledgeable other* is used in this chapter as it is more easily understood by teachers who are new to lesson study and is used in the literature.

In Japan, the whole structure of lesson study is well established, and it is considered "like air" in the professional life of the teacher (Fujii, 2014) and includes a specific role for a *knowledgeable other*. However in some countries outside of Japan, the role of a *knowledgeable other* has been more difficult to implement (Baldry & Foster, 2019). For the first experiences of doing research lessons, it may be that the team, in recognising the difficulties of planning and organising the research lesson, may be tempted to leave adding in the work of a *knowledgeable other* to a later time. That is understandable but the role of the *knowledgeable other* needs to be appreciated so that the team understands why it is deemed so important in Japan. This understanding will also help with how you select a *knowledgeable other* and the qualities the person will need, so you can plan to develop these in a colleague from within or from outside of your school. If you have not experienced a research lesson where a final comment is made by an experienced *knowledgeable other*, you may wish to make contact with a well-established lesson research community and find out if some of you can observe one of their research lessons.

Different *knowledgeable others* will operate in slightly different ways but you will see common strands in the role that they adopt. The *knowledgeable other* should be aware of

DOI: 10.4324/9781003375272-18

the particular context of the school and should assess and respond to the needs of the teachers involved (Watanabe, 2011). They will be raising questions and adding new perspectives to the outcomes of the research lesson (Lewis & Hurd, 2011). This can be challenging to teachers, but remember the *knowledgeable other* will make sure that their comments relate to the research lesson and not to the teacher who conducted the lesson. We often learn by having our thinking challenged and an experienced *knowledgeable other* will ensure their comments highlight positive points and use any other remarks to move the thinking forward. In this way, the *knowledgeable other* will help the school conduct effective discussions and reflections (Takahashi, 2014).

Seino and Foster (2020) identify seven categories in which a *knowledgeable other* may cluster comments:

- considering the didactical value of mathematical content
- use of representations
- fostering positive attitudes to learning
- incorporating students' ideas into whole-class discussion
- giving attention to what students write down
- giving attention to board-work
- teacher growth through reflection

The planning team will have considered these, and the observers at the post-lesson discussion will also have commented on such issues. The *knowledgeable other* could use these as a framework around which they might structure their thinking and reporting. Here, I suggest some prompts that might inform preparation for making comments using each of these categories:

Considering the didactical value of mathematical content

How is the teaching approach and any supporting materials contributing to the learners understanding of the mathematics? How are mathematical processes being identified and supported by the didactics that are being used? What methods and examples used are you considering? What evidence are you as *knowledgeable other* using to make these judgements?

Use of representations

How is mathematics being represented by both the teacher and the learners? Are manipulatives being used? Are the learners recording using symbols? How is everyone talking about the mathematics? In particular, note any evidence where a representation is causing confusion and when it is clarifying.

Fostering positive attitudes to learning

During the lesson, was there an emphasis on the teacher transmitting information by telling? To what extent were learners engaged in developing their own mathematical thinking? Did learners feel able to share something that they did not know? Was it recognised that not knowing was a good state to be in? Was there a conjecturing and convincing atmosphere with learners sharing ideas?

Incorporating students' ideas into whole-class discussion

To what extent did the plan for the lesson build in time for learners to share with each other and to present their thinking to the whole class? To what extent did the teacher use the ideas from the learners to explore mathematical thinking?

Giving attention to what students write down

Look at how learners record their work. Are they writing in note form or are there instances when they are communicating their thinking in a written form? How do learners use written work to share with others?

Giving attention to board-work

This links to incorporating student ideas into whole-class discussion. At the end of the lesson is there a record of the mathematics that different learners have shared with the whole class? Is the learner who shared their thinking identified on the board? How is the teacher engaging with the class to consider the different approaches? How is a wrong approach discussed to ensure that there is still a positive learning experience?

Teacher growth through reflection

The *knowledgeable other* needs to initiate protocols for teachers to reflect on their practice. This needs to be handled carefully as it must not become a criticism of the teacher but of the lesson structure. For worthwhile reflection, there needs to be evidence on which to reflect. Collect all the leaners written work, take note of what they were saying, take photographs of the board work. So long as the teacher feels comfortable with the process, take a video recording of the lesson. The *knowledgeable other* needs to provide articles and references to books that will support reflective thinking about the research aspects of the lesson. The Lesson Study lead teacher should be encouraged to provide opportunities for the lesson to become part of the professional development of the school.

When the importance of having a *knowledgeable other* has been recognised, how does the CLR group find the right person? They are looking for someone who has a broad understanding of mathematics education and can bring a perspective gained from teaching experience and, importantly, is experienced in CLR. This ideal person is likely to work at a university education department, be a member of a local authority mathematics team or be an experienced independent consultant who works directly with schools. You may well be able to make contact with an appropriate person through your contacts with other schools or an organisation like the Collaborative Lesson Research group in the United Kingdom or Lesson Study Alliance in the United States. You may identify your ideal person to fulfil the role of *knowledgeable other*, but these people are often very busy, and you should consider how you can build capacity for developing *knowledgeable others* from other sources. This is not a role that someone can take up without developing expertise and gaining much experience in CLR.

Someone from within the school could develop the necessary competencies but they would not bring the outside knowledge as they would be part of the school community. A good way to develop the role, is to partner with another school that is developing lesson study and for each school to identify a suitable person to gain the competencies needed allowing each to act as a *knowledgeable other* for their partner school.

The first stage in such a process is to find a person willing to engage with understanding the role of *knowledgeable other*. It may be a senior person in the school or someone who has recently retired from an educational institution. The important thing is for the person to immerse themselves in lesson study and to visit other research lessons and observe how the *knowledgeable other* typically conducts the final commentary. It will also be useful, if possible, to find videos of research lessons to observe how the *knowledgeable other* goes about fulfilling their role.

The second stage is for the prospective *knowledgeable other* to be part of a research lesson planning team. Until they have engaged with lesson study from the perspective of *knowledgeable other* directly, they will not fully appreciate the process. Now is the time to find a friendly and experienced *knowledgeable other* who will let the prospective *knowledgeable other* shadow them. They should join them for a consideration of the research plan, make their own notes during the research lesson and identify the points they would want to make. They should talk with the *knowledgeable other* following their commentary and understand how and why they took a particular approach; how did it compare with their notes? How did they make the points and how did it affect the teachers?

The points above will hopefully be convincing you that it is possible to build capacity for involving expert commentary by working with a recognised *knowledgeable other* to learn more about the role. A programme of action will be needed to build this capacity and it is useful to identify each criterion and consider how the prospective knowledgeable other can build an understanding of the role. In Chapter 3.5, six aspects of the role are identified; each of these is considered here.

Deep knowledge of the content

Whilst the *knowledgeable other* does not necessarily need to have studied mathematics to the highest academic level, they will need to understand mathematical processes and be confident with mathematical methods used in school mathematics. In a secondary school mathematics department, it can be assumed that an experienced mathematics teacher will have these capacities. In the primary sector, this may not be the case. However, the developing *knowledgeable other* will need to be someone who feels comfortable engaging with a mathematics problem. One way to build confidence is to identify the mathematics that is being considered for a research lesson and, if there are any uncertainties, for the person to make links with someone who is confident with the mathematics and can provide support. The prospective knowledgeable other will want to enjoy increasing their mathematical understanding; even if this is done in incremental steps as they work on different topics in research lessons.

Knowledge about content-specific pedagogy, including recent research

The title of the role, *knowledgeable other*, emphasises the need for an understanding and appreciation of mathematics pedagogy. They will be drawing on their own understanding of how children learn and a range of possible pedagogies to comment on what has been observed during research lessons. The person will, therefore, need to have studied mathematics education to a reasonable level and will have developed an interest in engaging with current thinking on how children learn mathematics. They will probably be members of a professional association and be reading journals and books. This is something that can be developed but the *knowledgeable other* will need to focus on the pedagogy that is being considered for each research lesson. It can be anticipated that the mathematics lead in either a secondary or primary school will have this attribute to some degree. However, they may already be the person who is leading the development of lesson study in the school and is not available to fulfil this role. This is a good time to look to make links with another school or engage with a university department or local authority team. You are looking to develop a relationship so that prospective *knowledgeable others* can develop by working with people with pedagogic experience and contribute to lesson research in another setting.

A broad perspective gained from teaching experience and observation of other research lessons

This is not so much about how long a prospective *knowledgeable other* has been teaching but how they have developed their approach to working with children by reflecting on how children learn and the role of the teacher. They will need to feel confident in using different learning opportunities. How to engage children in problem solving and how to encourage children to explain and share their thinking. Observing research lessons is a very good way to appreciate the *knowledgeable other* role. It is also important to have experience of being a member of a lesson study planning team.

Understanding the school context and research theme

There is important preparation work to be done in advance of the research lesson. Visit the school and meet with the planning team and any appropriate senior teachers. Understand why lesson study is being undertaken. How much experience do they have of conducting research lessons? How have they evaluated, or will evaluate, the role of lesson study in the professional development of the staff? What does the school see as the most important aspects of learning that need to be addressed and how do they know? How has this contributed to the research theme for the lesson?

Skill at observing students and using data from a lesson to support arguments about pedagogy and student learning

Whilst local authority personnel and university lecturers will have extensive experience of watching learners in different lessons, this may not be the case for teachers in a school. Senior members of staff will conduct appraisals of lessons, but the main focus is often the teacher rather than the lesson. To build capacity, sit in a number of lessons and make notes about the pedagogy and the interactions between teacher and learners and between learners. Then reflect on your own and recreate the whole lesson from your notes. Any points you identify will need to be supported by the evidence that you collect and will not be based on a general impression. Evidence can be discussed; opinion can just be disagreed with.

Tact

As a *knowledgeable other*, you may identify aspects of the lesson plan and the pedagogy that you want to criticise. You will certainly want to discuss how the research question was addressed. Remember, that the comments need to relate to the planning and the way the lesson progressed rather than a comment on the teacher presenting the lesson. It is useful to find aspects that worked well but it is important that the commentary identifies points where the lesson process could be improved; this will be important for the planning team and the observers to understand what happened and how they could rethink an approach. This needs to be done dispassionately by using evidence from the classroom to identify why a comment is being made; this is also a good time to introduce relevant research from the research literature. The *knowledgeable other* has a decision to make when such a comment is made; are you making a report that you will write up later or are you going to invite comments from teachers as you make each point? It will depend on the time available and the demeanour of the teachers. For some comments, the teachers will not be able to let the point pass without a response. This can be a useful opportunity for professional development as any comment will have been supported by evidence. There are occasions when a follow-up meeting between the planning team and the *knowledgeable other* will be of value. The comments and the evidence will have been reviewed by the team and any research articles read and discussed. This can be the most valuable part of professional development as part of the lesson study process.

Where to next?

The role of the *knowledgeable other* will play an important part in the success of professional development using lesson study. Building capacity for providing expert commentary will take time and you may find it advantageous to engage with planning and conducting research lessons as you are building capacity. If you can identify an experienced *knowledgeable other* to work with you, that would be an advantage both for the research lesson process and the development of a prospective *knowledgeable other*. If you want to get advice on where to find experienced people, contact the Collaborative Lesson Research Group UK at www.collaborative-lesson-reseach.uk, the Lesson Study Group at Mills College, www.lessonresearch.net, or the Lesson Study Alliance at https://www.lsalliance.org/.

References

Baldry, F., & Foster, C. (2019). Lesson study in mathematics initial teacher education in England. In R. Huang, A. Takahashi, & P. da Ponte (Eds.), *Theory and practice of lesson study in mathematics: An international perspective* (pp. 577–594). Springer.

Fujii, T. (2014). Implementing Japanese lesson study in foreign countries: Misconceptions revealed. *Mathematics Teacher Education and Development*, 16(1), 65–83.

Lewis, C. & Hurd, J. (2011). *Lesson study step by step*. Heinemann Portsmouth, NH.

Seino, T., & Foster, C. (2020). Analysis of the final comments provided by a knowledgeable other in lesson study. *Journal of Mathematics Teacher Education*, 1–20. 10.1007/s10857-020-09468-y.

Takahashi, A. (2014). The role of the Knowledgeable Other in lesson study: Examining the final comments of experienced lesson study practitioners. *Mathematics Teacher Education and Development*, 16(1), 4–21.

Watanabe, T. (2011). The role of outside specialists in Japanese lesson study. In C. Lewis & J. Hurd, *Lesson study step by step* (pp. 34–42). Heinemann Portsmouth, NH.

4.4 Building capacity in Initial Teacher Education

Rosa Archer

Lesson Study has, since 1999, been developed in the West, initially being used in the United States and Australia, and more recently in the United Kingdom (Hart, Alston & Murata, 2011). The Japanese model has been adapted in the West to suit different needs. In some cases, it has been adapted to such an extent that it can no longer be considered Lesson Study (Wood et al., 2019). We will look here at how Lesson Study can be modified to aid the development of practice of student teachers.

In Japan, Lesson Study is actively practised mainly by experienced teachers. There have been some attempts in Japan at using Lesson Study with beginning teachers (Chichibu, 2016), however, it is not common practice there to conduct Lesson Study with student teachers. Conversely, in England, lesson studies have recently been used to support the development of practice for student teachers (Wood & Cajkler, 2018). Here I present some evidence from the literature about the use of lesson studies in this way and report on a case study in which I was involved.

4.4.1 The value of Collaborative Lesson Research with student teachers

In England, Initial Teacher Education (ITE) courses for post-graduates compress a lot of material into nine months, preparing beginning teachers for a very pressurised and performative professional environment (Williams et al., 2014). In this climate, demands for evidence that teachers are meeting competence standards tend to be a deterrent to experimentation, an important component of lesson studies. However, within these constraints, lesson studies can offer a much-needed opportunity for collaboration, reflection, inquiry, and classroom research.

One of the main aims of university-based ITE courses is to prepare teachers to critically reflect on their practice. This can be achieved in various ways, including modelling good practice, participants keeping reflecting journals, practising reflection in action, etc. Lesson studies are potentially another way in which student teachers can develop such reflective skills. There is some evidence in the literature suggesting that lesson studies, or adaptations of the Lesson Study model, can be used successfully to develop reflective practice for student teachers: for example, see Radovich et al. (2014). Student teachers are often distracted by a myriad of things when teaching in early stages of their learning, for example managing students' behaviour, distributing resources, timing, setting homework and a host of other things. Lesson studies can encourage student teachers to pay close attention to learners' thinking and pedagogy rather than other lower-order distracting factors (Wood & Cajkler, 2018). It has also been observed that lesson studies can help beginning teachers to shift attention from what the teacher is doing to what learners are doing (Wood et al., 2019),

DOI: 10.4324/9781003375272-19

therefore allowing them to critically reflect on learning. It is in fact very common that when student teachers observe classes, they tend to focus on what the teacher is doing, while a research lesson will force the observation towards the learners in the room. A research lesson can also support student teachers to address the well-known issues in ITE of supporting teacher enquiry and bridging the gap between theory and practice (Cajkler & Wood, 2019).

Completing a Lesson Study cycle with beginning teachers presents some challenges, some of them of a practical nature. For example, Wood and Cajkler (2018) suggest that the success of a Lesson Study cycle in teaching practicum is highly dependent on the preparation and willingness of the school-based mentor to participate. In some cases, working with a mentor can diminish the student teacher's autonomy and confidence to evaluate lessons. If not carefully managed, student teachers might find the experience very stressful. School mentors might also feel undermined in their role or uncomfortable about accepting that the student teacher may have more expertise in the Lesson Study process.

4.4.2 Differences between Lesson Study with trainee teachers and with experienced teachers – Possible adaptations

In Japanese schools, it is not common practice to re-teach the lesson at the end of a cycle (see Figure 4.4.1) of Lesson Study. In fact, most Japanese teachers believe that re-teaching

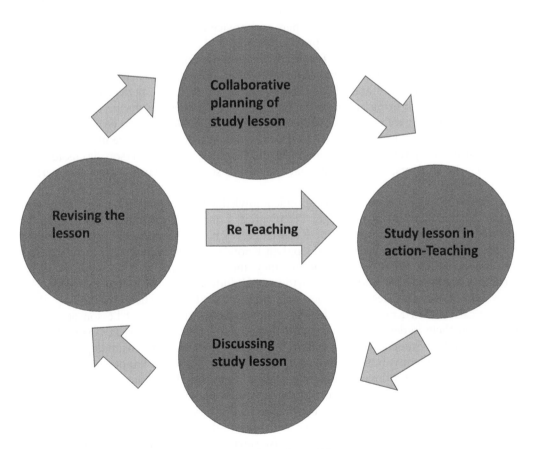

Figure 4.4.1 A representation of a Lesson Study cycle in ITE.

the lesson is not advisable. However, studies in England (e.g., see Radovic et al. (2014) and Wood and Cajkler (2018)) have suggested that re-teaching the lesson gives inexperienced teachers the ability to reflect on practice. Experienced teachers have acquired, during years of observing learners at work, rich knowledge about different types of situations, what we might think of as knowledge schemata. Given a problem, experts quickly have a solution strategy that matches the problem while beginners make progress more slowly. The re-teaching of a lesson helps novices to build these schema and to see themselves as the expert. This suggests that the re-teaching could be a significant adaptation when working with beginning teachers.

Notwithstanding the fact that student teachers are under pressure during ITE, the demand on their time is not comparable to that of fully qualified teachers. One of the advantages of working with student teachers is that they have more time for reflection and planning. In England experienced teachers often rush from one lesson to the next with little time for reflection in between. Any spare time is spent marking, writing reports, analysing data and very little time is left to develop pedagogy. Student teachers are free of some of these duties and have the luxury of being able to focus on pedagogy. Furthermore, student teachers are more likely to be willing to try new ideas. If established teachers make mistakes, they will have to respond to Heads of Department, parents, and potentially the school's Head Teacher, bring the class back to speed and possibly rebuild relationships and trust, while student teachers are only at a school on placement for a restricted period. Collaboration between experienced teachers and novice teachers has the added advantage of influencing experienced teachers' practice (Wood et al., 2019).

In Lesson Study cycles in Initial Teacher Education the university tutor, where possible, can take the role of the koshi or *knowledgeable other*. Indeed, University tutors have both knowledge of the research and of the classroom and are therefore perfectly positioned to act in this role and to bring attention back to the research question during the post-lesson discussion. However, we must observe that the role of the *koshi* needs to be adapted in this case since tutors have a responsibility to educate student teachers and are invested in their progress. University tutors when present during planning and post-lesson discussion can encourage the students, making sure that they don't see the research lesson as a performative activity.

Shulman (1986) delineated subject-specific knowledge for teaching into three categories: Subject Matter Content Knowledge, Pedagogical Content Knowledge, and Curricular Knowledge. Subject Matter Content Knowledge refers to the concepts and underlying structure of mathematics. Pedagogical Content Knowledge is the knowledge of how others learn mathematics, what misconceptions they may have and how to address them. Curricular Knowledge is knowledge of the curriculum and its associated materials. We have seen above how lesson studies can support student teachers to develop their Pedagogical Content Knowledge. Here we point to how experience of Lesson Study will also support them in developing Curricular Knowledge – in the *jyugyou kenkyuu* phase of the lesson studies. Student teachers can, in fact, study teaching materials in depth (kyouzai kenkyuu) independently, but they will have little idea of what might happen in practice and will certainly struggle to imagine possible student responses. Therefore, the re-teaching of lessons might be an important aspect of the Lesson Study cycle for student teachers. The *koshi* also has a very important role in lending a hand to student teachers and suggesting possible student responses. The teacher with day-to-day responsibility for the class, if present, also has an important role in this case since they have a strong knowledge of the class and of how they prefer to learn.

Another important outcome of lesson studies in Initial Teacher Education is to support teachers in developing their Subject Matter Content Knowledge. This will happen through conversations with the planning team. Some prospective teachers when working with young learners rely on a procedural understanding of school mathematics (Ball, 1990) and tend to teach the way they have been taught. Ma (1999) in an extensive project researching teachers' understanding of mathematics in China and in the United States found that in-depth analysis of school mathematics and task design allows them to develop their own Subject Matter Content Knowledge, and develop what Ma defined as Profound Understanding of Fundamental Mathematics. Other studies have confirmed that collaborative planning and discussion of teaching strategies can develop teachers' own Subject Matter Content Knowledge (Cavey & Berenson, 2005).

4.4.3 A case study working with student teachers

Now I turn to report on a Lesson Study experience with student teachers. In England, there are several routes into teaching, undergraduate and postgraduate courses, some are school based while others are university based. The students involved in this experience were following a postgraduate ITE course based in a university in the north of England.

A group of 50 mathematics student teachers were directly involved in Lesson Study in selected schools working collaboratively with experienced teachers and school-based mentors. I was present during the experience as their university tutor. I observed the planning, teaching and acted as *koshi* during the post-lesson discussions. We have discussed above how the role of the koshi needs to be modified when taken by a university tutor. Importantly, the tutors had to constantly emphasise to the student teachers that this was not a judgemental activity, which can often be the case when tutors observe student teachers. Experienced teachers and school-based mentors did not participate in the planning, which happened during an extended period for the students for them being based in university, but, in some cases, agreed to teach the lesson.

The experience was designed by the university team of tutors and rooted in our belief that Lesson Study can provide an opportunity to translate theory into practice and offers an opportunity for university teacher educators to model pedagogy. The model is influenced by the principles of transformative teacher education discussed by Darling-Hammond (2017), creating a culture of enquiry for teacher knowledge. The university tutors value research-informed intensive school experiences that are sustained over time via teachers' collaborative work in professional learning communities and we encourage student teachers to share these values. All through the Lesson Study experience participants were encouraged to respect everyone's contribution and engage in critical professional dialogue. This would not have been needed to be such a priority if working with experienced teachers. Student teachers, having planned the lesson, and having discussed it in detail saw themselves as the expert on the intended pedagogies while they recognised the class teachers as the expert in other areas, for their knowledge of the children and school procedures for example. This division of labour would have been very different if working with experienced teachers. As observed above the power dynamics of student teachers working with experienced teachers needs to be managed carefully.

One of the student teachers commented:

So having another experienced-teacher there, to say maybe "you haven't thought about that". It was more about the practical side of things, so "the lesson was good, but have you thought about distributing material …

Student teachers also reported on the value of collaborative planning. This is confirmed by a study by Wood and Carjaker (2018).

> because you have five different people's ideas and you don't want it to be a one person lesson necessarily, you want everyone to have an input, but everyone has a different view, and when you put the five people's ideas together it just doesn't work and you have to take some ideas out. And it took a lot longer to plan the lesson. But I think the evaluation of the lesson as a group went very well. And it just helped us to ... because there were things that I didn't notice ... I remember thinking how did I miss that!. So I think working as a group to evaluate how to make it better, it was very good, specially if you got a decent group dynamic

> I think reflecting with other people is useful, because, especially when you're teaching, you kind of have like blinkers on, and you see one kind of thing, and if someone else is stood at the back or took another part of the lesson, what they see may be different to what you thought you did (...) And discussing as a team helps to process it more, discussing it.

This experience gave the student teachers the opportunity to collaboratively develop their practice by constructing their pedagogical understanding. They worked on a "risky" lesson. In fact, it was agreed by the host schools that we did not have to follow rigid lesson structures and could experiment by emphasising problem-solving, collaboration and an active role for students. Experienced teachers at the host school were working together with student teachers, even if in some cases they took a less active role. In the cases where they invested substantially in the lesson studies the experience gave them the opportunity to also reflect on and develop their own practice. As stated above, re-teaching the lesson was deliberately chosen by the university tutors to make up for lack of experience and help student teachers reflect on expected responses. This essential component of our work with student teachers would have not benefited experienced teachers as much.

During the post-lesson discussion, a class teacher told the team:

> This lesson helped me realise that we don't take time to allow learners to ask questions and we don't teach them the importance of doing that. Students can answer questions but rarely have opportunities to use questioning to challenge their own understanding.

The tutors were also trying to encourage student teachers to develop their ability to observe learners. The impact of the lesson was analysed in the post-lesson discussion in relation to learners' responses. Wood and Cajkler (2018) argue that teacher reflection is centred on teachers' abilities to reflect on learner responses and modify their approaches accordingly. Lesson studies in ITE, therefore, seems to offer a great deal of promise by allowing student teachers to develop the habit of analysing and reflecting on learners' responses.

In this case, the research focus was on mathematical dialogue, and it was chosen based on our research experience and beliefs. We believe that dialogic lessons allow learners to develop thinking skills. We wanted to encourage student teachers to trust the ability of all learners to think independently. In the current climate in England, the use of traditional teaching methods, often through direct instruction, seems to be best suited to a system where disproportionate importance is placed on high-stakes testing (Williams et al., 2014). However, this is not always the most appropriate pedagogy for learners and their learning. Certainly, in some cases, repetitive practice might be necessary for securing memory, but we believe that for students to develop their understanding they need to be exposed to dialogical pedagogy. It is also important to note that by encouraging the student teachers to construct their understanding of their Subject Matter Content Knowledge, Pedagogical Content Knowledge, and Curricular Knowledge by having an open dialogue with colleagues during the Lesson Study cycle we were modelling to them what we believe to be a valuable approach in the classroom. We, the tutors, paid particular attention to supporting inexperienced teachers developing Pedagogical Content Knowledge, and Curricular Knowledge while this might have been less of a priority for experienced teachers.

To achieve an honest reflective dialogue with student teachers we worked very hard to ensure that the teachers and student teachers did not see the Lesson Study as a graded activity. As stated below we paid attention during observations on the learners rather than the teacher, as well as guiding the post-lesson discussion to be mainly focused on what students did, said and wrote in their books. This, as stated above, allowed student teachers to develop their ability to observe learners but also to gain more from the experience. By limiting performative anxiety, working in a collaborative, non-threatening climate allowed all participants to experiment with pedagogy and research their own practice away from external pressures.

Despite this being a very successful experience there are some aspects that we would like to continue reflecting on. Experienced teachers' involvement in the project varied in different schools. Some teachers invested time planning alongside the student teachers, others agreed to teach the lesson, even if they had spent little time planning, and yet others participated only as observers. Where participation from the host school's teachers was limited, mainly due to time constraints, the teachers were not able to participate in the lesson planning stage, and therefore they did not feel comfortable teaching the lesson or actively participating in the post lesson discussion. In this case lack of time to invest in the experience resulted in the more experienced teachers gaining less.

References

Ball, D. L. (1990). The mathematical understandings that prospective teachers bring to teacher education. *The Elementary School Journal*, 90, 449–466.

Cajkler, W., & Wood, P. (2019). Lesson Study in ITE: A family of approaches. In *Lesson study in initial teacher education: Principles and practices*. Emerald Publishing Limited.

Cavey, L. O., & Berenson, S. B. (2005). Learning to teach high school mathematics: Patterns of growth in understanding right triangle trigonometry during lesson plan study. *The Journal of Mathematical Behavior*, 24(2), 171–190.

Chichibu, T. (2016). Impact on lesson study for initial teacher training in Japan: Focus on mentor roles and kyouzai-kenkyuu. *International Journal for Lesson and Learning Studies*.

Darling-Hammond, L., Burns, D., Campbell, C., Goodwin, A. L., Hammerness, K., Low, E. L., ... & Zeichner, K. (2017). *Empowered educators: How high-performing systems shape teaching quality around the world*. John Wiley & Sons.

Hart, L. C., Alston, A. S., & Murata, A. (2011). *Lesson study research and practice in mathematics education*. Dordrecht: Springer.

Ma, L. (1999). *Knowing and teaching elementary mathematics*. Mahwah, NJ: Lawrence Erlbaum.

Shulman, L. S. (1986). Those who understand: Knowledge growth in teaching. *Educational Researcher*, 15(2), 4–14.

Williams, J., Ryan, J., & Morgan, S. (2014). Lesson study in a performative culture. In *Workplace learning in teacher education* (pp. 151–167). Dordrecht: Springer.

Wood, P., Larssen, D. L. S., Cajkler, W., & Helgevold, N. (Eds.). (2019). *Lesson study in initial teacher education: Principles and practices*. Bingley: Emerald Publishing Limited.

Wood, P. & Cajkler W. (2018). Lesson study: A collaborative approach to scholarship for teaching and learning in higher education. *Journal of Further and Higher Education*, 42, 313–326.

Part 5

Educators' learning from Collaborative Lesson Research (voices from the field)

5.1 What we learned by observing research lessons

Paul Crossley

5.1.1 Introduction and background

The faculty at The Redhill Academy, where I teach maths, has had strong links with the University of Nottingham maths education team since 2006. Members of the faculty have been fortunate enough to work with educational designers and researchers from that point forward and were delighted when offered a chance to get involved in a joint project with them and researchers in Japan.

In 2012, we were one of the original schools involved in the Bowland Maths Lesson Study Project.[1] This aimed to explore how the Bowland teaching resources[2] and assessment tasks[3] could be used, and improved, to explicitly teach problem-solving skills, whilst also training teachers in authentic Japanese Lesson Study. Mathematics education academics from Tokyo Gakugei University were all involved from the beginning, as were others who had been involved in the development of the Bowland Maths approach and materials from the outset.

Subsequently, we have continued to engage with Lesson Study through the Lessons for Mathematical Problem Solving (LeMaPS) project[4] and the ongoing work of the UK-based Collaborative Lesson Research[5] group.

During this time, I and a colleague had the benefit of visiting Japan to work with the Tokyo Gakugei research team. This has taken the form of both the IMPULS Immersion Programme (http://www.impuls-tgu.org/en/) and a bespoke visit with the Nottingham LeMaPS team. We have used our continued learning to make use of Lesson Study as part of Collaborative Lesson Research (CLR) in the professional development of maths colleagues across our multi-academy trust (MAT[6]) and teachers of all subjects within our schools.

This use of CLR has taken many forms over the years, from programmes of MAT-wide maths research lessons, out-of-school hours whole maths faculty research lessons and cross-curricular research groups. As it stands, at the time of writing, in the school in which I work, every member of the teaching staff is part of faculty-based collaborative research groups. These groups meet every six to eight weeks to collaboratively plan and carry out research lessons as part of our ongoing work in CLR. The details and learning from these lessons are recorded in a short-written summary that is then shared with all staff. This model of whole staff training has been taken up by several other schools within our MAT.

5.1.2 The importance of observation for staff development

Our involvement in CLR has enabled us to learn so many things about teaching maths. Without a doubt, one of those things has been the importance of observing lessons.

Teachers who train within the UK system, regardless of their training route, spend large amounts of time observing other teachers in their Initial Teacher Education (ITE). As soon

DOI: 10.4324/9781003375272-21

as these trainee teachers qualify and begin working as an Early Career Teacher (ECT), this all but stops. The additional 10% and then 5% of protected time (from teaching) that ECTs are allowed, in their first two years of teaching, is taken up planning and marking. It requires a very strong culture of taking responsibility for their own professional development for an ECT to use their precious hours observing others. As time goes on, the likelihood of a teacher observing a colleague only reduces. A teacher might not observe another teacher ever again, unless they seek promotion into a curriculum leadership role with specific responsibility for teaching.

One way in which this downward cycle may be broken is through observing ITE trainee teachers, who spend a considerable part of their course on practicum in one or more schools. We have worked with trainee teachers for many years. Our experience is that this is a good activity for stimulating you to reflect deeply on your own teaching, so that you can articulate to a trainee, or other member of teaching staff, what and how they might improve. Only through observation and subsequent discussion, can we develop many of the skills we use as teachers in our lessons.

Inspection of schools is one of the main quality control mechanisms we have in the UK education system. This is another area where classroom observation is carried out: Office for Standards in Education (OfSTED) inspectors visit and observe teaching of lessons. In preparation for visits by these inspectors, school leaders may mimic their visit observations, so for many teachers' observation becomes about judgments being made of their teaching. At Redhill, we introduced non-judgemental, teaching and learning focussed observations many years ago. To begin with, this was still carried out by staff with roles of responsibility. However, over time, we shifted this to peer observations. Initially, we offered faculty teams the option to carry out these teaching and learning observations in-house. A few faculties took that option. Others continued to be observed by staff with responsibilities and leadership roles. Feedback through meetings of Faculty Leaders quickly established that the positives gained through peer observations were even greater than the alternative. The following year, many more colleagues took up this offer. The feedback was so strong from this that it enabled us to convince our senior leadership team (SLT) that all faculties should work in this way from that point forward.

This shift to peer observations was the starting point for us to embed faculty-based collaborative research groups that are now carrying out CLR throughout the year in our school.

Our involvement with CLR has developed our experience and belief that observation and subsequent discussion is a hugely effective training opportunity if done properly. It has been the most sustained and impactful form of continued professional development we have experienced in the last five to ten years.

We have learned so much from all aspects of CLR but observation of teaching and learning in lessons has been the critical activity for our professional learning. In this way, we see Lesson Study as central to our professional learning.

5.1.3 Things we have learned

5.1.3.1 Observers as gatherers of data

As an individual teacher in a classroom of 30 students, we use a range of strategies to gather formative and summative data to assess the success of our teaching in achieving the intended learning for students.

Our experiences of CLR have been transformative in understanding the limitations of this. Working as a lone teacher, day-to-day, we have quite a limited evidence base from which we can work and make our teaching responsive to learning. If done well, "assessment for learning" (AfL) or formative assessment activities give enough information to inform our next planning steps. However, if we are seeking to develop curriculum resources that best support the intended learning for all students, we need more information than can be gathered by the lone teacher. By having multiple observers in the room, all with a clarity of the learning intentions and research goals, a huge range of rich data can be gathered. In our lesson observations, we have witnessed countless incidents where the teacher teaching the lesson has understood something about a students' understanding. However, in our experience, an observer, who was perhaps better placed, understood this very differently.

CLR is research. Research has (a) research question(s) as central and requires us to collect data so that we can answer this question. This question is developed in response to hypotheses that we have in relation to our teaching. In practice, there are a number of ways that observers of CLR can choose to collect data. It might be that they randomly select a group of students and observe their every thought and action throughout the lesson. This gives real depth for the CLR team, albeit with data gathered from a single group of students. If you have multiple observers working in the same way, this can draw together data from a relatively large sample of the available population and provide insight with real depth. Alternatively, we may specifically select a sub-group of students that fits the research aim: for example, we may specifically be considering learners who are having difficulty with expressing their reasoning. Alternatively, individual observers may choose to circulate the room to gather a wider sample of data, this gives them a more holistic overview of the learning taking place. We found that it is useful to be clear about the approach to be taken with the team before starting observations.

In gathering data, observers should consider how they will record their observations. Many observers take handwritten notes. This may be done by using a pre-designed proforma that is specific to the research question of the lesson. Taking photos and videos gives observers an accurate record of a moment for discussion. Many observers have followed the lead from our Japanese colleagues and made use of the LessonNote app[7]. The skilled use of this is a highly effective tool for recording and sharing observation data.

Regardless of the approach taken, in research lessons as part of CLR, we are trying to answer research questions. The data gathered is to inform the analysis and discussion around our original hypotheses and the success of the planned lesson on learning, in light of these. However, we are trying to gather data about how the planned lesson would go if it was a lone teacher with their class of students. As a result, it is imperative that observers do not interact with students or the teacher. They need to be as discreet as possible, not influence either the students' or teacher's thinking and yet, still gather useful data. They should act as researchers not teachers during the research lesson.

5.1.3.2 Task design

Through our exposure to authentic Lesson Study in Japan and through interaction with Japanese researchers, we have gathered much insight into the curriculum development process in Japanese education. The level of detail and thought that has gone into the design of problems and tasks is staggering. These details have been honed over many years through the evaluation of lesson plans using lesson study.

As an observer in a research lesson, the advantageous position you find yourself in affords you the opportunity to see the value in this.

A poorly planned task can easily lead to misconceptions for students which may hinder their learning and understanding both in the lesson and beyond. For example, a task may use a combination of numbers that leads a student to believe something is always true, when in fact, it is only sometimes true.

The time and depth afforded an observer of CLR research lessons, enables them to listen in on student-to-student conversations that reveal these issues in a way that the lone teacher could not. If this information is effectively highlighted in the post-lesson discussion and appropriate actions taken, improvements can be made to the lesson plan that will have lasting effects. Importantly, though, what we learn about the design of one lesson and its task design provides insight into how we might go about designing lessons more generally.

5.1.3.3 Clarity of research lesson aims

As eagerly as we signed up for the initial Bowland Project, we found the depth of the project challenging. To begin with, we felt we were learning about lesson study. Then, we thought we were learning about problem solving. Finally, we believed we were learning about teaching concepts through problem-solving. We often had a lack of clarity about what we were trying to achieve.

As observers, it is vital to prepare as effectively as the teacher. In CLR, lesson plans are effectively research plans/proposals. They identify what we aim to consider in the particular lesson but are part of a wider research agenda. This agenda needs to be carefully understood by all involved and lesson plans that clarify the research focus of a particular lesson should be shared in advance to give observers time to do this. Observers must have real clarity on what the research team is trying to achieve. This should include the learning intentions, success criteria, research question and any anticipated student responses or methods. Observers need to know their role in gathering data to support the collaborative answering of the lesson's research question at the end of the lesson.

5.1.3.4 Planned use of the board

Another feature of effective CLR is the way a research team plans the use of the board in a lesson. The Japanese art of *bansho* is a critical teacher skill. The recording of the story of the learning that the board work facilitates, as an always visible part of the lesson, reduces transient information and supports learning over time.

Observers should gather evidence to support the evaluation of this aspect of the lesson. They can do this by evaluating the record that is created but crucially, by listening to how students engage with it throughout the lesson.

At Redhill, we were fortunate to have a set of new classrooms built at a time when we had some influence over their design. To facilitate our teachers' use of boards in this way, each classroom was equipped with drywipe boards either side of an interactive whiteboard. In this way, staff could benefit from the interactivity that the interactive whiteboard offers, whilst also building a permanent record of the learning over the course of the lesson, on the drywipe boards.

5.1.3.5 Impact of language

Similar to the importance of task design is the use of language by teachers in their classroom work. We have found in our lesson planning process of effective CLR research lessons, that a great deal of thought and detail needs to go into the language we use as teachers. This results in the lesson being almost scripted for the teacher. This can apply to both whole-class discussion and one-to-one interactions with students. Throughout our observations, we have seen this significantly impact the direction of a student's learning. During a whole class session, teachers are often nervous due to the number of other adults in the room. This can lead to the teacher deviating from the language planned by the planning team. This in turn can lead to students developing misconceptions or taking a wrong turn through a problem. Scripted interactions on a one-to-one basis require careful planning and anticipation of student questions, misconceptions and approaches. If a teacher fails to prepare sufficiently, so they know the planned response to an anticipated student interaction, this can equally result in students taking an unintended direction during a lesson.

5.1.3.6 *Selecting appropriate work to spotlight*

As stated previously, real clarity is needed on what the success criteria are for a research lesson. Effective teaching involves communicating this to students in a way that they have the same level of clarity as the teacher. One way of successfully achieving this is highlighting or comparing student work. During our observations of research lessons, we have seen this done extremely effectively. However, we have seen that there is a real skill in selecting the most appropriate work to share so that the learning goes in the direction intended by the planning team. This skill is one that needs to be developed as part of a teacher's practice and is closely linked with their clarity of what success looks like.

As an observer, this is one of the areas we have found the most difficult not to get involved with during our classroom observations of lessons. Having seen a student's work, or overheard a conversation between students, the temptation to draw it to the attention of the teacher is very strong. However, observers must stand by the guidelines of being a discreet, independent data gatherer, or else the validity of the research lesson will be compromised.

For planning teams, considering possible student responses and potential ideal student work to share is crucial. To ensure the learning progresses as intended, planning teams should prepare for these in advance in case no 'ideal' work is produced by students during the lesson. In such situations, the teacher can introduce 'sample student work' that allows them to develop the whole class discussion in a direction that is helpful in supporting student learning. The research team at the University of Nottingham were helpful in discussing their thinking about this as it has been part of a major development they worked on, the Mathematics Assessment Project, in the United States. They describe the potential power of such working in an article in Educational Designer an online journal[8].

5.1.3.7 *Summary of observer behaviours*

Our experiences have led us to place observing lessons, and research lessons in particular, very highly on a list of effective professional development for teaching staff.

Observing research lessons, as part of CLR, is a very specific activity. If done well, these observations gather invaluable data on the success of the intended learning and enrich discussions about research questions.

In summary, in our experience, observing research lessons well involves

- having a strong clarity of the learning intentions, success criteria and research question through effective preparation and engagement with the lesson plan;

- approaching the lesson as an independent data gatherer. This may be done by focusing on a specific group of students or by gaining a holistic overview from many students. Effective note-taking, digital media and the use of Lesson Note are important means of recording observations.
- ensuring that when gathering data in the lesson that observers do not interfere with the research lesson. They must not interact with teachers or students and should be as discreet as possible. This includes not drawing the teacher's attention to interesting pieces of student work or discussion.
- being aware of, and sensitive to, the possible impact poorly selected tasks and aspects of the task (such as numerical values) can have on the lesson and identify any incidents of this during observations. We should also be aware of the possible impact of the language that teachers use during their student interactions and highlight any times where this may not align well with the learning intentions or research question of the lesson.
- considering and evaluating the effectiveness of the mathematical narrative of the lesson (including the board work (*bansho*)) and the impact this has on student learning.

Notes

1 https://www.bowlandmaths.org.uk/lessonstudy/
2 https://www.bowlandmaths.org.uk/projects/index.html
3 https://www.bowlandmaths.org.uk/assessment/index.html
4 https://www.nottingham.ac.uk/research/groups/crme/projects/lemaps/index.aspx
5 https://www.collaborative-lesson-research.uk/
6 In England Multi-Academy Trusts (MATs) are school collectives that have overarching aims and strategic leadership. They are often, but not always, geographically close and may include both Primary and Secondary schools.
7 https://apps.apple.com/us/app/lessonnote/id507466065
8 https://www.educationaldesigner.org/ed/volume2/issue7/article25/index.htm

5.2 What we learned by designing research lessons

Geoffrey Wake and Marie Joubert

Here we draw on our experience of designing research lessons as part of a large research study in England. For the research, we led the design of 15 lessons for an initial pilot and seven lessons for the main study. We structure our reflections by considering three levels of the design process: the strategic level in which we consider the overall research space; the tactical level where we consider the form of the lessons quite generally and the technical level where we focus on the detail of the lessons, their research questions and how these interrelate. First, we set the scene by providing minimal detail of the research project.

5.2.1 Context and background

The Centres for Excellence in Mathematics (CfEM) programme in England focused on students aged 16 or older, studying in Further Education colleges (post-16 colleges, primarily hosting students studying on courses leading to pre-vocational qualifications). These students had, at the time of the study, not achieved the required "pass" grade, grade 4 or above, in mathematics in their school-leaving examinations, the General Certificate of Secondary Education (GCSE). They were, therefore, required to attend mathematics lessons and re-take the GCSE examination at the end of the academic year.

In the CfEM programme's research trials some of the teachers, allocated to the intervention arms of the trial, were encouraged to use a teaching approach that emphasises understanding as well as fluency. This approach known as Teaching for Mastery (TfM), was designed based on five key principles that were developed by teachers and educators at the outset of the CfEM programme:

- Developing an understanding of mathematical structure
- Valuing and building on students' prior learning
- Prioritising curriculum connections and coherence
- Developing both understanding and fluency in mathematics
- Developing a collaborative culture in which everyone believes that everyone can succeed

The research might be classified as design-based research in that improvements in classroom teaching and resulting student outcomes were informed and supported by centrally designed lessons which then became used as research lessons in a modified Lesson Study cycle. In this way the research aimed to be able to determine to what extent the modified version of Collaborative Lesson Research (CLR) made a difference to teacher and student learning. Teachers participating in both intervention arms of the research trials were asked to teach the five lessons that had been written to exemplify the Teaching for Mastery

DOI: 10.4324/9781003375272-22

approach and to follow up this by adopting the approach in all their teaching. The lessons that were used in this way went through much modification between the pilot and main studies.

Overall, in the research, one group of teachers had access to the lesson materials, another had the same lessons but also took part in the modified CLR process and there was another group of teachers who went about their teaching as usual (the control group). The research examined student outcomes at a detailed level in the GCSE examinations and also explored the implementation of teaching and the CLR process.

The main modification to the CLR process, as used by one of the groups, was that the lessons were developed by the research team. The teachers spent time prior to the research lesson considering the design of the lesson, its structure and how it related to the key principles of Teaching for Mastery. In their Lesson Study cycles, led by "lead teachers", one teacher of the group taught the lesson and the other teachers observed and this was followed by a Lesson Study discussion guided by two research questions. The lead teacher of the group then introduced them to the next of the five lessons to be taught.

Here, we explain the thinking behind the design of the research lessons, as part of the wider research, and reflect on what we learned from our inclusion of CLR in our research.

5.2.2 Working strategically: The bigger picture of the CLR aspect of the research

As explained above and further in Chapter 2.2, the intention was that the lessons were taught within a randomised control trial, and that the students of teachers participating in the intervention arms of the trial all experienced mathematics taught in the same way. Clearly, this is impossible to achieve exactly, but our intention was that with teachers given fully scripted and explained lessons, their teaching of these lessons would be close to uniform.

The lessons needed to exemplify the Teaching for Mastery (TfM) approach and the accompanying documentation needed to provide explanations for the teachers to help them understand how the lesson activities fitted with the five key principles that underpinned the programme. Other design requirements included that the lessons:

• were accessible to all students who had previously been taught the mathematics using a wide range of didactical approaches and pedagogies
• were likely to last one and a half hours
• should include substantial periods of students working collaboratively and engaged in "productive struggle"
• should show how the mathematics just learned related to examination questions

There were two groups of teachers who had access to the TfM lessons and who, therefore, had opportunities to consider how they might align their teaching to the new approaches. Our final analysis considers if the CLR process contributes to a better understanding of the lesson design and therefore teaching that is more faithful to the lessons' intentions. We are interested in these teachers' engagement and likelihood to change their practice, and importantly in terms of impact on student outcomes.

In the rest of this section, we consider our experience of designing the TFM lessons for both groups of intervention teachers, particularly from the view of these being research lessons that may be used as part of CLR.

5.2.3 Working tactically: Informing our design of research lessons

At the start of the programme, the Centre for Research in Mathematics Education of the University of Nottingham produced a discussion paper on "mastery" in mathematics (available at the Centre's website[1]). TfM is being promoted across all phases of education in England, by the UK government: it was our aim, therefore, to develop an approach that is particularly meaningful for our target students who had still to master some of the mathematics important to becoming competent at GCSE level.

Together with other partners responsible for the CfEM programme, we ran a day-long meeting involving academics and Further Education practitioners, aimed at developing an understanding of what TfM might mean in this post-16 sector for these particular students. The outcome was the five key principles referred to above. These were eventually used to inform a Handbook that exemplified what Teaching for Mastery[2] would look like in the reality of college classrooms.

In terms of standard CLR practices, this phase of development relates to identifying and understanding the research theme that informs the focus of CLR lessons. Because of the large scale of the study we were undertaking, this process was carried out to a depth that might not always be possible, but on reflection, it seems particularly important to give some considerable attention to this process: the greater the level of agreement and understanding of Lesson Study participants of the intentions of the principles that inform their teaching the better. In our experience of observing Lesson Study in Japan, we should not forget that there is a widespread understanding of the model of teaching that underpins lessons that seek to teach through problem solving. It seems to us that this deep understanding of the approach to teaching that will underpin lessons is necessary, but not sufficient, for CLR research lessons.

In our research, we introduced these principles to all intervention teachers and the CLR process to those who would be involved. This was done through a number of online professional development sessions that we held at the outset of the year. Not only did we discuss these in online sessions but they were also carefully documented for all participants. We ran a further session at the midpoint of the teaching year, once the intervention teachers had taught two of the research lessons, to discuss the principles in more depth.

For the trials, seven research lessons were developed with Lessons A and B used in professional development for all teachers in the intervention groups of the trial. Lessons 1 to 5 were taught, during five time-limited windows, during the year of the research trial. These were the research lessons used in five cycles of CLR. In the full intervention of the trial all of the teachers taught these lessons to all of their appropriate classes and came together to observe one of their small CLR group teach it as a research lesson. The group then discussed the lesson seeking to answer two supplied research questions that focussed observations on specific aspects of the TfM approach. The research team, as part of their development of a number of case studies, observed some of the groups throughout all aspects of this process and also observed a number of teachers teach the lessons to their classes.

The research team developed six case studies focusing on teachers taking part in the full-intervention arm of the trials; they observed case study teachers teaching the lessons to at least one of their classes and all CLR meetings involving these teachers. Case studies of two teachers taking part in the partial intervention, and four in the control group were also developed.

5.2.4 Working technically: Designing the lessons

The University of Nottingham research team identified mathematics topic areas for the seven lessons and worked closely with an expert author of lessons who was commissioned to write the lessons. Each lesson went through several cycles of drafting and revision before being finalised by the programme partner responsible for publishing.

The design of the lessons was informed by an approach that took into account both the mathematics to be taught and ways of working in the classroom.

In terms of the mathematics; lessons

- address fundamental mathematical ideas/concepts
- highlight mathematical structure (e.g., by using context, representations, variation)
- foreground common misconceptions through an activity that provokes cognitive conflict
- provide for a range of likely solution methods and approaches
- connect different areas of mathematics where possible.

In terms of ways of working in the classroom (pedagogies); lessons include

- introduction through a context that is to be considered using mathematics (often but not always)
- drawing on, and valuing, students' prior learning (formative assessment)
- collaborative work and a culture in which everyone believes everyone can succeed (addressing issues of mathematics anxiety and resilience)
- active and collaborative student engagement on substantial tasks
- whole-class discussions which emphasise approaches to the mathematics rather than answer-getting and answer-checking
- opportunities to develop both understanding and fluency

The lesson resources provided to the teachers included a PowerPoint presentation, a lesson plan and all student resources such as worksheets[3].

The lesson plans explain to teachers what they should do at each stage of the lesson, how the various activities support the TfM approach and the thinking behind the design of the activities. They begin with a rationale, explaining why the topic was chosen and highlighting which aspects of the mastery principles are particularly emphasised. For example, in Lesson 4, the lesson is introduced as follows:

> Students usually know how to solve linear equations. However, they may have had little practice at modelling and representing relationships involving unknowns, and they often find questions involving unknowns inaccessible. The aim of this lesson is to develop students' algebraic thinking.

The lesson starts by introducing two contexts that are both horizontal in nature: building walls out of blocks and building train tracks. These contexts support students in developing an understanding of how bar models and other (commonly used) diagrams can be used to represent mathematical structure (Key Principle 1) and provide a "way in" for students, so that all students can make progress and have some success (Key Principle 5).

In all lessons, the students are actively and collaboratively engaged in a substantial task; the activities before the collaborative task involve ensuring that the whole class understands the mathematical context on which the task builds. In Lesson 4, in the main task the students work with four pairs of mathematical situations: each pair has one geometric and one worded scenario with the same mathematical structure.

The eventual lessons that emerge from planning are always bespoke to the needs of the students. However, we have found that it is important to work to an agreed format of lesson, agreed ways of working mathematically in the classroom and consequently accompanying pedagogies, as well as, and importantly, the mathematical narrative about how students should come to understand the mathematics, how it links to prior learning and how it will support future mathematical development.

In terms of lesson format, we note that the Japanese Teaching through Problem Solving (Takahashi, 2021) approach provides clarity about the different phases of the lesson, such as Hatsumon, Shikan-Shido, Neriage and Matome, how they are sequenced, their intentions and so on. In our research into Teaching for Mastery, we adopted a different design, but our lesson plans had different phases, namely: Introduction, Discuss, Explore, Review and Practice Question, throughout all of the lessons. In general, this seems an important factor in ensuring some uniformity in teaching over time: the important issue is that this is agreed, understood and that this fits well with teachers' values and aspirations for lessons.

Decisions about the format of the research lesson need to inform the different pedagogies that teachers may apply in their teaching. For example, in our programme, we wanted to have opportunities for students to articulate and work with what they already knew, understood, and could do and to collaboratively build on this. Our phases of Explore and Discuss supported this and was made real in classrooms with teachers thinking carefully how to activate these phases using particular pedagogies with which they thought would work best with their particular learners. Given that the students being taught were sometimes grouped according to vocational courses which they were following, such as plumbing or hairdressing, the issues, such as issues of motivation, that arose as a result were particularly stark in some of our research lessons.

Research questions that are bespoke to each lesson need to be identified. Of course, these are guided by the overall research theme of the sequence of CLR cycles. In successive lessons you may, as a CLR group, agree to have a series of lessons that probe particular aspects of your overarching research theme, and the design principles for lessons that have been established and agreed. In our work, we identified two types of research questions for each lesson: one had a pedagogic focus and one a focus on the mathematics. These questions for each lesson carefully reflected the overall research theme. For example, for Lesson 4 the questions were:

- Pedagogic focus: in what ways does the teacher develop and bring the lesson to a close to support a culture where everyone believes everyone can succeed?
- Maths focus: in what ways do students use representations to access the structure of mathematical problems?

You can see that these questions were derived from the principles that underpin our research. They might have been applicable in a number of different lessons that we have worked with. However, they were written specifically for Lesson 4 in that we expected that its design would provide instances where teachers at the research lesson would be able to observe students' behaviours that would allow the research questions to be discussed, if not answered.

It is important that the lesson design aligns carefully with the research questions in ways that ensure that there will be points in the lesson where those observing, and of course the teacher teaching the lesson, will have an opportunity to address the research question(s). In designing the lesson, this is where the teacher of the class can help considerably with their knowledge of exactly how their students are likely to respond to the lesson. For example, if the lesson is likely to be challenging to many of the class, it may be that it takes longer than the author might have thought likely and then the key moment that might best inform answers to a research question might not be reached. This is most likely when the lesson is being designed by an author for an imaginary standard group of students, as in the case of our research project. In the case of more localised lesson design for CLR research lessons this is less likely to happen but identifying opportunities to design key moments into research lessons needs to be considered carefully.

As has been discussed elsewhere in this volume it is important that the members of the CLR group are very familiar with the lesson plan for the research lesson and have considered the likely responses of students, and also how the teacher of the lesson will respond to these. Of course, we found that because teachers in the CLR groups were working with a centrally designed lesson script, they were less likely to engage meaningfully in this way. On the other hand, because of the particular context of the research, all teachers had one or more opportunities to teach the lessons themselves before the research lesson where they came together. The important issue here is one of ownership of the lesson: it is very important that the teacher and observers all have a clear idea of the exact focus of the research they are engaging in.

5.2.5 In conclusion

Overall, our experience of designing lessons that were used as research lessons in and across CLR communities lead us to emphasise the importance of:

- Designing lessons that are tailored as closely as possible to the needs, values and expectations of teachers and their learners
- Working to clear research theme principles that are widely shared and understood and which inform and underpin the research lesson design
- Having clear expectations about lesson structures, phases, and so on, and that these are consistent across research lessons
- Taking considerable care to ensure that lessons are designed with opportunities for the research lesson teacher and observers to be able to identify and observe key moments that will allow them to carefully consider the research questions of the lesson.

Notes

1 https://www.nottingham.ac.uk/research/groups/crme/documents/cfem-mastery.pdf
2 https://www.et-foundation.co.uk/wp-content/uploads/2020/03/CfEM_Mastery_Handbook.pdf
3 https://www.et-foundation.co.uk/professional-development/maths-and-english/cfem/cfem-resources-and-evidence/cfem-teaching-learning/cfem-mastery-lessons

Reference

Takahashi, A. (2021). *Teaching mathematics through problem-solving: A pedagogical approach from Japan*. Routledge. 10.4324/9781003015475

5.3 What can be learned by teaching research lessons

Luke Rolls and Mike Askew

Introduction

It is something of a truism to say that the relationship between teaching and learning is complex: no amount of breaking the curriculum down into small steps or providing clear explanations can ensure that desired learning outcomes will be attained. In our experience, teaching collaborative research lessons gets to the heart of examining and understanding the relationship between teaching and learning whilst recognising the need for both teachers and learners to maintain some autonomy. Attention to the teaching/learning gap – the gap between the intended and the attained curriculum – is a central aspect of Collaborative Lesson Research (CLR) and we have witnessed its transformative effect on the teachers involved in CLR through their attending to expected learner involvement, over and above teaching actions.

Over recent years, we have been developing the use of CLR involving teachers in a UK context to learn and reflect on the sort of conditions needed for transformative learning in maths both for children and for teachers. We document below some of our lessons learned and reflections on these.

5.3.1 Maths through problem solving

Throughout our involvement with CLR, there has been much debate in our community about the relationship between lesson research and teaching mathematics through problem solving, and in particular whether the two are inseparable. We understand that in Japan this is something of a non-issue: teaching through problem solving is so embedded in the textbooks and pedagogy, that conducting a lesson research cycle that was not based around problem solving seems not to be a possibility. In England, as we write, the situation is somewhat different: as a result of many policy drivers, teachers are encouraged to adopt a pedagogy of direct instruction first, with problem solving to be introduced only after core concepts and skills have been learned. Indeed, some policy makers and commentators have gone as far as stating that lessons should not start with a problem for which children have not previously been taught requisite skills.

We do not have the space here to set out all the arguments for or against teaching through problem solving (a starting point for the reader interested in these is Chen and Kalyuga (2020)) but briefly set out some of our reasons for working with teachers in designing research lessons based in problem solving.

First, we do not see the collaboration embodied in CLR as only being restricted to collaboration amongst teachers – we also view collaboration as important between learners, in line with the work of Cobb and Bauersfeld (1995): the view that mathematical meaning is not

DOI: 10.4324/9781003375272-23

intrinsic to the classroom experiences offered to learners but arises out of conversations about differing interpretations of those experiences. Offering learners problems to work on, make sense of, and find their own solutions to, allows different interpretations to emerge. Teaching through problem solving provides the "clay" from which teachers and learners together can mould mathematical meaning.

Second, we regard teaching through problem solving as a way to promote equitable classrooms. Providing problems to which all learners can find an entry point, and seek a solution, however informal, ensures that everyone is subsequently able to contribute to a dialogue about the different solution approaches, and means everyone has had a shared experience. The conversation can then focus on what happened within the lesson, rather than being largely dependent upon learners' prior experiences outside the lesson. Teaching through problem-solving levels the playing field in diverse classrooms.

Third, and linked to the point above, teaching through problem solving makes a virtue out of diversity. Dialogue about solutions best emerges when there is a range of different solution methods. We prefer the language of dialogue to discussion: as Bohm (2004) puts it, "dialogue" is about an exchange of ideas, as opposed to "discussion", which tends more towards participants holding to and arguing for a particular position. While teaching through problem solving may have a particular mathematical endpoint in view, a dialogic approach to working towards that endpoint again encourages equity.

Adopting a teaching through problem-solving approach does present challenges to teachers in England. One challenge is the shift in mindset from teaching that focuses on teaching TO solve problems to that of teaching THROUGH problem solving (Takahashi, 2021). With regard to the former, the focus on getting to a solution to a problem in an efficient manner can lead teachers to direct learners towards certain strategies with a resultant reduction in the range of solution methods that emerge. Teaching through problem solving not only requires teachers to, initially at least, take a less interventionist stance during the problem-solving part of the lesson, it also requires them to trust that the learners will come up with solutions via a range of different approaches that can subsequently be worked with. This is a mindset rather different to the direct-instruction-first approach that, as noted, currently dominates much of the advice teachers are getting in England.

A further challenge is that any collaborative research lesson is likely to explore introducing a mathematical concept in a way that is unfamiliar to teachers. For example, one of the lessons we conducted looked at exploring the distributive law by working on problems involving combining different arrays – while the teachers were familiar with the use of arrays to introduce multiplication, this use of them to explore underlying mathematical structure was less familiar to them. So CLR challenges teachers not only in terms of pedagogy; the how of teaching, but also in terms of didactics; the what of teaching.

5.3.2 Lesson design

Planning for teaching through problem solving is a deceptively complex endeavour for teachers, even those who are primary maths specialists. Planning requires structuring learning tasks that match desired learning outcomes, sequencing these effectively with what has previously been learned and what will be learned next, pitching the level of difficulty of the problem so that a "sweet spot" of challenge is created out of which bigger generalisable ideas and structures of mathematics can be drawn. This emphasis on "desirable difficulty" (Bjork & Bjork, 2020) and "productive failure" (Kapur & Bielaczyc, 2012) leads us to prefer to talk about lesson design, in the sense of some flexibility being built in, as opposed to the slightly more rigid idea of a lesson plan. In Japan, textbook materials and accompanying teacher guides lay out tried and tested tasks that have been developed through Lesson Study and developed iteratively over many years – an example of how curricula study and professional development can work in unison. In England, in contrast, fewer high-quality curriculum guidance materials are available to teachers. Resources that do lend themselves to teaching through problem solving tend to be from standalone maths subject association materials which are not widely accessed in primary schools. In contrast, there are many resources available online that teachers readily turn to but these tend towards providing worksheets of small tasks for learners to complete; such tasks thus often only requiring "surface-level thinking" (Hattie, 2012).

In England, there is also not a tradition of a self-improving model to improve curriculum materials, which are instead more often produced as one-off attempts, rather than going through an iterative process of development over time that is informed by researching their impact with children.

Having said this, in designing lessons through engaging teachers in CLR, we felt it important that we did not move too far away from resources and materials that the teachers were familiar and comfortable with. To that end, our starting point for developing problems to use in the lessons was to take nationally produced planning documents that presented sequences of teaching tasks. This process took place over three half-day collaborative planning sessions, involving the teachers, the school mathematics lead, and an "outside" expert. In the first of these sessions, the team examined the development of a unit of work (typically for three weeks of lessons), unpicked the intended mathematical learning and decided on what the focus for the research lesson might be and where it would fit in the sequence. In the second session, a problem, taken from the national planning documents, was chosen for the basis of the research lesson. In the planning documents, problems are most often presented after a number of direct instruction tasks: the teachers involved in our CLR community worked on examining what a lesson might look like if a problem taken from later in the sequence was used to introduce that sequence, how it might need to be modified so that learners could access the problem without having been taught prior skills and also how the problem might be adapted so that the underlying mathematical big ideas might be drawn out

After such dialogue, the problem designed to be offered to learners in one of our CLR cycles was:

> *I was chatting to a baker who had two baking trays next to each other, each with a different flavour, chocolate and blueberry. I saw that the chocolate muffin tray had 8 chocolate muffins in each row and there were 6 rows and the blueberry muffin tray had 8 blueberry muffins in each row and there I counted 4 rows. But because she was putting them in the oven, I didn't have time to count them. Can you help me work out how muffins there were altogether?*

In the third planning session, further attention was paid to anticipating children's responses, refining the problem further and finalising the logistics of the research lesson.

5.3.3 Anticipating children's responses

Pre-empting different representations and solutions children might come up with is a key tenet of the research lesson design stage. Translating ideas about what a planning group expects will happen in a lesson in comparison to what actually happens is, however, a challenging task, especially in relation to teaching a newly designed and untested lesson. Our experience was that while anticipating children's responses was an invaluable process, a list of possible solutions was not enough. As well as knowing these responses, teachers needed to see children's representations as they would be represented in their visual recordings and jottings as part of the lesson planning.

Box 5.3.1   Children's anticipated solutions to the multiplicative reasoning problem

Predictions of children's responses to the problem
Draw the two arrays and counting them
Draw an array which shows distributive property of multiplication
Drawing an open array
8 × 10
Calculate through jottings distribution of 8 × 4 and 8 × 6
Use repeated addition for both arrays
8 added to itself 4 times, 8 added to itself 6 times
Solve through skip counting
6 added to itself 8 times, 4 added to itself 8 times
Represent on a number line
8 × 2 doubled + 8 × 3 doubled and total.
8 + 4 + 8 + 6 =
Draw the muffins in a line or grouped (not in an array).
Use a tally/dots
Count or drawing piles of 8

5.3.4 Sequencing learning

Sequencing learning had to be considered at two levels: as noted above, where the research lesson might best come in a sequence of lessons and also, within the research lesson, how best to sequence a selection of pupils' solution methods.

Even having anticipated children's responses, the route to navigate through these within the research lesson was something that teachers typically found difficult. The group discussed the virtues and drawbacks of the varying options for sequencing children's responses:

- The most sophisticated response first allows children to compare their method to the one being presented
- The least sophisticated response first allows children to gradually build up their concept from an entry-level response
- Several carefully selected responses that expose different mathematical structures and lend themselves to comparison may focus attention on to specific ideas

5.3.5 Orchestrating dialogue

Given these complexities, however well-designed a lesson is, there is of course, the unpredictability of working with young mathematicians. In listening to learners' responses, ideas can be voiced which, whilst interesting and tempting to pursue, may not all progress the class's understanding towards the key learning points of the maths. Teachers found this distinction challenging; to assess in real time to separate unanticipated offerings that might provide a productive mathematical pathway and those that may turn out to be more like dead ends. In pre-lesson planning discussions, teachers needed clarity on what the maths was that they were in search of and which avenues of discussion they might or might not pursue. This approach contrasts with trying to elicit a maximum or equal number of responses from different children (which is perhaps unlikely to produce clarity about which responses are the ones to pay particular attention to). There is also the implication that teachers are actively finding out and listening when children are working on problems independently or collaboratively in order to know which examples to select and draw on.

Once the class had moved to discussing chosen solutions, landing on and then making explicit what the big mathematical idea was, became a key part of the lesson. This required another shift in mindset, from orchestrating dialogue that focused on what might be the most effective or efficient solution method, to using the solutions to draw out and make explicit the general mathematical structure being exemplified by the particular problem. Teachers engaging in teaching through problem-solving thus have to strike a fine balance between harnessing the diversity of children's ideas through elicitation against using these to bring the class to a new understanding. Teachers came to understand that "show and tell" alone does not lead to specific learning. The challenge for the teacher is to help children come to see how the problems they worked on exposed underlying generalisable structures of the maths – a more fundamental truth and moment of "aha".

5.3.6 Conclusion

Engaging in a CLR cycle brings to the fore the influence of pedagogical content knowledge and the awareness that, ultimately, there is no quick shortcut to addressing this. In a teaching through problem-solving approach, teachers need to make use of the ideas in their classroom as stimuli to focus on depth of understanding and create an ethos where everyone in the class looks beyond finding the correct answers to looking for the mathematics within. The teacher has to juggle many factors, including timings, pace, strategies for inclusion, classroom management and formative assessment whilst also helping children to engage with the didactial device (as elicited through the problem solutions) supporting them to build up their schema of understanding about the target concept of learning.

The learnings we have taken from working with teachers in a CLR cycle in large part speak to the importance of the planning stages beforehand. Teaching through problem-solving is a worthwhile but skilled endeavour and sits within the context of several factors:

- A classroom ethos with productive norms about what learning maths is about and what happens in a maths classroom
- Pedagogical knowledge about teaching through problem-solving
- Pedagogical content knowledge including how children progress in a particular concept
- Didactical knowledge of how the representational tool can be employed most effectively to expose the mathematical structure being attended to.

We found that these components have implications for the planning stage to include

- Storyboarding children's potential solutions as visuals – what will the children actually record and draw?

- Plan and rationale for sequencing the learning
- Routes of contingency to account for the unpredictability of a lesson and working with children!
- Helping the lead teacher to be really clear about what the progression of understanding is and what to aim for, what to generalise
- Opportunities for teachers to observe a TTPS lesson
- Discussion to bring out the parts of the TTPS approach that the teacher finds more difficult

References

Bjork, R. A., & Bjork, E. L. (2020). Desirable difficulties in theory and practice. *Journal of Applied Research in Memory and Cognition, 9*(4), 475.

Bohm, D. (2004). *On dialogue.* London: Routledge.

Chen, O., & Kalyuga, S. (2020). Exploring factors influencing the effectiveness of explicit instruction first and problem-solving first approaches. *European Journal of Psychology of Education, 35*(3), 607–624.

Cobb, P., & Bauersfeld, H. (Eds.). (1995). *The emergence of mathematical meaning: Interaction in classroom cultures.* Hillsdale NJ: Psychology Press.

Hattie, J. (2012). *Visible learning for teachers: Maximizing impact on learning.* London: Routledge.

Kapur, M., & Bielaczyc, K. (2012). Designing for productive failure. *Journal of the Learning Sciences, 21*(1), 45–83.

Takahashi, A. (2021). *Teaching mathematics through problem-solving: A pedagogical approach from Japan.* London: Routledge.

5.4 What we learned by facilitating research lessons (post-lesson discussions)

Ruth Trundley and Stefanie Burke

Our work on Lesson Study, as a maths support team in the South West of England, includes working with planning teams of teachers from different schools, as well as within a single school, with teams ranging in size from two to ten teachers and planning for both whole class and small group lessons. Sometimes the research lessons are observed by just the planning team and sometimes by a wider group; in all cases, we have found that the post-lesson discussion allows teachers the opportunity to recognise how their own beliefs and assumptions influence both their observations and their practice. Here we provide insight into what we have learned from our approach to facilitating post-lesson discussions in CLR when working with teachers in primary/elementary classrooms. We do this through 11 illustrative vignettes presented as case studies from our work.

We focus the post-lesson discussion on the impact on the learners of the teaching decisions made, both by the planning team in advance, and by the teacher in the moment. This is rooted in non-judgemental observations of what the learners did and said during the research lesson and it allows observers the opportunity to recognise the careful thinking of the planning team, interrogate why particular teaching decisions were made, and consider whether they had the desired impact on learners. These include decisions about choice of resources, numbers, and language; organisation of the class; writing on the board; and recording in books.

5.4.1 Positive and negative impact of "trivial" decisions

We have noticed teachers becoming aware of the positive impact of decisions that they may initially have considered trivial and inconsequential. When the planning team considered and discussed these decisions they may have thought it didn't really matter what they decided, as exemplified in Case Studies 1 and 2. In reality, the outcomes of these seemingly "trivial" decisions had a positive impact on student learning during the lessons. The post-lesson discussion can also expose the negative impact of decisions that were made in planning. We have frequently observed planning teams realise, during a research lesson, that decisions have been made without fully considering the options, and that they missed decisions that needed making. This is particularly the case in taking decisions about resources. The planning team often make the assumption that they are all imagining the same resource in their discussions and do not physically explore and create the resources together, as exemplified in Case Studies 3 and 4.

DOI: 10.4324/9781003375272-24

Case Study 1   Choice of paper

Following a lesson focussed on place value, teachers discussed how they wouldn't usually make a deliberate decision about the type of paper being used by students for recording their work. However, in this case, the choice of paper had a positive impact on how learners developed and revealed their thinking. They observed that the decision to use plain paper gave the children freedom to try out different things and show their mathematical thinking using a range of representations. The children were able to test out their thinking through their recordings which revealed how they were making sense of the mathematics, the place value composition of numbers and how this can be represented as an addition. It also revealed where further support was needed (see Figure 5.4.1).

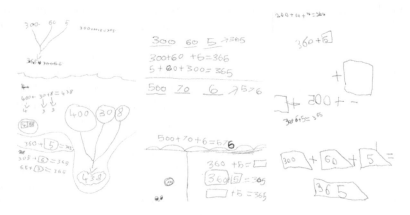

Figure 5.4.1 Examples of recordings on plain paper in Case Study 1.

Case Study 2   Choice of numbers

This lesson, with five- and six-year-olds, focussed on how lengths can be compared without measuring. The children were asked to consider a particular shell and decide whether it was 16 cm or 61 cm. The choice of 16 and 61, as the two lengths the children were asked to choose between, was deliberate and important; the children were able to use knowledge of the benchmark of a ruler being 30 cm to reason why the shell had to be 16 cm and not 61 cm **without measuring**. In the post-lesson discussion, it was observed that the children did not directly talk about their understanding of the value of the digits in the two numbers; this was because they were not comparing the numbers directly with each other but were comparing them with something else, their experience of the length of a ruler. They applied their understanding of place value in the context of length combined with the under-standing of a benchmark length.

Case Study 3   Choice of resources

This lesson explored the additive composition of five with five-year olds. The planning team chose to use the context of giraffes eating leaves on two different trees (one tall and one short); the children had been exploring a picture book on zoos in class, so they were familiar with giraffes. During planning the team chose giraffes because they knew they had lots of giraffes the same size available (see Figure 5.4.2); they didn't examine the resource together before the lesson. They also didn't agree how big the two trees should be for the children to distinguish between them using the desired language tall and short; one member of the team drew the trees (see Figure 5.4.3) and again, the team did not examine them together before the lesson. This meant they had not anticipated what might happen with the giraffes and the trees, which might have changed their decisions.

Figure 5.4.2 Giraffes used in the lesson.

Figure 5.4.3 Trees used in the lesson.

The impact of not fully considering these decisions was identified by all observers in the post-lesson discussion. The children immediately tried to stand the giraffes and they were unstable and fell over easily, causing a distraction, taking attention away from the mathematics. When asked what they noticed about the two trees, the children said they were green and had stalks and branches. None of the children referred to their size. When the language of tall and short was introduced, it was clear that the difference between the heights needed to be more obvious for the children to make sense of the language; one child suggested that they were the same size.

Case Study 4   Choice of resources

In a lesson on early multiplication, the planning team agreed that counters would be provided for the children to use, to represent chairs being set out in rows on a spaceship. They believed that having decided on using counters there was nothing else to discuss about the resource and that they did not need to get the counters out; they failed to consider that counters come in different sizes and different colours and whether this mattered. In the post-lesson discussion, it was observed that because the children had counters of different sizes and different colours (see Figure 5.4.4), the rows of ten they created did not look equal and therefore the representation did not support the mathematical understanding that was the focus of the lesson.

Figure 5.4.4 Counters used to show two rows of ten.

5.4.2 Decisions "in the moment"

Not all teaching decisions for a lesson can be agreed by the planning team in advance; the teacher must also make decisions in the moment, during the lesson, in response to the learners and the mathematical thinking they bring to the task. We have found that providing a clear lesson proposal, with space for making observations against the flow of the lesson (see Chapter 2.3), supports observers to notice when these "in the moment" decisions are made.

Sometimes these are decisions about how to use the students' responses to shape the lesson; whilst the planning team has anticipated responses, there may be responses that have not been anticipated, as in Case Study 5. Sometimes the teacher realises something additional is needed in a lesson, not because of a particular response, it is simply being in the classroom with the students prompts this realisation, and a decision is made in the moment, as in Case Study 6.

Case Study 5   Decision to use unanticipated student response

In a lesson on area, the planning team had not anticipated that students might split the shape ABCDEF into three identical rectangles (see Figure 5.4.5). During the lesson many children did use this method and the teacher decided to use it as the starting point for class discussion. In the post-lesson discussion, the teacher explained that they had made this decision because the method was used by so many of the class AND it provided a relevant starting point for considering methods that had been anticipated, building to the intended mathematical thinking, and understanding.

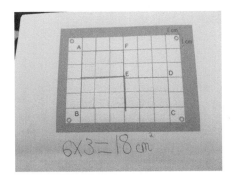

Figure 5.4.5 Shape ABCDEF split into three identical rectangles in order to find the area.

Observers then commented that it is impossible to anticipate everything that students might do and say and when something happens that hasn't been anticipated it is important for the teacher to decide what to include and what not to include based on the learning that is the focus of the lesson. There was agreement that it is definitely NOT a case of including everything; the focus needs to remain on the intended learning which is exactly what happened in this lesson.

Case Study 6   Decision to ask additional questions about the representation

In a lesson on early multiplicative reasoning, the planning team chose the context of forming teams to explore unitising, understanding equal-sized groups. The representation for this was strips of dots, with each dot representing one person in the team and the strip representing the team. Understanding of one dot representing one person was not in the plan but the teacher made the decision in the lesson to ask what one dot represented. The children suggested one dot represented: ten, the colour of the groups, one dot and then one child. The teacher then used a similar question with the strips of dots, linked to the context of teams. Identifying that a strip of ten dots represented one team of ten people was an important part of the understanding that was the focus of the lesson. In the post-lesson discussion observers identified how important these additional questions had been and the teacher explained that they recognised the need to ask these questions only when they were in the classroom with the children.

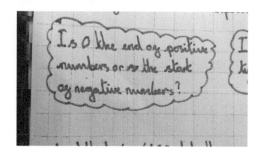

Figure 5.4.6 Student question about zero.

5.4.3 Student understanding

We have found that, as the observations of students are shared in the post-lesson discussion, teachers often express surprise, delight and puzzlement at things they have observed, and this prompts reflection on implications for teaching (Figure 5.4.6). Student interpretation of language has been a common theme in our post-lesson discussions; examples can be seen in Case Studies 7, 8, and 9, lessons on fractions as numbers, structured number lines and quadrilaterals .

Case Study 7   Understanding "one half"

For this lesson, the students were given a 0 to 2 number line and asked to decide where they would place the **number one half** (½) on the line. One child placed ½ halfway between 1 and 2, which had not been anticipated by the planning team, and explained "You have one and a half". She had recorded the number against the mark on the number line as 1½. This led to a discussion amongst the teachers, about the difference between the language "a half" and "one half", what children might understand and how a small change in language can reveal/hide the mathematics and expose limited understanding.

Case Study 8   Understanding "equal spaces"

In a teaching sequence introducing the number line as a measurement model, which began with exploring making journeys with equal steps, the research lesson included asking the students to consider the number lines in Figure 5.4.7 and to decide which of them should be used as a number line and why. They were asked: Where are the equal spaces? The teachers planned for this question to draw the children's attention to the experiences they had of journeys with equal steps.

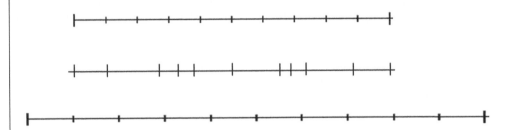

Figure 5.4.7 Lines with equal and unequal spaces.

In the post-lesson discussion, observers expressed surprise at responses given by some of the children, which included suggesting the bottom line should be used "because it is long" and suggesting the two above should be used because "they are the same length". This prompted discussion about what the children were understanding linked to their prior experience of the vocabulary used. The children who reasoned it should be the bottom line because it was long seemed to be attending to the word "space" and their experience that space is often used to indicate a big area. The children who suggested the two lines above seemed focussed on the word "equal" and identified these two lines because they were equal in length.

Case Study 9   Understanding "straight"

In a lesson for eight- and nine-year-olds, focussed on defining and then identifying examples and non-examples of quadrilaterals, the use of the word "straight" in the definition of a quadrilateral exposed a lack of shared understanding, as children identified straight sides of shapes as "not straight". The teacher asked what is used to draw a straight line in the classroom and the children identified a ruler so she used a ruler and drew a straight line and then held it up in different positions; some of the class thought as it was moved it went from being straight to being not straight, with some children saying "now it is diagonal". For many of the children only when the line was horizontal or vertical was it considered to be straight. The planning team had not anticipated this issue and in the post-lesson discussion teachers reflected that they would have assumed understanding of "straight" but that this revealed the importance of not assuming a shared understanding of vocabulary, especially when the same words are used to mean something different in everyday life.

Alongside recording observations of what the students say and do during the lesson, having students' work available for referring to during the post-lesson discussion, whether through photographs taken or books left on tables, is invaluable in terms of focussing on student understanding within the lesson. The opportunity to interrogate and make sense of student responses, looking at what has been recorded, sharing observations of what the students did and said, considering different perspectives, allows us to challenge assumptions about students, their engagement in mathematical thinking in the lesson and their understanding resulting from the lesson. For example, in Case Study 10, a lesson on understanding that comparison is subtraction, an assumption was made about one student not engaging yet her recorded reflections tell a different story, and in Case Study 11, a lesson on deriving multiplication facts, an assumption about student understanding of subtraction is exposed.

Case Study 10   Student reflections

This lesson with eight- and nine-year-olds focussed on understanding that comparing two prices, £2.60 and £2.39, and finding the difference between them, is represented by the calculation £2.60 - £2.39; none of the students had initially recorded this as the calculation to match the context although they had successfully found the difference. Following class discussion exploring the symbolic representation of difference, the children were asked to reflect at the end of the lesson. In the post-lesson discussion one observer identified a child they had noticed choosing not to talk to her partner during the lesson, who seemed little involved, and it was suggested this child had taken nothing from the lesson. When the child's written reflection was shared, it indicated far greater involvement and understanding than had been assumed, as she connected her method for finding the difference with the subtraction representing the problem (see Figure 5.4.8).

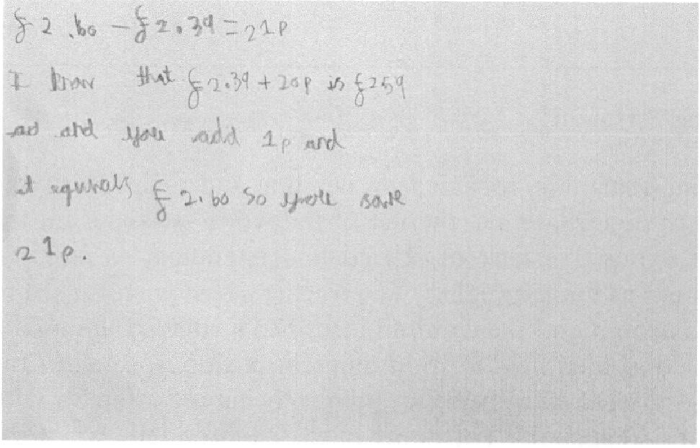

Figure 5.4.8 End of lesson reflections.

> **Case Study 11** In a lesson exploring deriving multiplication facts from known multiplication facts, children were asked to use the known fact $5 \times 10 = 50$ to derive 5×9. In the post-lesson discussion observations of many children counting in 5s from 5 to 45, in order to find 5×9, were shared and there was a realisation that the children who were choosing to count in fives from 5 to 45 to find 5×9 did not know what $50 - 5$ was and found this more difficult to solve than counting in fives to 45. The planning team had not considered that this might be the case; using $5 \times 10 = 50$ to solve 5×9 seemed obvious to the teachers but they had not appreciated that $50 - 5$ might appear difficult to the children.

5.4.4 Reflecting on lessons

Whilst much of the focus, in our post-lesson discussions, is on the detail of the lesson observed, we always take time at the end to step back from the detail and ask participants to consider "So what? What does this mean for you in your teaching? What are you taking away from this experience?" The opportunity for this sort of reflection allows those participating to look beyond the individual experience and connect it to the wider teaching and learning of mathematics, identifying more generally applicable ideas, and thinking. For example, the following reflections come from the same Year 1 (five- to six-year-olds) lesson with a mathematical focus on comparing groups, identifying and explaining more/fewer/same:

- Decisions had to be made to stop the context from complicating the mathematics and drawing attention away from the mathematics. If a context is being used to help the children make sense of the mathematics, then it needs to support understanding. Contexts can then be used to challenge understanding but when to do this needs careful planning.
- Resources can become a barrier especially where different properties such as colours are involved, or the resources are contextual but not related to the context being explored for the mathematics in the lesson (for example dinosaurs were available but the problem was about other animals). Cubes and counters are generally best kept in single-colour sets.
- The use of a grid for the independent activity (see Figure 5.4.9) allowed the children to demonstrate their understanding and has the potential to be used in a flexible way, in

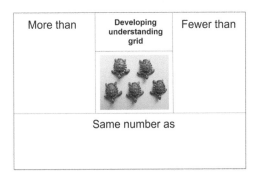

Figure 5.4.9 Developing understanding grid.

different areas of mathematics, allowing children to challenge themselves and teachers to provide for deep understanding.

- Having different resources available for children to choose from during their work allows them to demonstrate their understanding, make decisions and explain not only how they have chosen to represent the mathematics but also how someone else has. It allows for considering "what's the same and what's different?" At the end of this particular lesson, this question proved to be challenging, comparing two grids completed using very different resources.

- During the lesson the use of the stem sentence *There are fewer... than ...* supported the children to use new language and connect it to the context. Stem sentences and sentence starters (such as *I notice that ...*) can be used widely in mathematics to support understanding and talk. However, it is also important that the children express their thinking in their own words and are not restricted to the use of stem sentences. This particular lesson started from the children's own thinking; sentences used early on reflected the children's thinking and they were all able to repeat them easily. The lesson then built on this early language, with more complicated sentences reflecting more complicated mathematical ideas being introduced.

- Focussing on efficiency includes identifying when you do and do not need to count; it is important that children are making decisions in their mathematics, using what they know, and can explain why they have made decisions.

It is reflections like these that reveal just how powerful the experience of participating in Lesson Study can be and what a privilege it is to be involved.

5.5 What we learn by providing final comments

Jeffrey Goodwin

Lesson Study in the form of Collaborative Lesson Research (CLR), forms an important part of my professional life. My work in schools as an independent consultant and as an Associate Lecturer with the Open University gives me the opportunity to engage with teachers on the role that problem solving can play in mathematics education. I had been working with schools in North London for some twenty years when I was invited to contribute to a CLR and problem-solving project in a district of North London. This was my first experience of a form of Japanese Lesson Study and I was able to join a group of some fifty teachers in both primary and secondary schools where we were all embarking on a journey into Lesson Study together. I spent the first year being an observer at research lessons and had the opportunity to observe the way that experienced commentators/koshi/knowledgeable others[1] made final comments (see Chapter 1.2). I was interested in the different ways these knowledgeable others worked with the teachers and the different approaches they used to summarise the learning from the lessons.

As part of my experience towards taking on the role of knowledgeable other I was privileged to be an observer at a number of research lessons when experienced knowledgeable others from Japan made the final comments. Additionally, I have been on an IMPULS[2] online professional development course looking at the role of the knowledgeable other and am a member of the UK Collaborative Lesson Research group. A visit with members of this group to see lessons in schools in Tokyo made a lasting impression.

I have now had a long-term relationship with four schools and over time have observed how teachers have changed as a result of their engagement with CLR. More recently I have evaluated my role as a knowledgeable other by interviewing teachers to gain some understanding of how the final comments have influenced professional development and classroom actions. This long-term relationship has helped as we have developed mutual trust as well as confidence in our ways of working.

In this chapter, I reflect further on important aspects of making the final comments at research lessons and aim to provide insight into what I have learned from my experience as a knowledgeable other.

5.5.1 Collaboration and the knowledgeable other

Lewis and Perry (2010) note that "Teachers who participate in lesson study feel that learning with colleagues is effective and enjoyable more than do comparison teachers who do not participate". As a teacher in a UK school said of their experience of being involved in CLR, "I think the biggest thing there has been, is working with different people and having conversations". The teacher went on to say, "I just think that it is an amazing

DOI: 10.4324/9781003375272-25

opportunity we don't often get as teachers". Such opportunities can come from a range of different types of professional development but as Stigler and Hiebert point out in the book the Teaching Gap (1999), Lesson Study will improve teaching and learning through shared professional knowledge based on studying the outcome of a lesson.

There is much value in being a regular knowledgeable other to a research group. You get to know the teachers and how their approach to a research lesson is developing. This will influence the way that you prepare the final comments and how you will balance the mathematical and pedagogical points. Whilst in a secondary school, the comments may be more subject focussed, in a primary school this may need to be handled more carefully.

As another teacher said about working collaboratively with others, "... we don't often get that as teachers ... now what happens of course in lesson study is there is a particular procedure, and ... you've always got a research question to work with". I have found it helpful to understand how teachers are working with the research question as it helps inform my final comments. As the teacher went on to say, "... afterwards people say what happened and the, knowledgeable other, comes in at the end. It seems to me that this is a big part of lesson study ... [their] feedback to the rest of the group. I think that through the Koshiing and post lesson discussion you were able to bring all that in as well through your final comments, it provides really good learning for us". In making final comments, the knowledgeable other needs to give a focus for the teachers to have further meaningful discussions about the research lesson. One way I have found useful to do this is through providing reading in the form of both research and professional articles.

The collaborative process has the advantage that learning is examined through the lens of a number of teachers and commentators (Lewis & Hurd, 2011). As Peter Dudley points out (2015), in the West we tend to teach in isolation. In the final comments, the knowledgeable other needs to give the opportunity for a group of teachers to focus on a well-defined lesson and an identified research question. This is an important aspect of the final comments and the input from the knowledgeable other needs to focus on the outcomes that can be related to a particular experience that all the participants have shared (Takahashi, 2014). Identifying these experiences is an important part of the final comments. Have you understood from the research planning the focus that the teachers think is important? Have you identified important mathematical or pedagogic points that need to be considered further? During the feedback session, you need to be relating what happened during the lesson to the comments that are being made. This needs flexible thinking and, whilst you will have been considering your comments after viewing the research lesson plan and the research lesson, you will need to respond to points made, or not made, during the feedback.

5.5.2 Keeping your distance and being objective

As teachers engage with collaborative lesson research, they have invested time and commitment to the process. It is only natural to want to say how good the experience was and how it has made a change to classroom practice and learning. In this spirit, it is useful to be able to reflect on the whole process in a detached objective way that is based on evidence rather than impressions. A good place to start to work towards this is to evaluate your final comments and look at how these have identified issues, confirmed thinking, and provided positive professional development. One way to do this is to plan an evaluation process. In the lesson plan and the research question, what will be evidence of a change of thinking? Make a list and decide if everything on the list can be measured as part of the final comments; you will find that those that relate to teacher culture and how teachers are looking to approach working with learners can be identified and evaluated, taking account of both subject and pedagogic focus of the lesson. However, from the final comments, it will not be possible to understand any long-term changes in the way that learners are approaching problem solving. You will have an insight from looking at the work that the learners did during the research lesson, but teachers will need to observe learner behaviour in the classroom to evaluate any long-term change. As well as evaluating your own comments, it is important to engage with the teachers to understand changes to learner behaviour and the impact the research lessons are having on this process. For future final comments, if you are working with the group over a number of CLR cycles, you can refer to this and identify and comment on the way that CLR is changing the culture of lessons.

It is useful to find someone outside of the planning team and the lesson observers to stand back from any discussion and reflect on the processes and outcomes of the final comments. It will be important for this person to have a copy of the lesson plan beforehand, and important for the person to attend the research lesson to give context to any comments. Before the lesson, it is useful for this evaluator to meet with the planning team and to understand the list of outcomes that the team is looking for during the final comments. The evaluator should not be constrained by the lesson plan, or the outcomes listed by the planning team; these will form only some of the factors they will want to take into account.

The use of an evaluator is not necessary for every research lesson, but it is a useful way to understand what was learned from your final comments as knowledgeable other. The evaluation can be taken a step further and individual members of the planning team can be interviewed to understand how they have perceived the outcomes of the research lesson; a useful question is to ask which parts of the final comments are influencing their professional development. This can be a good way for the planning team to reflect on the way the final comments were structured and whether there needs to be more emphasis on some parts. This is a good opportunity to understand how the planning team is likely to respond to your comments as knowledgeable other.

5.5.3 Focusing on both teacher and student learning

It is important for the planning team to understand what has changed in the classroom in both teachers and learners because of CLR. As a knowledgeable other this provides another good reason for developing a long-term relationship with a CLR group. Such a commitment will allow you over time to understand the learning of both teachers and learners.

One teacher I interviewed was excited about how the learners were reacting to mathematics,

I think for the children, it has deepened their understanding of mathematical concepts. So, if you were to ask them a question, they don't just say the answer is 'four' then move on, they'll say, 'the answer is four because I did this because' and they will all start talking to you about their actual thinking.

This is an example of how the classroom culture had changed for this class when the planning team in the school had been concentrating on pedagogies for when learners are engaging in problem solving tasks. It is also important to evaluate how learners' understanding of mathematical concepts has changed. Is there a link between the research lessons, the mathematics in the research question and the outcomes of the final comments? Whilst some research lessons will focus more on pedagogy than mathematical understanding and others will have mathematical understanding to the fore; the final comments should be looking at the balance between the two and how it reflects the identified needs of the school and the overarching research theme. These needs will also be a reflection of the social context of the learners and the knowledgeable other needs to be aware of, and sensitive to, these when making final comments.

5.5.4 Capturing the work of the knowledgeable other

In previous sections, I have given some insight into the ways I have been working as a knowledgeable other and hope that this gives an indication of the level of commitment needed to ensure that final comments made as a knowledgeable other can have the potential to make a real difference. In general, it is useful to have a clear record of the work of the CLR group, both to assist with ongoing professional learning, but also as a way of demonstrating the value that a knowledgeable other with expertise beyond that of the group can add to their work.

We know that there are both financial costs and time commitments that need to be allocated to CLR and that these need accounting for. The support of the senior team, particularly the head teacher, and other stakeholders such as the governing body (in the United Kingdom), parents and teachers, is very important for a well-supported and re-sourced CLR project. It is important that there is good communication between all inter-ested groups and that convincing arguments can be made for the continuation of lesson research. It is helpful if the planning team has a programme of actions that keeps all parties informed and that there is convincing evidence of the value of research lessons. Presentations with information sheets are useful ways of informing the school community about the value of the work of the CLR team. One aspect that needs explaining, for ex-ample, is the amount of time spent by a group of teachers to plan one lesson. Video can prove a useful way of conveying what is happening during a research lesson. Clips of teachers from the school and other visitors during the lesson can emphasise how the school is being viewed by others. An edited video of the final discussion and the comments of the knowledgeable other are a powerful way of explaining the professional development opportunities and, of course, provide a permanent record of a particular research lesson. Having video evidence of the way that learners in the classroom are excited at doing mathematics and are confident mathematicians is very convincing. Link this to the Lesson Study process from planning to delivering the research lesson to the final comments and you will have positive messages to deliver.

As a knowledgeable other, you will, for better or worse, have an impact on the CLR process and its outcomes. Your final comments play an important role in this and you need to ensure that you are evaluating and learning from each final comment that you make. You need to engage with the teachers and understand how their CLR journey is pro-gressing. How will you tailor your comments to take account of this and how will you provide a supportive atmosphere for the critical points that you will need to make? When reviewing and evaluating a final comment, check that it was the lesson and not the teacher that you were making comments about. Take every opportunity to engage with the CLR group and understand how and why your final comments made a difference. Think about providing articles and references to support further discussion by the CLR team. Refer to these in the final comments. In general, immerse yourself in the work of the CLR team. Make sure that you fully understand what their long-term aims and goals are, how the research lesson reflects these and how the research questions for the lesson will help them explore their intentions. Make sure that you consider both the learning of teachers and students. And finally, enjoy the privilege that the role brings: it is an important and wonderful opportunity to join in the professional learning of the whole team.

Notes

1 The role of these "experts" is described more fully in Chapter 1.1. Here, henceforth I will use the term *knowledgeable other* to refer to the person with this responsibility.
2 IMPULS: Improving Math-teacher Professionalisation through Lesson Study. Project at Tokyo Gakugei University http://www.impuls-tgu.org/en/

References

Dudley, P. (2015). *Lesson study: Professional learning for our time*. London and New York: Routledge.

Lewis, C., & Perry, R. (2010). *Building a knowledge base for teaching: Design and test of research-based toolkits to support lesson study*. Paper presented at the annual meeting of the American Educational Research Association, April 2009.

Lewis, C., & Hurd, J. (2011). *Lesson study step by step*. Portsmouth, NH: Heinemann.

Stigler, J., & Hiebert, J. (1999). *The teaching gap: Best ideas from the world's teachers for improving education in the classroom*. New York: Free Press a division of Simon & Schuster.

Takahashi, A. (2014) The role of the Knowledgeable Other in lesson study: Examining the final comments of experienced lesson study practitioners. *Mathematics Teacher Education and Development*, *16*(1), 4–21.

5.6 What we learned by researching Lesson Study

Matt Woodford

A distinguishing factor of CLR is that it used to develop mathematical thinking in students (Lewis, Perry, & Murata, 2006) rather than trying to produce a perfect demonstration lesson (Huang et al., 2017). Here, I reflect on some important lessons that I have learned in my research. These relate in particular to two phases of the CLR cycle and I illustrate these by drawing on a recent CLR cycle completed with a mathematics department from a secondary school (students aged 11–18) in England. The adapted CLR cycle that we followed is shown in Figure 5.6.1 with each of the four sessions scheduled to fit within the mathematics department's monthly 1-hour development time. In addition, the diagram also highlights how we were explicit in recognising that our educational values (Fujii, 2014) feed into each of the phases. In brief, the planning team met together for three sessions prior to the live research lesson, before meeting together in the fourth session to discuss it. Here, I explore the role of educational values in the context of the phases of *identifying a research* theme (session 1) and carrying out the groundwork for the lesson design through *kyouzai kenkyuu* (session 2).

5.6.1 Learning about the research theme

In the first session, the planning team were introduced to the CLR process before we sought to identify a research theme and a topic. From my experience, identifying a suitable research theme can be a difficult task to complete. For example, I have participated in Lesson Study cycles where the research theme was retrospectively copied from the mathematical objectives of the lesson. So, a lesson on angles between parallel lines might be given a research theme of: *students should be able to find the angles between parallel lines.* Takahashi and McDougal (2018) see this as the first layer of a research *focus*, but it would be considered insufficient without an accompanying research theme. In isolation, the first layer risks placing an emphasis on the perfection of a lesson rather than on the development of student thinking. With the addition of a research theme, the focus of the Lesson Study moves from perfecting a lesson to considering the learning of students. This research theme adds a second layer to the research focus which seeks to address a common school issue (Takahashi & McDougal, 2016) and subsequently allows a suitable lesson to be identified. Takahashi and McDougal (2018) suggest that a good research theme for a lesson should include both a desired outcome for students and an entry point by which it may be achieved. Few of the schools I have worked with have a pre-existing common issue that they wish to work on and without careful design the research theme can be ignored. Giving time to discuss the educational values of the school, and how these values practically apply to students in mathematics, places emphasis on the importance of student thinking. A successful strategy utilised in this planning team was the

DOI: 10.4324/9781003375272-26

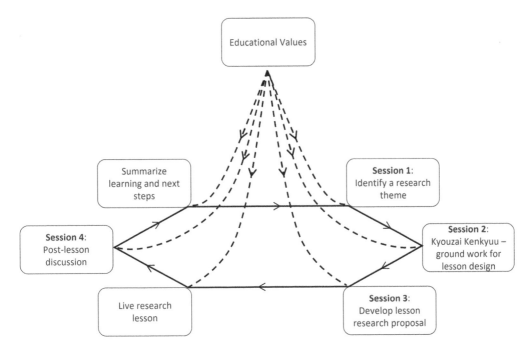

Figure 5.6.1 The CLR lesson cycle adapted from Takahashi and McDougal (2016) with the addition of educational values from Fujii (2014).

creation of a set of cards (see Figure 5.6.2) to prompt discussion around the research theme. These cards consist of three *What?* statements based on the school's values and three *How?* statements summarising the aims of the mathematics national curriculum for England (Department for Education, 2021).

The planning team used these cards to help identify a suitable *What?* and *How?* combination for the research theme. Through discussion we decided to focus on encouraging respect for others (the what) through providing opportunities to reason and follow a line of enquiry (the how). This led to an agreed research theme of: *how does a lesson that provides opportunities to develop reasoning through engaging with alternative explanations help to develop respect in students?* Consequently, we decided to adopt a Teaching Through Problem-Solving style lesson (Takahashi, 2021) on the topic of angles between parallel lines as a research lesson. In particular, we decided to adapt a lesson with a long history of use in Japan which was included in the 1999 TIMMS video study[1] and is also discussed with respect to board use by Baldry *et al.* (2022).

To summarise the lesson, students are asked to find as many different strategies to solve the problem in Figure 5.6.3 as they can during ten minutes of individual problem solving. The teacher then orchestrates the sharing of strategies so that students can learn different ways of thinking from each other. In addition, the teacher also has the opportunity to draw attention to the range of angle facts that can be utilised. Finally, the lesson progresses by students being asked to individually adapt the problem and then work through the solution to the new problem with a partner. The reader may like to see how many different strategies they can find to solve the problem in Figure 5.6.3 before proceeding with their reading.

From my experience, selecting a research theme is most effective when there is an explicit consideration of the educational values that the school wishes to develop. This explicit

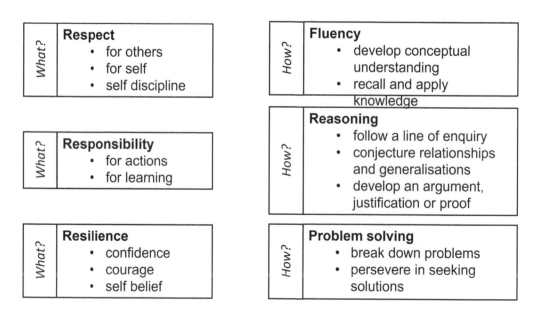

Figure 5.6.2 The What? and How? cards used to develop a research theme.

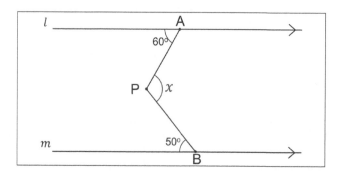

Figure 5.6.3 The main problem from the research lesson.

consideration consequently leads to an understanding of the type of lesson that should be used for live research. Creating a lesson before considering the research theme, or making the research theme about the mathematics of the lesson, risks placing an emphasis on trying to perfect a lesson rather than on developing students' mathematical thinking. CLR appears most effective when the lesson research proposal can be designed with the intention of providing opportunities to make the research theme visible.

5.6.2 Learning about Kyouzai Kenkyuu

In the second phase of the CLR cycle, *kyouzai kenkyuu* (the groundwork for lesson design) takes place. Lerner and McDougal (Chapter 3.5) note that the Japanese term of *kyouzai kenkyuu* is used in CLR since the English translation does not capture the full meaning. However, the concomitant danger of retaining the Japanese term is that it provides little clarity around what should take place in this phase. I have found that this lack of clarity can be unhelpful in that there can be a wide variety of interpretations of what should take place. I have seen *kyouzai kenkyuu* phases that include reading research papers, include information giving and even the actual process of designing the lesson. Watanabe, Takahashi, and Yoshida (2008) suggest that effective *kyouzai kenkyuu* allows the development of a clear vision of what students should understand and should come before planning a lesson. For me, this phase has been most effective when it is seen as an opportunity to *envision student learning*. Whilst this may not be a sufficient translation to capture all that takes place within the *kyouzai kenkyuu* phase, it provides helpful clarity for the focus of the phase. Therefore, I see this phase as focusing on the research of instructional materials (a more literal translation of *kyouzai kenkyuu*) *in order* to envision what students could learn. In my experience, this has often involved providing the planning team with opportunities to gain a deeper understanding of the mathematics prior to planning the lesson so that we can raise questions about what we want the students to learn.

Therefore, for the angle between parallel lines lesson, during session 2, the teachers were asked to individually solve the problem in as many ways as possible, share and discuss their strategies, and then classify the strategies into similar methods. A copy of some of the cards that were used to facilitate the classification of methods can be seen in Appendix A. They are not provided as an exhaustive set of strategies but as representative of a range of possibilities. By carrying out this task the planning team were able to consider their values around mathematics problems, and what they want students to be aware of. Taking part in this activity led to the planning team discussing the following points:

- Should learning focus on students knowing a single strategy to solve this problem? Does this avoid confusing students with many competing possibilities?
- Should learning focus on students seeing that there are many ways to solve a problem and building connections between them?
- Should learning focus on students knowing that there are four general methods that all involve the addition of an auxiliary line?
- Should learning focus on students realising that the addition of an auxiliary line enables a range of angle facts to be used?

These discussions revealed much about individual's, and the group's, educational values. The activity placed attention on the kind of mathematical thinking that we want students to experience and adopt.

There is often discussion in planning teams around whether a live research lesson should be based around existing material or designed from scratch. For me the choices that we make place a different emphasis on what is done in the *kyouzai kenkyuu* phase. If a department chooses to design a lesson from scratch then this phase can become dominated by thoughts around pedagogy. If the planning team is not careful then this can result in an inadvertent focus on creating a perfect lesson. In contrast, using a lesson that has already been designed frees the planning team to focus on developing mathematical thinking. (There are many sources of well-designed lessons that can be used, including https://www.mathshell.org/ and https://www.nottingham.ac.uk/maths-for-life/teacher/classroom-materials.aspx.) This is not to say that designing a lesson from scratch is wrong but that we should be aware of the possible implications. Just as within the phase of planning a research theme, a consideration of educational values keeps this phase centred on what we want students to be thinking about. Session 2 (and phase 2 of the cycle) now leads naturally to session 3 and the development of a lesson research proposal that focuses on developing student thinking rather than on perfecting a lesson.

5.6.3 Conclusion

Space does not permit a discussion of session 3 where the lesson research proposal was completed. However, the same underpinning principle as the first two phases is important – that a consideration of educational values enables a lesson research proposal to be focused on developing mathematical thinking in students. However, it would be remiss not to briefly mention the mathematical thinking that students in year 8 (ages 12–13) demonstrated during part of the live research lesson. Figure 5.6.4 includes some of the strategies demonstrated by students when given the time to individually solve the problem and come up with as many strategies as they could. Whilst not all strategies are correct each one provides the class teacher with an opportunity for whole-class discussion and the sharing of thinking. The reader may wish to consider what is revealed by the thinking of each student's work shown in Figure 5.6.4.

Following the live research lesson, a discussion between observers took place in session 4. During this discussion, one teacher who watched two students during the lesson stated:

> *My main observation is that they didn't quite have the confidence or the resilience to take that first step [in solving the problem] but they gained it when the first method was drawn up [by another student].*

It is worth noting that the teacher fell naturally into using the language of the research theme. The time spent in session 1 led to a focused awareness of what should be observed and what should be discussed in this session.

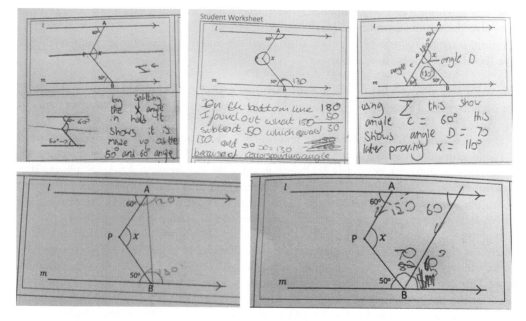

Figure 5.6.4 A selection of strategies in response to the main task of the lesson (Figure 5.6.3).

In summarising their reflections on the lesson, the class teacher stated:

Normally I let them [the students] sit where they want, give them a problem, and they get down to it, but what I think is that the better mathematicians take the opportunities of the weaker, whereas this time [in the research lesson] I was surprised at the people [the weaker students] that went for it.

What we see in this quote is a recognition that whilst group work can be beneficial for students, there is also a place for individual problem solving which can feed into whole class discussion. The class teacher could see that the students he saw as weaker sometimes need time to develop their mathematical thinking. Once given this time they are better equipped to participate in the respectful listening and sharing of ideas with the whole class. Even in the post-lesson discussion, educational values and the development of student mathematical thinking are at the forefront.

Finally, in researching CLR I have been drawn to notice the following two points. First, the phases of the CLR process are most effective when facilitated by careful design. Whilst this can be difficult with time pressures it could be a role that a knowledgeable other (Lewis et al., 2006; Watanabe & Wang-Iverson, 2005) can take to support the planning team. Second, explicit attention on educational values throughout all phases increases the likelihood that the phase will focus on the development of mathematical thinking in students. Whilst here I have only looked at two phases of the CLR cycle in detail, I have found that the same principle applies within every phase. Indeed, it is this focus on educational values which mediates the development of student mathematical thinking that distinguishes CLR from other forms of Lesson Study.

Note

1 http://www.timssvideo.com/jp1-finding-the-value-of-an-angle

References

Baldry, F., Mann, J., Horsman, R., Koiwa, D., & Foster, C. (2022). The use of carefully planned board work to support the productive discussion of multiple student responses in a Japanese problem-solving lesson. *Journal of Mathematics Teacher Education*, 1–25. 10.1007/s10857-021-09511-6

Department for Education. (2021). *National curriculum in England: Mathematics programmes of study*. Retrieved 29 August 2022, from https://www.gov.uk/government/publications/national-curriculum-in-england-mathematics-programmes-of-study/national-curriculum-in-england-mathematics-programmes-of-study

Fujii, T. (2014). Implementing Japanese lesson study in foreign countries: Misconceptions revealed. *Mathematics Teacher Education and Development*, 16(1), n1.

Huang, R., Fang, Y., & Chen, X. (2017). Chinese lesson study: A deliberate practice, a research methodology, and an improvement science. *International Journal for Lesson and Learning Studies*, 6(4), 270–282.

Lewis, C., Perry, R., Hurd, J., & O'Connell, M. P. (2006). Lesson study comes of age in North America. *Phi Delta Kappan*, 88(4), 273–281.

Lewis, C., Perry, R., & Murata, A. (2006). How should research contribute to instructional improvement? The case of lesson study. *Educational Researcher*, 35(3), 3–14.

Takahashi, A. (2021). *Teaching mathematics through problem-solving: A pedagogical approach from Japan*. Routledge.

Takahashi, A., & McDougal, T. (2016). Collaborative lesson research: Maximizing the impact of lesson study. *Zdm, 48*(4), 513–526.

Takahashi, A., & McDougal, T. (2018). Collaborative Lesson Research (CLR). In: Quaresma, M., Winsløw, C., Clivaz, S., da Ponte, J., Ní Shúilleabháin, A., & Takahashi, A. (Eds.), *Mathematics Lesson Study Around the World. ICME-13 Monographs.* Springer, Cham. 10.1007/978-3-319-75 696-7_8

Watanabe, T., Takahashi, A., & Yoshida, M. (2008). Kyozaikenkyu: A critical step for conducting effective lesson study and beyond. *Inquiry into Mathematics Teacher Education, 5*, 131–142.

Watanabe, T., & Wang-Iverson, P. (2005). The role of knowledgeable others. In P. Wang-Iverson & M. Yoshida (Eds.), *Building our understanding of lesson study* (pp. 85–91). Research for better schools.

Appendix A

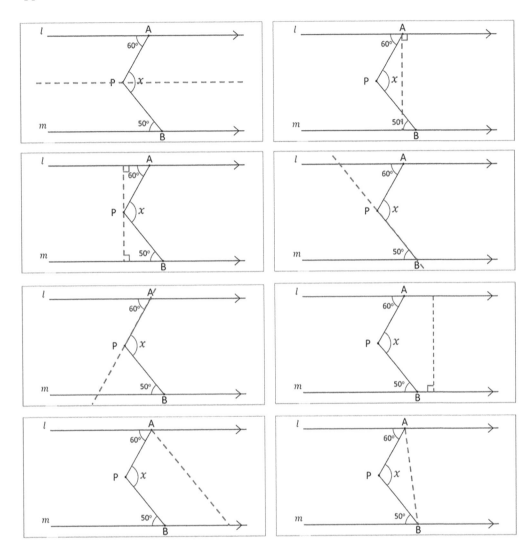

Part 6

Recommendations

6.1   Recommendations

Geoffrey Wake and Akihiko Takahashi

As editors of a book such as this that brings together the writing of a large number of contributors, we would like to comment on the immense privilege it has been to gain insight into the work and thinking of all the contributors. We count them as colleagues and fellow enthusiasts for CLR. We each know some of them well, and indeed have collaborated with them in a number of ways over the years, but drawing their thinking together in one place has provided us with not only fresh insights into the thinking of individual contributors, but also an opportunity to see emerging themes and issues. One issue stands out above all: every contributor values and wishes to support and embed teachers' professional learning as part of the fabric of their day-to-day work. They see CLR as providing a workable model around which to coalesce and support such an endeavour. Here, in one volume, we have managed to capture contributors' insights and experiences from years of engagement in their personal journey into and through CLR. There is much to learn from this, and it may be that you have found this by reading the volume from beginning to end, or maybe from time-to-time you dipped into certain sections to stimulate your thinking. Maybe if, like many of us do, you have come first to the final section, to consider our recommendations. In that case, our first recommendation is that, over time, as needs arise, you read all of the wisdom and advice that is offered here.

In this chapter, we provide something of a summary of the outcomes of the final collection of contributions and make some recommendations for both those getting started with, and those already somewhere along their journey in, CLR.

We make some comments around themes of (1) getting started and developing a workable model of CLR, (2) thinking about learning, and (3) embedding and sustaining CLR.

6.1.1 Getting started and developing a workable model of CLR

In reading the different contributions that our authors make it becomes apparent that CLR is not a simple activity; it is complex and has many interacting facets that need careful attention. In Japan, as *Jyugyou kenkyuu*, often translated as Lesson Study, it is not an addition to the usual work of teachers, it is integrated so that it is part of the whole (Fujii, 2014, p. 68). In other countries as a new addition to our daily work, this does provide both challenges and opportunities: although it is easy to feel that the challenges do outweigh the opportunities. We would like to encourage you to try to find ways to make it work *for you* (and colleagues).

Following the publication of *The Teaching Gap* (Stigler & Hiebert, 1999) many educators from around the world were alerted to Japanese Lesson Study as an important factor in the high levels of attainment of Japanese students in the Organisation for

DOI: 10.4324/9781003375272-28

Economic Co-operation and Development (OECD)'s Programme for International Student Assessment (PISA) mathematics tests. You may read quite widely about how Lesson Study is implemented in Japan (e.g., see Fernandez & Yoshida, 2012; Isoda, 2007; Makinae, 2010; Murata, 2011).

Attempts to implement Lesson Study in other countries soon became widespread and partnerships between Japanese educators and those in other countries were established. There are many studies that you may wish to seek out and read, especially those that were developed in educational settings most like your own – although as we recognise elsewhere in this volume (Chapter 1.2) having sensitivity to your own specific setting's unique features will ensure that you maximise the potential to get a workable model.

Elsewhere some studies give something of a survey of practices across countries: notably, Seleznyov (2018) and Fujii (2014), whilst others are more focussed on describing and providing insights into adaptation of Lesson Study in other countries. For example, Seleznyov (2019) considers challenges in adapting CLR for use in England, Lewis (2006) and Perry and Lewis (2009) consider Lesson Study in North America, and Groves et al. (2016) focus on their experiences in Australia. Important in reading any of these articles we need to bear in mind that at issue is not only the implementation of what is a new activity for all concerned with a focus on teacher learning, but also we may be attempting to change the structures of lessons, teachers pedagogies, and importantly expected ways of working of students. We are setting a challenging agenda for change.

Many of the contributors to this volume point to how they have made adaptations that attempt to remain true to an idealised model of CLR, but do take account of local and national cultures, systems, and structures. The contributors here, primarily, come from the United States and United Kingdom and naturally their experiences and examples are situated within these countries. However, their examples are indeed just specific manifestations of solutions to general problems. We ask that you view them in that light and consider how the experiences that are detailed might inform your own adaptations.

Our recommendation is that as a potential and putative CLR group, you start out by considering carefully what will work and how. How can you adapt the general CLR model in ways that will work to the benefit of teachers and ultimately learners in your particular context? We suggest that you set these discussions and deliberations as the focus of a special meeting(s) where you pay attention to not only general intentions but also the specific details that need to be considered. Whilst you will need to recognise difficulties and challenges the aim is to identify these and consider how they can be circumvented or overcome.

In addition to some of the literature referred to above, there is much to learn and consider here in this volume across all chapters that might help with your deliberations, but especially the insights that are developed in Parts 1 and 2.

6.1.2 Thinking about learning

The joy of CLR is being involved in *collaborative* professional learning. Perhaps this is particularly the case in the West, where teaching can be quite an isolated activity. Although teachers are very busy, both inside and outside of their classrooms, it seems that there is not always a lot of time and space in which to engage with fellow professionals to discuss what goes on in their teaching and students' learning. There are many contributions here that provide insightful insights into both.

We recommend that as a CLR group you make time as part of your agenda to consider and make explicit your intentions in relation to three aspects of learning – (i) students,

(ii) teachers' professional learning in relation to teaching, and (iii) the group's learning about CLR as a process.

i Students

Clearly, the learning of students is paramount in our work as teachers. It is central to our CLR planning, teaching and post-lesson discussions. As a number of contributors here suggest, it is important to identify what we wish to achieve in terms of student learning in CLR research lessons, both in relation to the overarching research theme (see Chapter 1.1 and for further discussion Chapter 5.6). There needs to be a shared vision of what the sequence of CLR cycles is hoping to achieve, as well as clarity about the specific focus on mathematical concepts and understanding in particular lessons.

ii Teachers' professional learning

As part of your discussions as a CLR group ensure that you make time to identify at a research theme level, as well as for specific lessons what you hope to be your own learning as teachers. A number of UK contributors, for example, write about their experiences of working on improving their teaching, and students' learning of problem solving. It is worth having a discussion about what this means in terms of teaching and not only what teachers might expect to learn, but also to consider what the outcomes were for them as they worked through a number of cycles.

iii The group's learning about CLR as a process

In Section 6.1.2 we recommend that you make explicit your intended adapted model of CLR. The group needs to take ownership of this and as we suggested attention is paid to the overall model as well as the detailed aspects. There is much reading in this volume that can inform your thinking about this learning: for example, chapters of Parts 4 and 5 provide much to consider about each of the different phases of the process. We recommend that whilst monitoring your overall progress in CLR, you make time to consider such detailed aspects of your work. For instance, you might want to set time aside in a meeting to consider the value of including final comments from a knowledgeable other. You may consider including in your deliberations someone who has undertaken the role for you and have a full and frank discussion about what is and isn't working.

Again, there is much literature that you may find helpful to stimulate your thinking in these areas. We suggest that as a developing CLR community you put in place a library of useful sources of learning and inspiration. It may be that you include a book club style, discussion group as part of your activities. We would particularly draw your attention to a volume that similar to this draws on authentic voices from the classroom: Educators' Learning from Lesson Study: Mathematics for Ages 5–13 (Takahashi et al., 2022). Other articles that focus on teacher and student learning through Lesson studies include Shuilleabhain (2016), Wake et al. (2016), Wake and Seleznyov (2020).

6.3.3 Embedding and sustaining CLR

One-off professional development events are known to be ineffective at bringing about much in the way of change to professional practice (Guskey & Yoon, 2009). Fundamental to CLR is the expectation that CLR is sustained over time in a way that embeds it as part of professional practice. This may turn out to be the most difficult aspect of initiating CLR in your particular context. If we accept that there is a cost to CLR, if only in terms of a time commitment from participants, then it is important that the emerging CLR community at the outset considers how they will facilitate and manage this. There is also much else to consider to put in place and maintain the infrastructure of a CLR community. Whilst it is obvious to consider the essential aspects of CLR as a new activity at the outset, what might be less obvious is the need to consider how these will be sustained in the long run. Monitoring and discussion of the group's capacity to maintain their activity needs to be considered on a regular basis.

There is also a need to consider how to build capacity in leadership of the group, and also in other key roles associated with the different components of the CLR cycle, for example, in providing the outside expertise that knowledgeable others provide. Issues in relation to capacity building again are scattered throughout contributions to this volume, but Part 4 in particular considers this issue and how CLR can be embedded and sustained.

Further to the work reported here, a number of educators and researchers have considered the issues that arise when trying to ensure that CLR is sustainable, minimally in the medium term, but hopefully in the long term (see e.g., Adelman & Taylor, 2003; Akiba & Howard, 2021; Cheng, 2020; Fang & Wang, 2021).

One way to think about the problem is to move thinking on from considering CLR as a project. Having said this I draw attention to a project in the United Kingdom that considered the sustainability and scalability of a Lesson Study model[1]. Although the research team was funded, it was a deliberate policy not to fund teachers from the participating schools: the CLR communities that developed had to find their own models of funding the time needed for participation. The project's final report made recommendations in relation to policy and practice, and at both system and school levels. As has been suggested at times in this volume the organisational and governance systems and structures we work within don't always act in ways that easily facilitate or support our CLR endeavours. Here we draw attention to the following issues that the report identified as important that you might like to consider addressing with policy makers if the opportunity arises:

- Acknowledging, celebrating and rewarding expertise in teachers' classroom practice in subject teaching.
- Developing a culture in the teaching profession in which teachers at all stages of their career expect to work with colleagues in and across schools to inquire into and develop expertise in teaching their subject.
- Expectations that universities are resourced to contribute to supporting research informed development of the teaching profession and subject expertise.
- CLR is used in collaborative research partnerships that inform future iterations of curriculum design (as in Japan).
- Initial Teacher Education initiates new entrants to the profession into CLR practices in schools that work with high-quality principles.
- Professional associations and others are supported to contribute to the initiation, development and sustaining of networks of expertise and experts in CLR and subject teaching.
- Strategic development of a network of acknowledged expertise and experts in the lesson study process and research-informed subject expertise in teaching and learning.

Further to this at the school level we highlight these issues that need attention:

- School policy and management should value and reward the development of expertise in subject teaching.

- Schools should support a culture of inquiry into what constitutes subject teaching expertise and focus this by establishing specific research themes within the school for periods of time.
- Schools should devote time and energy to the process of CLR.
- Schools should collaborate with each other to ensure cross-fertilisation of ideas.
- Schools should draw on expertise from outside of Lesson Study groups to ensure that groups can benefit from research and professional knowledge and state-of-the-art practice to stimulate future work of the group.

We recommend that the leadership of a CLR community pays careful attention to not only the initial stages of setting up their operational processes and structures but that these need revisiting and careful attention over time with a view to ensuring sustainability of the group.

One source of inspiration and energy, and opportunities to meet with like-minded professionals are overarching organisations such as Collaborative Lesson Research – UK[2] and Lesson Study Alliance[3] in the United States that operate at a regional and/or national level. We as editors are involved with these organisations and find they can help provide high-level direction and a community of CLR advocates and leaders. **We recommend** that you invest some time and energy in supporting such organisations so that they might develop their status so as to potentially influence policy at a system level.

Finally, no matter what your experience to date, **we recommend** that you continue to engage with, and enjoy your journey in, CLR and the professional learning that results. There is no doubt that there are often major cultural expectations in relation to teaching, learning and schooling that can seem like potentially insurmountable barriers. For example, there are often expectations of "classroom privacy" (as teachers these are "our" spaces and we have our own unique way of operating and interacting with learners), there are multiple initiatives that we may be involved with at any one time (many of them very valuable, but what space is there for CLR, in such a landscape?), our time is precious and all accounted for. However, as we have indicated previously, we need to turn challenges into opportunities that not only sneak CLR into our work but might also address other issues that are of concern. CLR provides a model for teachers of how to engage deeply with what lies at the heart of teaching and learning, our work in classrooms. Addressing challenges like those raised above requires work, it often requires ingenuity, maybe even sleight of hand, but as the accounts of much work written about here demonstrate, it is very much worthwhile.

Notes

1 https://www.nottingham.ac.uk/research/groups/crme/documents/lemaps-report.pdf
2 https://www.collaborative-lesson-research.uk/
3 https://www.lsalliance.org/

References

Adelman, H. S., & Taylor, L. (2003). On sustainability of project innovations as systemic change. *Journal of Educational and Psychological Consultation*, 14(1), 1–25.

Akiba, M., & Howard, C. (2021). After the race to the top: State and district capacity to sustain professional development innovation in Florida. *Educational Policy*. pp. 1–44, doi: 10.1177/ 0895 9048211015619.

Cheng E. C. K. (2020). Knowledge management strategies for sustaining lesson study. *International Journal for Lesson and Learning Studies*, 9(2), 167–178.

Fang, Y., & Wang, H. (2021). Trends of and implications for the diffusion of lesson study: thematic analysis of WALS2019 conference presentations. *International Journal for Lesson and Learning Studies*, 10(1), 61–74.

Fernandez, C., & Yoshida, M. (2012). *Lesson study: A Japanese approach to improving mathematics teaching and learning*. New York: Routledge.

Fujii, T. (2014). Implementing Japanese lesson study in foreign countries: Misconceptions revealed. *Mathematics Teacher Education & Development*, 16(1): 65–83.

Groves, S., Doig, B., Vale, C., & Widjaja, W. (2016). Critical factors in the adaptation and implementation of Japanese lesson study in the Australian context. *ZDM Mathematics Education*, 48(4) (this issue). doi: 10.1007/s11858-016-0786-8.

Guskey, T. R., & Yoon, K. S. (2009). What works in professional development? *Phi Delta Kappan*, 90(7), 495–500.

Isoda, M. (2007). *Japanese lesson study in mathematics: Its impact, diversity and potential for educational improvement*. World Scientific 2007.

Lewis, C. (2006). Lesson study in North America: Progress and challenges. In M. Matoba, K. A. Crawford, & M. R. Sarkar Arani (Eds.), *Lesson study: International perspective on policy and practice* (pp. 1–15). Beijing: Educational Science Publishing House.

Makinae, N. (2010). The origin of lesson study in Japan. *5th East Asia Regional Conference on Mathematics Education: In Search of Excellence in Mathematics Education*, Tokyo. Vol. 15.

Murata, A. (2011). Introduction: Conceptual overview of lesson study. *Lesson Study Research and Practice in Mathematics Education*, 1(12), 1–11.

Perry, R., & Lewis, C. (2009). What is successful adaptation of lesson study in the US? *Journal of Educational Change*, 10(4), 365–391.

Seleznyov, S. (2018). Lesson study: An exploration of its translation beyond Japan. *International Journal for Lesson and Learning Studies*, 7(3), 217–229.

Seleznyov, S. (2019). Lesson study: exploring implementation challenges in England. *International Journal For Lesson And Learning Studies*, 9(2), 179–192.

Shuilleabhain, A. (2016). Developing mathematics teachers' pedagogical content knowledge in lesson study: Case study findings. *International journal for lesson and learning studies*, 5(3), 212–226.

Stigler, J., & Hiebert, J. (1999). *The teaching gap: Best ideas from the world's teachers for improving education in the classroom*. New York: Free Press.

Takahashi, A., McDougal, T., Friedkin, S., & Watanabe, T. (2022). *Educators' Learning from Lesson Study: Mathematics for Ages 5–13*. London and New York: Routledge.

Wake, G., Swan, M., & Foster, C. (2016). Professional learning through the collaborative design of problem-solving lessons. *Journal of Mathematics Teacher Education*, 19(2–3), 243–260.

Wake, G., & Seleznyov, S. (2020). Curriculum design through lesson study. *London Review of Education*, 18(3), 467–479.

Index